THE BEDFORD SERIES IN HISTORY AND CULTURE

Conservatives in Power: The Reagan Years, 1981–1989

A Brief History with Documents

Related Titles in
THE BEDFORD SERIES IN HISTORY AND CULTURE
Advisory Editors: Lynn Hunt, *University of California, Los Angeles*
David W. Blight, *Yale University*
Bonnie G. Smith, *Rutgers University*
Natalie Zemon Davis, *Princeton University*
Ernest R. May, *Harvard University*

The Era of Franklin D. Roosevelt, 1933–1945: A Brief History with Documents
Richard Polenberg, *Cornell University*

The Rise of Conservatism in America, 1945–2000: A Brief History with Documents
Ronald Story, *University of Massachusetts Amherst*, and Bruce Laurie, *University of Massachusetts Amherst*

The Age of McCarthyism: A Brief History with Documents, Second Edition
Ellen Schrecker, *Yeshiva University*

The Movements of the New Left, 1950–1975: A Brief History with Documents
Van Gosse, *Franklin and Marshall College*

Lyndon B. Johnson and American Liberalism: A Brief Biography with Documents, Second Edition
Bruce J. Schulman, *Boston University*

American Cold War Strategy: Interpreting NSC 68
Edited with an Introduction by Ernest R. May, *Harvard University*

Jimmy Carter and the Energy Crisis of the 1970s: The "Crisis of Confidence" Speech of July 15, 1979: A Brief History with Documents
Daniel Horowitz, *Smith College*

THE BEDFORD SERIES IN HISTORY AND CULTURE

Conservatives in Power: The Reagan Years, 1981–1989

A Brief History with Documents

Meg Jacobs

Massachusetts Institute of Technology

Julian E. Zelizer

Princeton University

BEDFORD / ST. MARTIN'S   Boston ◆ New York

To Nathan and Claire

For Bedford/St. Martin's

Publisher for History: Mary V. Dougherty
Director of Development for History: Jane Knetzger
Executive Editor: William J. Lombardo
Senior Editor: Heidi L. Hood
Developmental Editor: Debra Michals
Editorial Assistant: Jennifer Jovin
Production Associate: Ashley Chalmers
Executive Marketing Manager: Jenna Bookin Barry
Project Management: Books By Design, Inc.
Index: Books By Design, Inc.
Text Design: Claire Seng-Niemoeller
Cover Design: Donna Dennison
Cover Photo: *President Reagan Addresses Congress and the Nation on the Program for Economic Recovery from the U.S. Capitol* (first speech after the assassination attempt). 4/28/81.C1681-21A. Courtesy Ronald Reagan Library.
Composition: Achorn International
Printing and Binding: RR Donnelley & Sons Company

President: Joan E. Feinberg
Editorial Director: Denise B. Wydra
Director of Marketing: Karen R. Soeltz
Director of Production: Susan W. Brown
Associate Director of Editorial Production: Elise S. Kaiser
Manager, Publishing Services: Emily Berleth

Library of Congress Control Number: 2010928026

Manufactured in the United States of America.

5   4   3   2   1   0
f   e   d   c   b   a

For information, write: Bedford/St. Martin's, 75 Arlington Street, Boston, MA 02116 (617-399-4000)

ISBN-10: 0-312-48831-9
ISBN-13: 978-0-312-48831-4

Acknowledgments

Document 1: Courtesy of the Eureka College Archives. Used with permission.

Document 6: Gingrich Communications, Inc.

Document 12: © 1981 William Greider, as first published in *The Atlantic*.

Document 22: Reprinted with permission of the Heritage Foundation (heritage.org).

Document 60: This article first appeared in *Salon.com*, at http://www.Salon.com. An online version remains in the Salon archives. Reprinted with permission.

Foreword

The Bedford Series in History and Culture is designed so that readers can study the past as historians do.

The historian's first task is finding the evidence. Documents, letters, memoirs, interviews, pictures, movies, novels, or poems can provide facts and clues. Then the historian questions and compares the sources. There is more to do than in a courtroom, for hearsay evidence is welcome, and the historian is usually looking for answers beyond act and motive. Different views of an event may be as important as a single verdict. How a story is told may yield as much information as what it says.

Along the way the historian seeks help from other historians and perhaps from specialists in other disciplines. Finally, it is time to write, to decide on an interpretation and how to arrange the evidence for readers.

Each book in this series contains an important historical document or group of documents, each document a witness from the past and open to interpretation in different ways. The documents are combined with some element of historical narrative — an introduction or a biographical essay, for example — that provides students with an analysis of the primary source material and important background information about the world in which it was produced.

Each book in the series focuses on a specific topic within a specific historical period. Each provides a basis for lively thought and discussion about several aspects of the topic and the historian's role. Each is short enough (and inexpensive enough) to be a reasonable one-week assignment in a college course. Whether as classroom or personal reading, each book in the series provides firsthand experience of the challenge — and fun — of discovering, recreating, and interpreting the past.

Lynn Hunt
David W. Blight
Bonnie G. Smith
Natalie Zemon Davis
Ernest R. May

Preface

This is a history of what happened when conservatives came to power in the United States in 1980. Although many historians, intellectuals, and journalists have pointed to the 1980 election as the beginning of a new conservative era and the 1980s as a renaissance for conservative politics, we suggest that the realignment to the right was not as complete as previously thought. The introductory essay and the documents that follow show the challenges and limitations conservatives faced once they were in office. By reading these primary documents, students can observe firsthand how conservatives dealt with the demands of governance.

Many interpretations of recent American history tell the story of the "rise of the right." They show the intellectual origins of conservatives in the cold war of the 1950s. They trace the emergence of a grassroots conservative movement in the 1960s and 1970s as a reaction against New Deal and Great Society liberalism. These narratives culminate in the election of President Ronald Reagan in 1980, a landslide victory that seemed to usher in a new conservative age.

This book examines the obstacles conservatives encountered after they won control of the White House and the Senate in 1980. No longer in the opposition, they now had to respond to the difficulties of governance and soon discovered many of the limitations of their agenda. For one thing, liberalism proved much more durable than they had expected. In spite of the appeal of antigovernment rhetoric, Americans actually liked many of the liberal objectives, such as Social Security pensions and a cleaner environment. In addition, conservatism as a movement turned out to be more fragile and fragmented than they had originally thought. Holding together a coalition of businessmen, fiscal conservatives, and the religious Right proved hard to do.

Ronald Reagan is a pivotal figure in understanding the transition of American conservatism from the period of opposition to the period of governance. Reagan's political career also is emblematic of the post–World War II conservative movement. Early in his career, he was shaped by the writings of conservative intellectuals such as William F. Buckley and circulated among many of the key activists who founded the movement. He participated in Senator Barry Goldwater's 1964 presidential campaign, which was the first Republican campaign to embrace right-wing conservatism. As governor of California from 1967 to 1975 and as president of the United States from 1981 to 1989, Reagan, more than any other conservative, had to translate conservative ideas into a blueprint for governance. As the documents reveal, that was not as easy task. Most of the challenges that he confronted during his time in the White House remain central issues that conservatives continue to grapple with today.

The introductory essay in part one uses Reagan's political career as a window on the development of the modern conservative movement when it came to Washington. It moves from Reagan's origins to his election to the White House and then explores the issues he grappled with in domestic politics and foreign policy. The introduction shows how, during his years in power, conservatives recalibrated their priorities and found new tactics to achieve their goals. They were able to make many gains during the 1980s, such as a historic tax cut and an arms reduction agreement with the Soviet Union, while they also abandoned certain issues, such as Social Security reform. The essay concludes by looking at the legacies of Reagan's time in office.

The documents in part two offer a firsthand account of these years. The sections follow the same organization as the introduction, moving chronologically from conservatism's origins, through domestic politics and foreign affairs, and finally to legacies. The first section captures Reagan's early years in California as a private citizen and politician, when he developed his antigovernment, anti-Communist ideas.

In the sections on domestic politics, the primary sources show Reagan was committed to tax cuts and rolling back government intervention while also wrestling with the difficulties of building a new stable governing coalition. The documents reflect how hard it was to move policy and politics to the right. The recession of the early 1980s created political uncertainty for Reagan, but the recovery in 1983 led to his reelection in 1984. After this victory, Reagan's conservative supporters pushed even harder to advance their positions on cultural issues.

The next group of documents looks at national security, demonstrating similar challenges in implementing a conservative foreign policy. Reagan articulated a vision of peace through strength, which meant assuming a tough attitude toward the Soviet Union and an increase in defense spending at home. Here, too, he had to recognize the limitations of support, as Americans were fearful of nuclear war and also unwilling to sacrifice and spend for anti-Communist policies in Latin America. As on the domestic side, Reagan used behind-the-scenes tactics to advance his agenda, in this case negotiating with the Soviets to reach an arms agreement and authorizing covert missions in Latin America that circumvented legislation passed by Congress. In his second term, Reagan and conservatives faced a setback with the Iran-contra scandal, although his arms treaty with the Soviets helped improve his popularity with the American public.

The documents in the last section reflect the legacies of the Reagan years. They capture how conservatives came to live with the limitations they faced by recasting their goals and relying on new strategies of governance.

In the appendixes, we include study materials to help students learn more about this period and pursue additional research. The chronology begins with Reagan's birth in 1911, charts his rise to national power in 1980, and extends through his death in 2004. The questions for consideration raise issues for students to think about and discuss as they read through the introduction and the documents. And the selected bibliography points students in the direction of additional scholarship on the various topics covered in this volume.

A NOTE ABOUT THE TEXT

Most of the documents come from the archives at the Ronald Reagan Presidential Library in Simi Valley, California. From memos and personal letters to policy papers and celebrated speeches, they give students a flavor of how politicians and policymakers grappled with issues at the time. The documents from the archives appear as the authors wrote them—typos, errors, and all. In the speeches, we corrected typos and misspellings, since these documents are merely printed records of what the speakers said. Students can find additional documents, as well as the complete texts of speeches excerpted here, online at the Reagan Library, www.reagan.utexas.edu/.

ACKNOWLEDGMENTS

We would like to thank the participants of seminars and panels at the University of California, Santa Barbara, the Policy History Conference, and Boston University for their comments on earlier drafts of this volume. We would also like to thank the reviewers of this book for their helpful input in shaping the final manuscript: Brian Balogh, University of Virginia; David Farber, Temple University; Laura Kalman, University of California, Santa Barbara; John Putman, San Diego State University; Bruce Schulman, Boston University; and Jason Scott Smith, University of New Mexico. Finally, we would like to thank William Lombardo, Mary Dougherty, Jane Knetzger, Heidi Hood, and Jennifer Jovin at Bedford/ St. Martin's and developmental editor Debra Michals for their editorial assistance, along with Jamie Pietruska for her research assistance.

Meg Jacobs
Julian E. Zelizer

Contents

PART ONE

Introduction: Mr. Conservative Comes to Washington

In May 1981, a few months after Ronald Reagan's inauguration as the fortieth president of the United States, Richard Nixon laid out his wish for the political future. At a Republican party fund-raiser in Seattle, Nixon, the former Republican president, said that because of "'the Reagan Revolution,' the whole direction of the country is going to change."[1] Reagan had won the 1980 election in a dramatic fashion, setting the stage for what many on the right were hoping would be a new era of Republican rule and conservative dominance.

Yet, as conservatives understood in the 1980s, undoing at least half a century of liberalism would be difficult. In April 1981, when President Reagan addressed the Congress—where Republicans had taken control of the Senate for the first time in more than twenty-five years and had made major gains in the House—he laid out the historical challenge confronting conservatives. The actor turned politician stated the problem as he saw it: "Our government is too big and it spends too much." In addition, Reagan worried that American international power had waned since the Vietnam War. The nation, he said, was scared about standing tough against communism.[2]

Ultimately, what would come to be known as the Reagan Revolution met with mixed results. Successful as a campaign platform in 1980 and 1984, and soaring as political rhetoric, Reagan's antigovernment and anti-Communist ideology was hard to translate into a lasting shift to the right in American politics and policy and in the popular mind-set. Richard Nixon, whose two presidential victories in 1968 and 1972 had set the stage for a rightward move, was deeply familiar with the difficult challenges that Reagan and his cohort of conservatives faced. At the Seattle fund-raiser, Nixon warned that the Reagan Revolution would encounter serious obstacles, especially on Capitol Hill. Republicans would have their work cut out for them as they attempted to reverse the liberalism that had been born in the 1930s during President Franklin Roosevelt's New Deal and had come to maturity in the 1960s under President Lyndon Johnson. Despite Reagan's tremendous skill as an orator, Nixon astutely explained in 1981 that the newly elected president and his congressional allies would need "at least eight years" to roll back what a Democratic-controlled Congress had done in the past quarter century.[3]

Members of the Reagan administration were aware that the 1980 election did not constitute a popular mandate for a conservative revolution. As governor of California in the late 1960s and early 1970s, Reagan had learned firsthand that it was easier to talk about dismantling government than actually doing so. Since the New Deal, which had ushered in a period of liberal Democratic governance and political strength, conservatives had been building grassroots organizations and an ideological and policy agenda. In the 1950s and especially in the 1960s, their ideas began to attract a political following that gradually gained momentum in the mainstream. Yet liberal politics and policies were very much entrenched in America. For this reason, conservatives immediately felt pressure to sell the nation the idea that the 1980 election had signaled a decisive turn to the right. Promoting the idea of a Reagan Revolution, a phrase used first by Reagan insiders, became a central part of the administration's political strategy.

Upon his election, Reagan gladly accepted the mantle as the leader of the conservative movement. Reagan and his supporters saw it as their duty to hasten communism's decline and to trim the role of the federal government in people's lives. Hedrick Smith, a reporter for the *New York Times*, captured the historic significance of Reagan's inauguration on January 20, 1981: "The nation today arrived at a fascinating and quite remarkable moment in its political history: A 69-year-old citizen-politician who spent most of his working life in another profession has entered the White House and won the opportunity to lead a conservative political renaissance. . . . [Reagan] is a crusader, the first missionary conservative to be elected with the aim of reversing the liberal New Deal revolution of governmental activism and Democratic Party dominance established by Franklin D. Roosevelt nearly half a century ago."[4]

Whether Reagan and his conservative allies could fundamentally reform American government and politics, however, remained an open question.

Through Reagan, this book focuses on the era when conservatives came to power in Washington. During the 1980s, conservatives learned that liberalism had not died as a political force and the liberal policies they inherited were much more durable than they expected. Republicans, once in control, also discovered that as elected officials, they would be under pressure to provide long-established government benefits to voters to solidify their electoral position, much as Democrats had done when they were in office. Reagan and fellow conservatives spent these crucial years — as they adjusted from being an oppositional force to being a governing one — rethinking their expectations and recalibrating their agenda. In control of the White House but facing formidable foes in Congress, they relied on and developed tools of governance outside the legislative arena, including the use of executive power, bureaucratic warfare, and judicial appointments, to bring about political change.

FROM MOVEMENT TO GOVERNANCE

Conservatism became an organized force in American politics as early as the Great Depression of the 1930s. When Franklin Roosevelt was elected president in 1932, he set in motion a dramatic growth of federal power. The New Deal saw the creation of Social Security pensions, unemployment compensation, union rights, and minimum wages. The New Deal also established many regulatory agencies, such as the Securities and Exchange Commission and the Federal Deposit Insurance Corporation. All of these programs and regulations expanded the size and role of the federal government in the economy in an attempt to bring stability and prosperity. Although Roosevelt won election four times and the New Deal had millions of supporters, by 1938 a conservative coalition of southern Democrats and Republicans coalesced in Congress in opposition to the New Deal. There were also businessmen who had started to mobilize against federal intervention in markets.[5] When Harry Truman became president after Roosevelt's death in 1945, the conservative coalition had grown strong enough to block efforts to pass additional New Deal measures in the postwar years.

The cold war between the United States and the Soviet Union strengthened the power of conservatives in American politics. Although they had been allies in World War II, after the war these two superpowers, one democratic and the other Communist, opposed each other as enemies in a cold war that would last half a century. In 1947, President Truman declared the Truman Doctrine, which committed the United States to a policy of containment of Soviet power, dedicated to limiting the spread of communism in Europe and Asia. Truman and other Democratic leaders were devoted cold warriors, supporting the creation of a national security state, including the establishment of the Central Intelligence Agency (CIA), the National Security Council (NSC), and the Defense Department. But conservatives in the Republican and Democratic parties said that the Truman administration was not doing enough to fight communism in Asia or the threat of Communist subversion within the United States. When China fell to communism in 1949, Republicans claimed that this Communist revolution in Asia offered proof that Democratic cold war policies were failing. Conservatives also used anti-Communist rhetoric to defeat liberal domestic programs, such as Truman's proposal for national health insurance, as being socialistic.

An informal network of philanthropists, journalists, and organizations formed in the 1940s and 1950s to promote the conservative anti-Communist critique. Many of the ideas circulating among America's growing right wing could be read on the pages of the *National Review*, a magazine that William F. Buckley Jr. founded in 1955 when he was just thirty years old. Buckley's father had lost his oil fortune during the Mexican Revolution, in 1911, and the experience taught his son that Marxist-inspired revolutions were a threat to religion, private property, and freedom. In 1951, a year after graduating from Yale, Buckley published *God and Man at Yale*, attacking the entire "eastern Establishment" for a decline in morality and an insufficient defense against communism. Buckley then started the *National Review*, which he famously announced was meant to stand "athwart history, yelling Stop, at a time when no one is inclined to do so." It was one of several right-wing publications from the period and would become a mainstay of conservative politics in the decades that followed. Intellectuals such as Buckley and philosopher James Burnham depicted the United States as the last force standing between a free society and communism.[6]

Reagan's Origins

Ronald Reagan's path to conservatism was not inevitable. Reagan was born on February 6, 1911, in Tampico, Illinois, to a shoe salesman named John Edward Reagan, who had a drinking problem, and his wife, Nelle Wilson Reagan, an active member of the Disciples of Christ Church. In 1920, the Reagans moved to Dixon, Illinois, where young

Ronald attended high school and became notable as a town lifeguard. The 1930s were hard for the family. John found employment in several New Deal programs, which led his son to admire President Roosevelt.

As much as the New Deal helped his father, the future president's own life lessons pointed toward self-reliance, hard work, and rugged individualism. Graduating from Eureka College, a small religious school, in 1932, the young Reagan got a job as a radio sports announcer in Des Moines, Iowa. While in Los Angeles to cover the Chicago Cubs, the charismatic and talented Reagan took a screen test and secured a movie deal with Warner Brothers. With income from films, he soon bought his parents their first home. Reagan starred in several B movies, the most famous of which was *Knute Rockne All American* (1940), in which he played the famous college football player George Gipp. That same year, Reagan married actress Jane Wyman. Like many young men of his generation, Reagan was called to serve in World War II, but his less-than-perfect eyesight prevented him from being sent into combat. Instead, he was assigned to an Army unit that made propaganda and training films.

After the war, Reagan became more involved in politics. He was elected president of the Screen Actors Guild (SAG) in 1947, just as cold war tensions were pitting conservative anti-Communists against liberals. In his capacity as president, Reagan cooperated with federal investigators by sharing the names of alleged Communists in Hollywood and quit liberal organizations suspected of Communist infiltration. Reagan divorced Wyman in 1948 and four years later, in 1952, married actress Nancy Davis. That same year, Reagan voted for the Republican presidential candidate, Dwight Eisenhower. Though still a registered Democrat, Reagan expressed contempt for most of his party's leaders.

The Speech

Reagan finished his leadership work with SAG and in 1954 signed a contract with General Electric (GE) to host a television show, *General Electric Theater*, which became one of the highest-rated television shows of the time. As part of his job, GE paid Reagan to deliver promotional speeches in factories around the country about the virtues of private markets and the dangers of the Communist threat. This was part of a GE public relations campaign to undermine union support by improving the company's public image.[7] Through these speeches, Reagan refined his ideas. He became increasingly vocal in his criticism of liberal domestic policies such as progressive taxation and developed a series of arguments challenging the foreign policy of containment, which was based on accepting the permanence of communism in certain parts of the world. Instead, he supported the concept of rollback, promoted by conservatives such as James Burnham and John Foster Dulles, which stated that the United States should seek to destroy Communist regimes rather than contain them. Reagan's politics continued to shift rightward. He believed that private markets could handle most problems, other than national security, more effectively than the federal government.[8]

In almost all of Reagan's public appearances, anticommunism served as his key theme (Document 1). He said, "We are engaged in a great war to determine whether the world can exist half-slave and half-free."[9] Reagan insisted that the cold war was not a strategic geopolitical fight but, rather, a moral struggle between good and evil. Reagan posited four arguments about communism. The first was that the Soviet economy was too fragile to withstand the cost of an accelerated arms race. The second was that the Soviet Union remained in power in Eastern Europe only as a result of brute force. Third, Reagan believed that most Americans would support a substantial increase in defense spending as long as the government demonstrated a genuine desire to achieve peace in the long run.[10] Finally, Reagan detested nuclear weapons and sincerely hoped that one day they could be totally abolished.[11] In his mind, the only way to eliminate nuclear weapons was for the United States to develop a sufficiently intimidating arsenal that would force the Soviet Union to accept substantive concessions and ultimately for the Soviet Union to collapse altogether.

Like many conservatives, Reagan rejected the bipartisan strategy of mutual assured destruction (MAD), which held that the only deterrence against nuclear war was the fear of massive retaliation if one superpower attacked first. According to Reagan, the success of MAD depended on neither country pulling the trigger, which was an enormous gamble. MAD, Reagan argued, did not offer protection from a technical accident or an attack by a madman. He frequently compared MAD to "two westerners standing in a saloon aiming their guns to each other's head—permanently."[12]

Conservative Republicans, or the Republican Right, as they were called, became a growing concern for Democrats in the early 1960s. Besides anticommunism, some conservative organizations and politicians were capitalizing on racial tensions that were dividing the Democratic party. During the 1948 presidential election, a group of southern Democratic delegates bolted from the Democratic convention when Truman endorsed a strong civil rights plank. South Carolina Democrat

Strom Thurmond headed a third-party campaign. Although Thurmond lost his bid for the presidency, the tensions were difficult to contain. In northern cities such as Detroit, citizen organizations consisting of working- and middle-class white Americans—most of whom were Democratic and beneficiaries of New Deal programs—mobilized to protect racial segregation in residential zoning and industrial employment.[13] The Supreme Court stirred these emotions in 1954, when it ruled in *Brown v. Board of Education* that segregated schools were unconstitutional. Virginia and Arkansas shut their school systems for a year rather than comply with desegregation. Average citizens resorted to verbal intimidation and physical violence to block progress. In 1956, 101 congressmen and senators signed the Southern Manifesto opposing the Supreme Court's *Brown* ruling. In the 1960s, the civil rights legislation of the Kennedy and Johnson years, combined with the grassroots mobilization led by Martin Luther King Jr., further alienated many white southerners from the Democratic party and triggered a conservative backlash.

At the same time, grassroots right-wing activists were starting to develop more of a political presence. One organization that received considerable attention was the John Birch Society, which was formed in 1958 by a Massachusetts businessman named Robert Welch. The Birchers were on the extreme end of the political spectrum, castigating liberals for their weakness in the fight against communism and protesting against civil rights legislation. The Birchers distributed half a million copies of pamphlets with titles such as *The Black Revolution Is the Red Revolution*, suggesting that the civil rights movement was Communist inspired.[14]

On college campuses, Young Americans for Freedom organized conservative students. In the 1960s, this group grew as fast as, if not faster than, the more well-known Students for a Democratic Society (SDS), an organization of New Left activists who called for an end to cold war hostilities and an expansion of civil rights. In addition, there were pockets of the country, such as Orange County, California, where middle-class Americans were flocking to conservative candidates and organizations. Well-educated and upwardly mobile Americans who were beneficiaries of the booming southwestern economy were attracted to the free-market arguments of the right.[15]

This budding conservative movement crystallized in the Republican candidacy of Senator Barry Goldwater in the 1964 presidential election. During his campaign against Lyndon Johnson, who had become president after John F. Kennedy's assassination in November 1963, Goldwater tapped into the energy of conservative organizations. He promoted

Ronald Reagan's Speech at the International Hotel, Los Angeles, 1964.
Ronald Reagan gained national prominence through his support for Barry
Goldwater. While Goldwater was too radical for many voters, Reagan offered
an appealing voice for conservatives.

Courtesy Ronald Reagan Library.

conservative themes such as the privatization of Social Security and the use of tactical nuclear weapons in Vietnam. Reagan cochaired the Citizens for Goldwater chapter in California.

Reagan played an important role in the campaign, which brought him national attention as a potential candidate. On October 27, 1964, Goldwater's campaign broadcast a commercial that featured Reagan delivering a staged speech. In an address to an audience of conservatives, formally called "A Time for Choosing" and later known as "The Speech," Reagan urged Goldwater's supporters to embrace their political values proudly (Document 2). Reagan railed against liberal programs, using specific statistics and facts to challenge the assertions that Democrats had been successful at improving society. To illustrate his point, Reagan recounted the story of two friends who were speaking to a Cuban refugee who had escaped Fidel Castro's Communist regime. As they spoke, Reagan said, one of his friends remarked, "We don't know how lucky we are" to live in the United States. The Cuban said, "How lucky you are? I had someplace to escape to." Reagan added, "This is the last stand on earth. And this idea that government is beholden to the people, that it has no other source of power except the sovereign people, is still the newest and the most unique idea in all the long history of man's relation to man. This is the issue of this election: Whether we believe in our capacity for self-government or whether we abandon the American revolution and confess that a little intellectual elite in a far-distant capitol can plan our lives for us better than we can plan them ourselves." Reagan was even willing to harshly mock liberal ideals, criticizing Johnson-era Great Society antipoverty programs. Refuting the existence of widespread poverty, Reagan said, "We were told four years ago that 17 million people went to bed hungry each night. Well that was probably true. They were all on a diet." The combination of a polished Hollywood delivery, details and statistics, and lofty rhetoric proved attractive to members of a nascent movement that had been dismissed as unintelligent, irrational, and politically marginal.

The Gubernatorial Years

Two years after Goldwater's failed election bid, and at the urging of close confidants and businessmen, Reagan decided to run for governor of California in 1966. His campaign lashed out against the excesses of the 1960s and portrayed the Democratic incumbent, Pat Brown, as a symbol of liberalism's failures. The Great Society, a reform campaign Lyndon Johnson announced in 1964, had sought to eliminate poverty and combat racial injustice. Although Johnson signed historic civil rights legislation, many civil rights advocates called for greater reforms to tackle issues such as police brutality and discrimination. Charges of police brutality led to rioting in several American cities, including the Watts section of Los Angeles. While many supported civil rights, urban unrest and the persistence of poverty fueled anxieties about the negative consequences of the Great Society. Reagan's campaign played to these fears with arguments that the streets were no longer safe as a result of liberal judicial rulings and government policies.[16] Reagan also criticized the civil rights and anti–Vietnam War student protesters at the University of California at Berkeley, who insisted on their right to free speech, for undermining law and order on the campus (Document 3).

During the campaign, Reagan faced the dilemma of trying to balance the support of right-wing organizations with the need to attract moderate Republican voters. This was a challenge he faced throughout his political career. Reagan distanced himself from extreme right-wing organizations such as the John Birch Society but was always careful not to alienate their members.[17] His victory over Pat Brown revealed that voters in the Sunbelt, especially white, suburban, middle-class voters, were warming to the conservative message of smaller government, law and order, and traditional values[18] (Document 4).

During his governorship, Reagan had considerable difficulty fulfilling his promises to conservatives. He faced a Democratic legislature, where Speaker of the Assembly Jesse Unruh turned out to be a strong political opponent. Reagan agreed to numerous compromises with Democrats, a political instinct he retained throughout his years as a politician. Governing this large state gave Reagan insights into the adaptations that conservatives would have to make once they held power. To resolve the fiscal crisis facing California — a $200 million deficit — he agreed to the largest tax increase in the state's history. George Deukmejian, a Republican state senator, observed, "A lot of people, including me, thought he would be ideological. We learned quickly that he was very practical."[19] Moreover, Reagan's budgets increased state spending, and he backed off a number of proposed cuts, including those for mental health facilities, when they triggered a political backlash. Reagan also signed a liberal abortion rights law that was anathema to many conservatives.[20]

During his governorship, Reagan continued to test the national waters. He entered several Republican presidential primaries in 1968. Although he won in California, former vice president Richard Nixon had secured all the necessary delegates to be the party's nominee. As a shrewd political tactician who hoped to shift the country in a conservative direction,

Nixon attempted to build a new Republican majority in his run for president. This new coalition would attract white southerners who were fleeing the Democratic party, as well as northern working-class voters who felt out of step with the Great Society. The not-so-subtle appeals to racial antagonism—usually through law-and-order rhetoric about the rioting in places such as Watts and Detroit—helped Nixon undercut some of the appeal of Democrat George Wallace, the segregationist Alabama governor who made these themes central to his third-party campaign. Nixon also appealed to Americans who were dismayed by antiwar activists. With the Democrats in disarray, Nixon won the 1968 election.

Hoping to diminish some of the frustration that emerged with the compromises he had made in Sacramento during his first year in office, Reagan took a strong stand against student protesters. The governor ordered the National Guard to end student protests at Berkeley. The Guard stayed on the campus for seventeen days until they were able to restore order. Ending what Reagan saw as the chaos at Berkeley enhanced his popularity, and he won reelection in 1970, defeating Jesse Unruh, who proved to be weaker as a candidate than as a legislator.

Like many conservatives, Reagan did not think highly of President Nixon's record. He was unhappy when Nixon eased relations with China in 1971 and 1972 and signed the SALT I arms limitation agreement with the Soviets in 1972. Conservatives believed that SALT I would be dangerous for the security of the United States. Reagan also criticized Nixon for allowing the federal budget to expand dramatically to pay for programs such as Social Security and federal welfare. Nixon's involvement in the Watergate break-in and subsequent scandal led Reagan to conclude that the president was not a respectable person, although he publicly supported Nixon throughout the scandal.[21] The most important positive accomplishment for conservatives had been Nixon's landslide reelection in 1972, since he had achieved victories throughout formerly Democratic southern states, a hopeful sign that the electorate was up for grabs and possibly moving to the right.

A Conservative Movement Comes of Age

During the 1970s, the conservative movement grew stronger.[22] The movement consisted of several factions, not all of which fit neatly together. Business conservatives and libertarians pushed for deregulation of markets and lower taxation. Midwestern Republicans continued to espouse traditional claims of fiscal conservatism and limited overseas involvement. An emerging group, neoconservative Democrats, offered another hopeful sign. This group comprised intellectuals and political elites who had become frustrated with their party's domestic and foreign policies in the 1960s. Similarly, racial busing programs in cities spawned local community opposition to the liberal Democratic civil rights agenda in the North as well as in the South.

Other conservative groups organized to promote a return to what they saw as traditional cultural values. The Supreme Court's 1973 *Roe v. Wade* ruling legalizing abortion motivated many conservative activists to engage in politics. Conservative activists also challenged some of the key platforms of the era's feminist movement. Phyllis Schlafly, a leading conservative who had supported Barry Goldwater, headed the campaign against the Equal Rights Amendment, which Congress passed in 1972 and sent to the states for ratification. Evangelical Christians were among the most aggressive and well-organized participants in the newly emerging conservative movement. Under the direction of evangelical preachers such as Billy Graham and Jerry Falwell, they became politically involved and created an industry of television and radio shows, books and magazines, and personal events to spread their gospel.

There was also a concerted campaign to expand the intellectual presence of conservatives. The movement sought to counter liberal strength in the media and think tanks by forming and strengthening their own institutions, such as the American Enterprise Institute and the Cato Institute. One of the most influential of these operations was the Heritage Foundation, funded in 1973 by beer magnate Joseph Coors. A network of conservative philanthropists poured money into allied foundations to underwrite its ideological campaign.[23]

In 1975, conservatives were openly frustrated with President Gerald Ford's administration, which they saw as too moderate. Ford, the Republican vice president who succeeded Nixon after he resigned in 1974, started off on the wrong foot with conservatives by nominating the liberal Republican Nelson Rockefeller as vice president. Then the conservatives felt that Ford did not do enough to cut government spending. Further, the White House continued Nixon's policy of détente with the Soviet Union, attempting to ease tensions through arms negotiations. *National Review* publisher William Rusher went so far as to call for the replacement of the Republican party with a more conservative third party. It was accurate to say that Ford, Reagan explained in a 1975 interview with United Press International, was a "caretaker president."[24]

More than any other politician of the 1970s, Reagan tapped into the energies of the conservative movement. Out of office in 1975, Reagan returned to radio broadcasting, delivering daily political addresses

Portrait of the Future President, 1976.
Ronald Reagan appealed to Americans' romance with rugged frontier individualism. A skilled actor and politician, Reagan carefully used images, like this
iconic portrait of him wearing a cowboy hat on his ranch, to project his values
to American voters. The West was an important region for the new Republican
majority.

Courtesy Ronald Reagan Library.

that reached ten million to fifteen million listeners nationwide. Writing these speeches himself, Reagan honed his anti-Communist, antigovernment arguments. Free from the confines of government, Reagan could espouse his political views in an undiluted fashion. The editors of the *Wall Street Journal* thought that Reagan's ideological drive was fresh in a political system that favored pragmatism.[25]

Reagan decided to challenge Ford in the 1976 Republican presidential primaries. He began his campaign by focusing on domestic issues such as welfare reform and called for a massive $90 billion cut in federal spending, eliminating the federal role in welfare, education, Medicare, and other programs. State and local governments could provide services if they wanted to, he said. When asked what would happen to the poor in laggard states, Reagan responded that they were free to move. "You can vote with your feet in this country," he said. "If a state is mismanaged, you can move elsewhere."[26] Despite the political costs incurred by Barry Goldwater for taking on the issue in 1964, Reagan suggested that part of the Social Security Trust Funds should be invested in the stock market or in industrial bonds.[27]

Reagan's campaign used sophisticated media techniques to sell the candidate. Reagan held "citizens' press conferences" at local institutions such as schools, where he answered questions from "average" citizens. Reporters were allowed to cover the events but not ask questions. Reagan prepared for the types of questions that he normally received from the local citizens. The campaign then broadcast clips from the conferences as commercials on television stations, making them appear as news stories. Through these tactics, the campaign hoped to overcome the challenge of voters seeing Reagan as an actor and thus someone who might be disingenuous or not up to the job.[28] Still, Reagan lost in the early primaries, and pundits speculated that he would have to drop out of the race.

Facing the possibility of defeat in March, Reagan turned almost all of his attention to the issue of national security. He believed in peace through strength, an argument he had honed since the 1950s. He was not against negotiations with the Soviet Union in the future, but he insisted that the United States was making bad agreements and allowing the Soviets to advance in military and territorial strength. He also warned that Ford was negotiating with the Panamanian government to give back the Panama Canal. These national security issues resonated with conservative voters, especially in the South (Document 5). In North Carolina, Reagan received support from the state's first Republican senator of the twentieth century, Jesse Helms, who had developed close ties to the grassroots conservative movement, including its more extremist elements. Young Americans for Freedom, the American Conservative Union, and other allied organizations on the right mobilized North Carolinian voters.[29] Reagan won the North Carolina primary on March 23, followed by a string of victories in Texas, Alabama, Georgia, Nebraska, California, and Indiana.

In the end, Ford won the Republican party nomination, but Reagan's victory came in both defining the terms of the contest and influencing the GOP's agenda. Reagan's primary wins had caused Ford to move to the right. "Reagan was the dominating presence of the 1976 campaign," concluded William F. Buckley Jr., "even though Ford was the formal victor."[30]

The general election proved difficult for Ford. The country's memories of Nixon and the Watergate scandal haunted his campaign, especially Ford's decision to pardon the former president. Economic stagnation and high inflation left citizens disillusioned with Ford's economic policies. At their convention, Democrats selected Georgia governor Jimmy Carter, who presented himself as an "outsider" who could restore trust in government after Watergate. His southern upbringing offered the possibility of appealing to Democratic voters in the South who had fled to the Republicans. Carter conducted an effective campaign that played on the portrayal of him as someone who could heal the country while also securing core Democratic votes.

Carter won the election by one of the narrowest margins in U.S. history. The former governor received 50.1 percent of the popular vote and 297 electoral votes to Ford's 48 percent of the popular vote and 240 electoral votes. (Reagan received one electoral vote.) The Democrats retained control of Congress. One of the most important developments in the campaign was the GOP's shift to the right. Conservatives had gained traction in the party and started to vanquish the memories of Goldwater's 1964 landslide defeat.

Carter's Malaise

During the next few years, while Jimmy Carter was in the White House and Democrats controlled Congress, conservatives continued to solidify their movement. In 1978, conservative activists used the debate over the Panama Canal to mobilize Republican support in Congress. Carter had signed treaties with Panama in which he agreed to turn over the canal by the end of the century, and he worked hard to win Senate ratification. Carter also launched a new round of arms limitation talks with the Soviet

Union, called SALT II, which conservatives said were proof that he was weak on defense. In 1978, evangelical Christians were livid when the Internal Revenue Service threatened to alter the tax-exempt status of private religious schools, strengthening their support of conservatives.

At the local level, conservatives were making their mark in a number of areas, including taxation. The specific problem that working- and middle-class Americans were facing was "bracket creep," in which inflation pushed taxpayers into higher tax brackets without any real gains in income. In California, businessman Howard Jarvis headed a campaign to cut property taxes through ballot initiatives. In 1978, California voters passed Proposition 13 by large margins, which cut property taxes by 57 percent and triggered a debate about all types of taxes.

Dejected over his loss to Ford, Reagan maintained a political action committee, called the Committee for the Republicans, which distributed unused funds from his presidential campaigns to conservative congressional candidates[31] (Document 6). During the Carter years, Reagan continued to host a weekly radio show and write a syndicated newspaper column emphasizing his signature themes of stronger defense and smaller government. Through such activities, he continued as a vital and visible force for a growing conservative movement.

Carter's problems as president facilitated this conservative mobilization. The economy was in shambles. High inflation and high unemployment, which contemporaries called stagflation, continued to shackle Americans' well-being. The corrosive inflation of the 1970s stemmed from Vietnam War deficits, a surge in oil and commodity prices, and poor economic management. A fiscal conservative who sought to fight inflation by trimming government, Carter disappointed traditional liberals and organized labor, who called for New Deal–style spending. The president also frustrated those who had hoped he would be a greater advocate for civil rights and feminist causes. Alienating liberals without winning over conservatives, Carter was in political trouble.

Carter's approval rating sank to a new low in the summer of 1979, when the Iranian Revolution and a second round of oil price increases by the Organization of Petroleum Exporting Countries (OPEC) — the first being in 1973 — led to gasoline shortages and long lines at the pump. On July 15, 1979, Carter delivered a controversial speech that became known as the "Malaise" speech. The president's pollster, Patrick Caddell, had convinced him to address a psychological and moral crisis facing the nation. He characterized the "fundamental threat" to American democracy as a "crisis of confidence." He laid blame on a society oriented toward a culture in which Americans valued themselves based on "what one owns" rather than "what one does." "Too many of us now tend to worship self-indulgence and consumption," Carter said. The president explained his energy proposals to the nation and asked Americans to "take no unnecessary trips, to use carpools or public transportation whenever you can, to park your car one extra day per week, to obey the speed limit, and to set your thermostats to save fuel." Many Americans felt that he was blaming them rather than offering a solution, and the speech in effect highlighted his own weaknesses as well as the nation's.[32]

In addition to the oil crisis, twin foreign policy crises plagued the Carter administration. The taking of American hostages by Iranian revolutionaries in the fall of 1979 and the Soviet invasion of Afghanistan later that year made it appear as though the White House had lost control of international events. Even when Carter tried to act like more of a hawk, conservative Republicans and neoconservative Democrats dismissed the president's change of tone as insincere.

As Carter stumbled, the conservative movement was gaining strength. In the summer of 1979, the Reverend Jerry Falwell announced the formation of the Moral Majority. This organization brought together conservative evangelical Protestants who had gradually become more involved politically in an effort to promote conservative social issues such as school prayer and opposition to abortion and homosexuality. The existence of this and other grassroots conservative groups, along with a rise in unemployment and record-high inflation, meant that Carter would face a tough race for reelection.

The Election of 1980

In 1980, the Republicans nominated Reagan as their presidential candidate. Appealing to conservative movement activists and party leaders, Reagan defeated the establishment candidate George H. W. Bush in the primaries; Bush would run as Reagan's vice president. From the start of his campaign, Reagan focused on the theme of national decline under Carter. In contrast to the gloomy demeanor that Carter displayed in his "Malaise" speech, Reagan, the optimistic former governor of California, promised to restore American confidence without asking for sacrifice from citizens.

Reagan's campaign stitched together different strands of the conservative movement. He attacked the inefficiencies of domestic programs such as welfare and announced his support for steep tax reductions. Reaching out to the Moral Majority, he criticized abortion. Although he continued to avoid the explicit racial politics that were embraced by some on the right, Reagan did make speeches that touched on racial tensions in America. He began his presidential campaign in 1980 at the Neshoba County Fair in Mississippi, not far from the site where white supremacists killed three civil rights activists in 1964. In his speech, Reagan endorsed states' rights, a rhetorical phrase that challenged federal commitment to civil rights and potentially appealed to southern white voters who opposed federally mandated integration (Document 7). Critics said that the speech aimed to send a tacit message to southern racists that Reagan would be friendly to their cause. During the campaign, Reagan also went after Carter on foreign policy, targeting the president's willingness to negotiate with the Soviet Union and his tolerance of left-wing forces in Latin America.

Reagan drew on campaign tactics that he had perfected over the years. On September 15, 1980, for instance, his team put together the Capitol Steps Event, in which he, Bush, Republican leaders in the House and Senate, and 150 Republican candidates congregated on the Capitol steps and made a series of promises that included cuts in spending and income taxes, incentives to encourage private investments, and "stepped-up" efforts to strengthen foreign policy. According to one reporter, "Republican presidential nominee Ronald Reagan and GOP congressional leaders staged what amounted to a family portrait day on the Capitol steps yesterday—a picture of well-disciplined harmony to contrast what Reagan called the 'legislative chaos' of the Democrats."[33]

Despite his antigovernment rhetoric, Reagan made it clear that conservatism was not really a debate about government versus no government. Rather, the debate was about reordering priorities. Conservatives wanted to place more emphasis on spending for defense and federal subsidies for industry (either directly or via tax breaks) and less on social programs. They were also committed to a massive tax cut as a way to spur economic growth.

Besides Reagan, Carter had to fend off a challenge for the Democratic party nomination from the liberal icon Senator Edward M. Kennedy, who was farther to the left politically than Carter. Kennedy won several major primaries, including New York, Pennsylvania, Michigan, and California. Carter barely beat out Kennedy for the nomination, and the contest undercut much of the enthusiasm of liberal Democrats. Patrick Caddell wrote to the president that "the country's general mood remains much as it has since late 1978. The public is anxious, confused, hostile, and sour." Carter faced a tough opponent in Reagan, he added.

But he warned, "Reagan cannot be made an evil person—unlike a decade ago, age has taken the harshness off the image."[34]

Above all, the Carter campaign could not figure out how to overcome Reagan's charisma. The former actor appealed to voters personally. Whereas Carter had done well in 1976, when "character" was the issue in the wake of Watergate, in 1980 the issue was leadership. And Reagan—strong, handsome, athletic, full of confidence—was a leader. His campaign of rebirth and renewal contrasted with Carter's image as an inept president who could not respond to international crises or economic decline. Carter offered sobering realism, whereas Reagan sold hope about restoring American strength without great sacrifice. Americans, after a decade of economic troubles, wanted the latter. In a campaign speech in Jersey City, New Jersey, with the Statue of Liberty in the background, Reagan told a crowd of white ethnic workers, "A recession is when your neighbor loses his job. A depression is when you lose yours. Recovery is when Jimmy Carter loses his."[35]

For much of 1980, Carter's attention was focused on the U.S. hostages in Iran. Beginning on November 4, 1979, terrorists held fifty-two hostages captive for 444 days, an ordeal that ABC's *Nightline* featured each night. The White House conducted around-the-clock negotiations in an effort to get them freed. The single military operation to rescue the hostages resulted in the deaths of eight U.S. military men and ended in failure. The president's inability to obtain their release played into Republican attacks on him as ineffective.

Even with all of Carter's problems and Reagan's appeal, the race was neck and neck throughout September and October. Polls showed that the candidates were even, including in the South. The power of incumbency and the strength of the Democratic organization in key parts of the country meant that Carter was still hard to beat.

The race didn't swing dramatically to Reagan until the final weeks of the campaign. During the single presidential debate that Carter agreed to, which took place one week before the election, Reagan fared well. Carter used the debate to paint Reagan as an extremist—for example, reminding voters that Reagan had opposed Medicare upon its creation in 1965. Reagan used the debate to demonstrate how out of touch and negative Carter was. Carter sounded more like a professor than a president when he provided a detailed argument about the problems of health care in America. Viewers could see Reagan on camera literally laughing as Carter spoke. Reagan simply shook his head at Carter and said, "There you go again." Reagan delivered the knockout punch in his closing remarks when he asked viewers, "Are you better off than you were four years ago? Is it easier for you to go and buy things in the stores than it was four years ago? . . . Is America as respected throughout the world as it was?"[36]

Reagan took forty-four states to Carter's six. He had built a broad coalition of conservative factions, bringing together social conservatives, pro-business/antitax voters, and foreign policy hawks, and effectively linked the Republican party to the conservative movement. Millions of evangelical Christians contributed to Reagan's victory, and he made major inroads in the South and Southwest, where Democrats traditionally prevailed. According to political scientists Earl Black and Merle Black, "Reagan's presidency built the firmest grassroots base of Republican partisans ever to appear in the region."[37] He also gained ground among northeastern and midwestern blue-collar voters, who were formerly loyal Democrats but now became known as "Reagan Democrats." As one white carpenter in Brooklyn, New York, put it, "The liberals and the press look down on hard hats like me."[38]

While the popular vote was not a landslide, the Electoral College tally and the congressional election results told a different story. Reagan received 43.9 million popular votes and 489 electoral votes. Carter received approximately 35 million popular votes and 49 electoral votes. Independent party candidate John Anderson received nearly 6 million popular votes. The Democrats retained control of the House, but the Senate shifted to Republican hands. The GOP picked up a net gain of 12 Senate seats with a 53 to 46 majority. Nine Democratic incumbents targeted by conservatives were defeated. In the House, Republicans picked up 35 seats, giving them 191 seats to the Democrats' 242. Southern conservative Democrats also recorded significant gains, adding strength to the conservative coalition.

DOMESTIC POLITICS

From the moment of his victory, Reagan sought to transform his win into a decisive event in American history. Since the 1950s, Reagan had supported free enterprise, low taxes, and deregulation. In his 1981 inaugural address, Reagan said, "In this present crisis, government is not the solution to our problem; government is the problem. From time to time we've been tempted to believe that society has become too complex to be managed by self-rule, that government by an elite group is superior to government for, by and of the people" (Document 8). Enough was enough, proclaimed Reagan. But what did that mean? What would happen when conservatism finally arrived in Washington?

Cutting Taxes

The first order of business for the Reagan administration was to press hard for a dramatic tax cut. The members of the administration, along with their critics, would judge their success by whether they could win on this issue. Reagan had long had an antipathy toward taxes. In the 1940s, when he went from rags to riches as a result of his Hollywood career, his income put him in the highest tax bracket, where 94 percent of his earnings went for taxes. Since his GE days, he had promoted tax cuts. As a presidential hopeful, he was primed to hear an intellectual rationale that buttressed his beliefs. That came from economist Arthur Laffer, who argued, in what became known as the Laffer Curve, that high taxes work as a disincentive for businesses and individuals to invest money and produce. In 1977, Jack Kemp, a conservative congressman from upstate New York, latched onto Laffer's ideas and, along with William Roth of Delaware, translated them into the Kemp-Roth tax cut bill. Kemp maintained that cutting federal income taxes by 30 percent would uncork the "creative genius that has always invigorated America" but remained "submerged, waiting like a genie in a bottle to be loosed."

This supply-side theory held that tax cuts geared toward the upper income brackets and corporations would stimulate investment, which would trickle down to benefit those in lower income brackets. Early in the 1980 primaries, Bush denounced Reagan's supply-side theories as "voodoo economics," challenging the claim that tax cuts would boost economic growth and diminish deficits. But according to Jude Wanniski, the *Wall Street Journal* editorial writer who became a leading spokesman for supply-side economics, the Laffer Curve "set off a symphony" in Reagan's imagination, and upon learning about it, he believed "instantly that it was true and would never have a doubt thereafter."[39]

As soon as he was elected, Reagan's team swung into action. Edwin Meese, the conservative lawyer who had served as Reagan's chief of staff when he was governor of California, handled the transition into the White House. Meese then assumed a role as presidential counselor, guaranteeing a right-leaning perspective close to the president. As deputy chief of staff, Michael Deaver, who also had worked with Reagan since his years as governor, crafted the president's public image, using Reagan's skill as an actor to build a rapport with the public and thereby enhance his political capital. As David Gergen, the communications director, would later explain, Deaver was a "master of political theater. . . . He brought an imagination and an eye and a sense of the country to the presidency."[40] Together, these old California hands worked with James A. Baker III, Reagan's more moderate chief of staff, to make cutting taxes the top priority. While Baker may not have been as conservative as Reagan, he understood the centrality of the tax cut in securing the Republicans' success.

Reagan's staff promoted the tax cut as the remedy to the nation's ills. The cut capitalized on the popular perception of big government as inefficient and counterproductive and also promised to relieve the pinch in the pocketbook that millions of Americans were experiencing as a result of bracket creep. Double-digit inflation caused real economic hardship, especially for millions of Americans whose fixed incomes and salaries did not keep up. Although tax cuts were traditionally seen to trigger further inflation, the Reagan administration packaged this policy as a cure for the country's economic and political problems. After a decade of stagflation, from which politicians had been able to offer little relief, Reagan's tax cut represented an appealing solution.

The tax cut was the centerpiece of a larger policy agenda that favored the market instead of the government as the guarantor of prosperity. Deregulation had begun under Carter, but Reagan would extend its reach. Throughout his years in office, Reagan pushed to end or curtail federal regulation of welfare, affirmative action, unionization, and industry and finance, the last of which would result in a speculative boom in the savings and loan industry and on Wall Street.

Reagan's support of market-oriented policies and smaller government was part of a larger cultural shift in the early 1980s. The president's deregulatory policies privileged a notion of individual advancement and personal achievement, as did much of the popular culture of the era. In the early 1980s, the number-one-ranked television show, *Dallas*, which told the story of a Texas oil family, celebrated wealth, greed, and ruthless competition. While realizing that not everyone could achieve that kind of lifestyle, Americans became fascinated by stories of fabulous riches and spectacular success, which they could see highlighted on television shows such as *Lifestyles of the Rich and Famous*. In much of his rhetoric, Reagan suggested that success was attainable for all Americans, not just the elite, through hard work, faith, and moral courage, provided that government got out of the way.

Under Reagan, the Republican party assumed a new position as defender of the average American. Since the days of Richard Nixon, the GOP had sought to capture the loyalty of white, ethnic, traditionally Democratic, working-class voters who had once seen the liberal state as their friend and ally but had become disillusioned. Feeling left out and resentful of the Great Society programs aimed at helping the poor and minorities, these voters were up for political grabs. The Reagan White House, with assistance from young acolytes such as Peggy Noonan, one of Reagan's favorite speechwriters, attempted to win over voters to the Republican party. Noonan was part of what she called the "quiet realignment of the eighties, in which what had seemed in my youth the party of rich dullards became, almost in spite of itself, the party of the people."[41]

Noonan's personal political journey from Democrat to Republican captured the sincere hope and anticipation that a young, right-leaning cadre of reformers brought with them to the Reagan White House. As working-class Irish Catholics from Brooklyn, New York, Noonan, her parents, and her grandparents were loyal Democrats. In the 1960s, as a young child, Noonan bought two goldfish in Woolworth's and named them Jack and Jackie after the Kennedys. Her family moved to Long Island and then to New Jersey, where Noonan graduated from high school in 1968. As they traveled from city to suburb, the Noonans barely managed to make ends meet and keep up with mortgage payments. After high school, Noonan looked for a job. As she explains, "I didn't go to college after high school. I went to Newark, to work as a clerk at the Aetna Insurance Company." She worked to put herself through college, attending classes at night. Noonan felt out of step with the radicalism on college campuses. "It was Jersey, and we were first-in-our-family college students, and we were working and studying and partying, and only rich kids wanted to occupy a dean's office; normal kids just wanted to not get called on the carpet there."[42]

David Stockman, who became Reagan's director of the Office of Management and Budget, had a similar awakening, traveling an even greater distance from his days as a radical college student in the 1960s to a Christian fundamentalist to a free-market true believer. As he would later recall about the early Reagan years, "I began to feel as if I was part of a movement. My revolutionary fires had been rekindled once again."[43] Stockman had perhaps the most sophisticated ideological and long-term view. In spite of the supply-side logic, which reasoned that tax cuts would pay for themselves by stimulating economic growth, Stockman knew ahead of time that a massive tax cut would most likely spawn deficits. As he saw it, the deficit that was likely to result would be like, as one journalist described it, a "tightening noose around the size of the government." Deficits would make additional government spending difficult, a strategy Stockman would later refer to as "starving the beast."[44]

Economist Milton Friedman had helped to popularize this notion of a minimalist government. Winner of the 1976 Nobel Prize, Friedman was better known to the average middle-class American through his regular column in *Newsweek*, which he had been writing since 1966. Throughout the economic turmoil of the 1970s, a decade that saw the failed efforts of wage controls, price freezes, and oil allocations, Friedman had laid before the public a simple proposition: If the government got out of the way, the economy would once again flourish. In 1980, Friedman and his wife, Rose, published the best-selling *Free to Choose* as a free-market manifesto, which was turned into a ten-part miniseries on public television. Others, such as Jude Wanniski and George Gilder, also espoused market ideas for popular audiences with a moral, almost religious fervor. Wanniski believed that taxation and government regulation encouraged illicit economic activity such as prostitution and crime. Gilder, who also wrote for the *Wall Street Journal*, saw capitalism in religious terms: "Faith in man, faith in the future, faith in the return of giving, faith in the mutual benefits of trade, faith in the providence of God are all essential to successful capitalism."[45]

Reagan, of course, played the leading role in promoting the tax cut (Document 9). On February 18, 1981, Reagan explained his plan to Congress and the nation. Much like Franklin Roosevelt soothing a frightened populace scarred by unemployment in 1933, Reagan worked to ease the minds of a citizenry wracked by uncertainty, doubt, and anxiety. The tax bill would slash federal income and business taxes by 30 percent over three years; cut capital gains, estate, and gift taxes; and speed up depreciation allowances for business investments. The bill also would eliminate bracket creep. Reagan additionally pushed for reduced federal spending and sought to cut the budget by $47 billion. His budget bill called for eliminating or scaling back regulations while also trimming welfare programs from Social Security and Medicaid to food stamps, public service jobs, education, and child nutrition.

To apply pressure on legislators, Reagan tapped into a network of grassroots conservatives. Lyn Nofziger, White House political director, and his deputy Lee Atwater relied on these well-organized conservatives, who had become a formidable right-wing base. As Atwater put it, "He's got more people committed to him than anyone else. They're ready, able and willing to go into action at a moment's notice."[46] The tactics that conservative activists had employed in the 1964 and 1980 campaigns, such as Richard Viguerie's use of direct mail to reach millions of citizens who had displayed some interest in the conservative cause, were now put into operation to influence legislators. Reagan also worked behind the scenes and, in the four months before the bill's passage, met with congressmen about seventy times, paying special attention to the forty-seven conservative southern Democrats in the House of Representatives whose help he would need to get his measures through.

Reagan's economic package gained momentum after John Hinckley Jr.'s attempted assassination of the president on March 30, 1981. This episode frightened Americans, who had been traumatized in the 1960s by the assassinations of John F. Kennedy, Robert Kennedy, and Martin Luther King Jr. Reagan, though shot in the lung, made a quick recovery and got a boost in his popularity ratings. His press secretary, James Brady, was not so fortunate, suffering permanent paralysis as a result of one of Hinckley's gunshots. Addressing Congress in a nationally televised speech, Reagan assured the nation of his health and used the occasion to push hard for his tax cut, equating his personal recovery with that of the nation.[47]

On Capitol Hill, budget director David Stockman spearheaded the effort to win the necessary votes and, with Republican help, keep the package intact (Document 10). If Reagan was the public face of the tax cut and used his bully pulpit accordingly, Stockman was the main tactician formulating legislative strategy, especially on budget cuts. Some years later, he wrote, "It would be up to me to design the Reagan Revolution," and "if the others weren't going to get his administration's act together, I would."[48] Corporate lobbyists and New Right activists complemented his efforts by pressuring legislators. Thomas P. "Tip" O'Neill, the powerful Democratic Speaker of the House, who would lose on this issue, said, with only a trace of humor, that companies such as Exxon and Philip Morris "turned over their switchboards" to lobby on behalf of the president's bill. This was, as O'Neill described it, a "telephone blitz like this nation has never seen."[49] As early as May, O'Neill could tell that the president had won over the nation. The administration had sweetened the legislation's appeal by allowing Democrats to add their own provisions that would benefit constituents in their districts.

On July 29, 1981, six months after Reagan had been sworn in, Congress passed the Economic Recovery Tax Act. On August 13, Reagan signed the bill. At the same time, he also signed the Omnibus Reconciliation Act, which cut spending by $35 billion. Although the final tax bill reduced taxes by 25 percent instead of 30 percent, it was still a major victory and the single largest tax cut in American history. Just as important to the conservative agenda, the measure lowered the overall tax rates to a range of 11 to 50 percent. Reflecting the challenges of conservative governance, the administration was unable to find support for all the budget cuts it sought, which meant the deficit would increase dramatically. But the passage of the tax cut filled Reagan with confidence, as this was seen as his signature legislation.

Simultaneous with this success, Reagan scored another political triumph in his confrontation with organized labor. On August 3, 1981, thirteen thousand members of the Professional Air Traffic Controllers Organization (PATCO) — one of the few unions that had endorsed Reagan in 1980 — went on strike. Although PATCO bargained and functioned much like other unions, these workers' standing as federal employees prohibited them from striking. Reagan gave them forty-eight hours to return to work or be fired. Two days later, he made good on his word and in a single gesture transformed postwar labor relations (Document 11). Since the New Deal, the Democrats had supported and protected the rights of organized labor, and even Republican administrations had accepted unions and their right to strike as legitimate means of negotiation. With the firing and replacing of these striking workers, Reagan dealt a serious blow to the political power and economic clout of an already waning union movement.

This move against organized labor came against the backdrop of an equally dramatic shift in monetary policy. Throughout the 1970s, the appearance of inflation and unemployment at the same time presented policymakers with a difficult choice. They could attempt to fight inflation with higher interest rates and risk higher unemployment, or they could stimulate the economy and face higher inflation. In 1979, President Carter had appointed Paul Volcker as chairman of the Federal Reserve. Volcker was devoted to ending inflation and was willing to push the nation into a recession to do so. Under Reagan, he got the necessary political support and took tough actions. With Reagan in office, Volcker limited the expansion of the money supply and insisted on high

---

(Opposite) *National Address on Tax Cut Legislation, July 27, 1981.*
Besides anticommunism, supply-side economics was at the heart of Reagan's political philosophy. In his first year, Reagan pushed through a historic tax cut, which would be one of his lasting legacies.
Courtesy Ronald Reagan Library.

interest rates to stabilize the economy, even as that cost Americans their jobs.

The challenge to organized labor, the tight money policy, and the tax victory, along with substantial increases in the defense budget, signaled a new direction—"more guns, less butter," as contemporaries labeled it. But the key question was, would Reagan's success last?

The Persistence of Liberalism

In assessing the chances for further conservative victories, there were three main questions: First, did the 1980 electoral victory signal a genuine realignment of voters to the right? Second, how much would achieving the tax cut carry over to other conservative agendas? Third, would supply-side economics actually succeed in bringing economic growth?

First, did the successes of 1981 stem from Reagan's popularity as "the Great Communicator" during a honeymoon phase of his presidency, or did they reflect a new conservative mood of the country—a Reagan Revolution? Much of the administration's appeal was Reagan himself. In spite of the low opinion many critics had of this seventy-year-old, cowboy-hat-wearing actor, Reagan proved to be a highly skilled speaker, and his team made sure to use his talents to maximum advantage, staging all his performances and even suggesting camera angles. This carefully choreographed strategy of Michael Deaver's worked well in a television age. In the 1980s, as the readership of daily newspapers fell substantially from 73 percent to 50 percent, more Americans got their news from TV.[50] Reagan also witnessed a surge in his popularity after the failed assassination attempt. He made Americans feel good about themselves and their country, and that talent redounded to his political advantage.

But conservatives had to confront the persistence of liberalism and the popularity of big government programs such as Social Security and Medicare. Reagan learned that the hard way. By the early 1980s, politicians and budget experts began to worry about the future solvency of Social Security. Initially, David Stockman wanted to cut benefits for those who took early retirement. That solution was ideologically consistent with a conservative philosophy but politically risky. Sensing an opportunity for victory, House Democrats jumped on the president, pointing to the proposed cuts as evidence of Reagan's harsh views toward the elderly. Speaker Tip O'Neill said the proposal was a "rotten thing to do." Eager not to be outmaneuvered and wanting to avoid angering constituents, Senate Republican Bob Dole, chairman of the Finance Committee, pushed through a resolution denouncing the plan, which the Senate supported by a vote of 96–0.[51]

Liberals also continued to play a powerful role in politics, with Democrats retaining solid control of the House of Representatives. Beginning in the 1970s, the nation had witnessed the gradual weakening of the New Deal coalition of workers, liberals, intellectuals, minorities, Catholics, and Jews that had given the Democrats political strength since the 1930s. But weakening did not mean disappearance. Public interest groups flourished in the 1970s, representing middle-class causes such as environmentalism and consumer protection. Organizations associated with these issues raised significant amounts of money and developed sophisticated interest group operations.[52] On Capitol Hill, congressional reforms of the 1970s created more space for these groups to assert their power. Reforms weakened the control of committee chairmen and strengthened the influence of the rank and file over party leadership. As Democratic legislators outside the South generally became more liberal during the 1970s, Speaker O'Neill understood that to maintain his power, he had to champion their issues.[53]

Republicans also had a hard time solidifying a new governing coalition to support a continued shift to the right. The rise of suburbia meant the rapid expansion of new middle-class voters who were not as attached, as an earlier generation was, to urban political machines and had no fixed party identities. Americans were increasingly liberal on social issues and retained high expectations of what they should get in return for their tax dollars.[54] According to public opinion polls from the 1980 election, the majority of Americans supported Reagan's candidacy because they believed "it's time for a change." Only 11 percent said that they chose Reagan because "he is a real conservative."[55]

It was not even clear that their support of the Reagan tax cut signaled a rightward shift. Cutting taxes worked as policy for conservative governance because it combined an ideological vision of small government with tangible benefits for voters. That is, smaller government meant a smaller tax bill. But was antitax sentiment really, as Democratic pollster Patrick Caddell called it, a "revolution against government?"[56] Kevin Phillips, a leading Republican party strategist, did not think so and believed that Reagan and his advisers had misread the voters in 1980. Phillips thought that Americans, particularly middle-class Americans who populated the new suburbs in the South and Southwest, were more populist than conservative. As he pointed out, in these "frontier[s] of *frustration*" Americans "are hostile to the rich and to big business at the same time as they dislike minorities and the liberal politicians who seem to favor minority interests over those of the white working class." According to Phillips, the White House should not jump to the conclusion that Americans shared a conservative antigovernment ideology. He suggested that if Reagan's economic policies failed, voters might want the government to bail them out.[57]

The second question regarding conservatism, which stemmed from the question of the genuine conservative nature of voters, was how much the tax cut victory would extend to social issues such as abortion, busing, and school prayer. Unlike the issues of taxation, spending, and regulation, Reagan himself had not invested a lot of time in these issues in his public life. As governor of California, he had taken positions that angered conservatives, such as his support for a bill that liberalized abortion. Out of the hundreds of radio addresses Reagan delivered between his time as governor and his run for the presidency in 1980, he devoted only a few to social issues and delivered only two speeches on abortion. He spent the bulk of his time discussing communism, the economy, and the size of the federal government.

In his first years as president, many factions of the conservative movement expressed concern that they were not being heard in the White House. Richard Viguerie, the inventor of direct-mail grassroots conservative organizing, openly complained that the administration practiced politics as usual after having won an election based on the promise of change.[58] The tensions between conservative activists and Reagan dating back to the compromises he made while governor of California were amplified once he was in the White House (Documents 15 and 17).

Third, Reaganomics, the promise that supply-side tax cuts could boost economic growth and reduce the deficit, had not yet been fulfilled, and its failure could undermine Reagan's political popularity. As much as commentators described Reagan's tax victory as signaling the biggest policy change since Roosevelt's Hundred Days, they also acknowledged the challenges posed by tax cuts in the presence of a large federal budget and increases in military spending. In spite of the hopes of committed conservatives such as Stockman, the president and Congress lived in the real political world, where it was difficult, if not impossible, to cut spending. In 1982, spending for entitlement programs such as Medicare and Social Security—where people were guaranteed benefits in exchange for having paid into the system—accounted for 48 percent of the budget. Defense spending, accounting for 25 percent, was also growing under Reagan, while interest on the national debt constituted another 10 percent. All told, roughly 80 percent of the budget was nearly impossible to cut. Most cuts would continue to come, if they came at all, from smaller Great Society programs that benefited low-income Americans. As Stockman complained in an interview with *Washington Post* reporter William Greider, "The system has an enormous amount of inertia." "You can only do so much," he added (Document 12).[59]

By the fall of 1981, the most immediate impact of Reaganomics was a huge increase in the federal deficit. Throughout Reagan's time in office, budget cuts never went deep enough to offset decreasing revenue, and the result was a dramatic surge in annual budget deficits, which reached as high as $200 billion. (When Carter left office, the deficit was $80 billion.) The signs of an economic downturn were clear as the year drew to a close, and the need to finance the growing deficit was not welcomed by Wall Street investors worried about economic stability.

The recession of 1982 complicated the political future of Reagan's presidency. In the fall of 1982, unemployment reached 10.8 percent, the highest rate since the Great Depression. Smelling political blood, Democrats embarked on a concerted strategy to link the president to economic decline. According to Democratic party operative Kirk O'Donnell, "The economy is no longer our burden; it is a Republican economy." Democrats constantly spoke about the "Reagan recession" and what appeared to be the administration's lack of "fairness" in the economy.[60] Reagan responded aggressively (Documents 13 and 14). When asked by reporter Sam Donaldson whether he shared responsibility for the economic problems he was blaming Democrats for, the president quipped, "Oh my yes. I share responsibility—I was a Dem. for years."[61] Nevertheless, Reagan's popularity slipped to 44 percent in May 1982.

The budget deficit started to emerge as one of the big issues in public debate. The deficit was quickly becoming the guiding factor in making decisions about taxing and spending, undercutting the flexibility of liberals and conservatives alike. In August 1982, under pressure, Reagan signed the Tax Equity and Fiscal Responsibility Act, which increased taxes on businesses and added new excise taxes on tobacco, alcohol, communications, and airports. The *Conservative Digest* lambasted the president for having sold out the conservative agenda by accepting an increase in taxes.[62] But as the economy worsened, the White House would come under more pressure to reevaluate its economic plan (Document 16).

The 1982 midterm elections were a political setback, and commentators started to deliver funeral orations for the Reagan administration. Historically, the party in power experiences losses in midterm elections, but there have been some notable exceptions. In 1934, Franklin

Roosevelt cemented his political fortunes, and by extension those of the New Deal, with Democratic victories in the midterm elections. In 1982, Reagan and the conservatives were less fortunate. The Republicans lost twenty-six seats in the House, leaving the Democrats firmly in control. For a brief moment, Reagan seemed as ineffectual as Carter had been. Reagan strategists began to think about how to rebuild the president's support, including that among women, who as a group seemed to favor Democrats (Document 18). But the damage was undeniable. *New York Times* reporter Tom Wicker concluded, "There is no Reagan Revolution."[63]

Morning in America

Although Reagan was wounded, it was too soon to count him out. The administration received a boost when the economy started to recover in 1983. Recovery was uneven across the economy, as the manufacturing sector continued to slide, especially in certain industries such as steel, resulting in significant job losses.[64] Throughout the 1980s, income inequality expanded, with only the top 20 percent of families making gains and the rest of the population declining or stagnating. In general, workers who lost their manufacturing jobs fared poorly. But significant parts of the economy experienced real growth. Businesses added fifteen million jobs to the economy, mostly in the service and technology sectors, and many of these jobs were for professionals with college degrees, who were well compensated. Reagan eagerly claimed credit for the recovery, pointing to tax cuts, deregulation, the anti-inflationary policies of the Federal Reserve, and the private spending stimulated by those policies. The major increase in deficit spending and huge defense budgets also played a large role in recovery, as was clear in the high-tech, defense-related booms in the Boston area and on the West Coast. Much of the public gave Reagan credit for the return of growth while not worrying about the deficit.

Reagan's political pragmatism and the lessons of his first two years pushed him to avoid controversial stands on domestic policy. Reagan also recognized that he might have to compromise again on taxes, this time to address the problem of Social Security solvency. Reagan wanted to retain the support of working- and middle-class Americans who depended on receiving future benefits, but he also needed to avoid alienating his conservative base, which opposed higher taxes. The president appointed a bipartisan commission on Social Security to study the problem, and after the 1982 midterm elections, the commission recommended increasing payroll taxes and limiting cost increases, which Reagan endorsed. This tax increase, combined with increases in state taxes, meant that in spite of Reagan's historic tax cut, the average American family was paying the same taxes as it had before. The Social Security Amendments of 1983 shored up the short-term finances of Social Security and expanded coverage. Reagan appeared as an effective statesman who could rise above partisanship, reform a politically popular entitlement program, and yet deflect criticism for raising taxes.

Throughout, Reagan praised the values of the free market and offered the optimistic view that anyone could make it in America. *The Yuppie Handbook*, published in 1984, best captured a culture consumed with upward mobility, success, and striving. The word *yuppies* referred to young urban professionals, who, as *Time* magazine explained, "are dedicated to the twin goals of making piles of money and achieving perfection through physical fitness and therapy." Even if they lived better than most Americans, they represented a new cultural norm. *Newsweek* proclaimed 1984 the "Year of the Yuppie."[65] Reagan embraced this market culture of entrepreneurialism and hard work. He claimed that his favorite television show was *Family Ties*, a popular sitcom in which Alex P. Keaton (played by Michael J. Fox), a young Republican and Reagan supporter, rejected the values of his hippie parents.

Reagan matched his espousal of market values with a commitment to conservative social values. He filled several key cabinet positions with figures, such as Secretary of the Interior James Watt, who were closely connected to the right wing of the Republican party. In addition to being friendly to the interests of logging, mining, and oil companies, Watt articulated the concerns that were important to social conservatives at the time. In a 1983 commencement speech at Jerry Falwell's Liberty Baptist College, Watt called on his listeners to lead a "Christian revolution" in the country. Advocates of abortion "seek to destroy life for the convenience of others," Watt warned. The United States "is a hurting nation," he said, "a nation that needs help." Shortly after this speech, Watt banned the Beach Boys from playing at the National Mall in Washington, D.C., on the Fourth of July, denouncing their fans as "riffraff."[66] Outspoken and often controversial, Watt helped to mobilize and win support from the religious Right, although ultimately Reagan would have to let him go after he said about his staff, "I have a black, a woman, two Jews and a cripple. And we have talent."[67] Although Reagan did not expend major political capital on these social issues, rhetorically he signaled his support of traditional families, prayer in school, and anti-homosexuality, all key issues for the religious Right.

In the 1984 presidential election, Democrats would try to win back support from working-class Americans, the elderly, and minorities. Liberals argued that Reagan's economic policies were exacerbating social inequality and creating an economic recovery that left millions of Americans behind (Document 19). At the 1984 Democratic convention Reverend Jesse Jackson warned of the consequences of Reagan's economic policies. He and other liberals rejected the idea that Democrats should move toward the center in response to Reagan. Instead, Jackson called upon the party to live by its traditional principles and build a broad coalition of blue-collar workers, feminists, African Americans, immigrants, and more.

These Democratic appeals were no match for Reagan. Reagan's skill at building a personal rapport with the public and portraying himself as the champion of the average American redounded to his great success in the 1984 presidential election. In a highly effective political advertisement that featured Americans going to work, the narrator boldly proclaimed that it was "morning again in America" (Document 20). Walter Mondale, the Democratic candidate, had trouble matching Reagan's charisma on the campaign trail. His honest assessment during a debate that if he was elected president, he would have to raise taxes, fell flat. Reagan overwhelmed Mondale, securing 54.5 million popular votes to the former vice president's 37.6 million. Mondale won only his home state of Minnesota (and the District of Columbia) — and just barely. Only Jews and blacks gave more support to Mondale than to Reagan. Those who had fared best economically — suburban, middle-class, professional voters in the high-technology sector — strongly supported the president.

Second-Term Stalemate

By the time of Reagan's second term, American politics had settled into a stalemate. Although Reagan remained popular, the media, pundits, and intellectuals began to express concern about what became known

---

(Opposite) *President Reagan Accepting His Party's Nomination at the Republican National Convention in Dallas, August 23, 1984.*
By the time he ran for reelection, Reagan emphasized to voters the economic recovery and a sense that America's standing had improved around the globe. It was morning again in America, Reagan told the country.
Courtesy Ronald Reagan Library.

as policy gridlock. With a Republican in the White House and a Democratic House (and Senate after 1986), divided government could undermine the ability of the nation's leaders to solve the country's problems. The problem went beyond large Democratic numbers in the House. More striking was that the number of centrists in both parties started to diminish in both the House and the Senate. As Republicans captured southern Democratic votes and Democrats won over most northeasterners, the number of moderates continued to decline. After 1982, Reagan faced a House in which there were more Democrats and fewer who were willing to reach a deal with him. At the same time, Republicans continued to shift to the right (Document 21). It became more difficult to achieve bipartisan legislative compromises.

Unable to come together to fix problems such as the mounting deficit, Congress passed various measures to force compromises, including the Gramm-Rudman-Hollings Balanced Budget and Emergency Deficit Control Act of 1985. Senators Phil Gramm (R-Tex.), Warren Rudman (R-N.H.), and Ernest Hollings (D-S.C.) sponsored the measure with the hope of requiring Congress to move beyond gridlock. By mandating a balanced budget, the act was intended to impose either spending cuts or tax increases. As Rudman explained, it "forces resolution of . . . policy differences." But almost everyone recognized that the reform would have limited impact, because legislators would figure out ways around the imposed deficit ceiling.[68]

Although critics derided divided government, the close competition of the parties could sometimes work in favor of reform, as was the case with the Tax Reform Act of 1986. Not wanting to give the other party credit for the act, which simplified the tax rate structure and closed many loopholes but did not raise or lower revenue, both parties signed on to this measure, as did Reagan, demonstrating the success of bipartisanship.

Yet overall these kinds of victories were not fulfilling the high expectations and hopes that conservatives had in the 1970s about fundamentally remaking government. Rather than overturning social provisions

---

Opposite: President Reagan with Congressman Newt Gingrich, May 30, 1985.
On Capitol Hill, a young group of Republicans, led by Congressman Newt Gingrich of Georgia, formed the Conservative Opportunity Society. This caucus pushed the Republican leadership to the right and championed conservatism in Congress. Gingrich used hardball tactics against the Democratic majority and even against the GOP leadership, which at times caused problems for Reagan and his efforts to preserve a coalition.
Courtesy Ronald Reagan Library.

such as the minimum wage, for example, conservatives had to settle for blocking increases of benefits or coverage. As Congress failed to update the level of benefits in key social programs such as the minimum wage, their real value steadily diminished. The programs remained in place but did not grow.[69] On social policy, too, conservatives encountered roadblocks. Republicans sold themselves as the party of family values, which meant upholding what conservatives saw as the traditional family. Reagan supported a constitutional amendment to ban abortion and put pressure on Congress to prohibit federal funding of birth control and abortion. But here, too, he saw limited gains.

The 1986 midterm elections ended any hope that conservatives had for making progress on domestic policy through the legislative process. Democrats regained control of the Senate, taking a 55-to-45-seat majority. The Democratic advantage in the House rose to 258 to 177, as the Democrats picked up five seats.

New Strategies

The experience of being in office led conservatives to formulate new strategies for enacting their agenda. The most important component of their strategy was the presidency itself. To counter the obstacles presented by Congress, conservatives pushed for the buildup of executive power. Reagan's staff could undertake this effort in the 1980s in large part because Reagan had strengthened the popularity of the presidency. By gathering power in the White House, conservatives could exert greater influence in how government functioned and push policy to the right.

Under Reagan, administrative agencies were staffed with bureaucrats who did not believe in the regulatory intent of the offices they served. For example, Clarence Thomas, who was appointed by Reagan to the Equal Employment Opportunity Commission and served as chairman, stalled on resolving class-action lawsuits charging racial discrimination in hiring. Similarly, the Justice Department did not pursue violations of voting rights. Instead, under the direction of Attorney General Edwin Meese, the department sought to undo what its conservative appointees saw as the "reverse discrimination" against white males of affirmative action laws. Secretary of the Interior Watt and Energy Secretary James Edwards deliberately subverted the regulatory powers of their offices.[70]

The White House relied on the heads of executive agencies to avoid enforcing their mandates.[71] Reagan named committed deregulators to head the Federal Communications Commission, the Federal Trade Commission, the Occupational Safety and Health Administration, and many other departments.[72] Assistant Secretary of Housing and Urban Development (HUD) Emanuel Savas used his time at work to write a book, *Privatizing the Public Sector: How to Shrink Government*. Stockman, with Reagan's blessing, cut HUD's budget by more than half, making this Great Society agency relatively impotent.

The head of the Environmental Protection Agency (EPA), Anne Gorsuch Burford, was also hostile to the regulatory powers of her office. As a result of prodding from the White House, Congress cut billions of dollars from the budgets of agencies such as the EPA, which in turn made enforcement more challenging. The EPA faced a budget cut of 25 percent and a staffing cut of 20 percent.[73] Burford did not resist these cuts and, for example, put Rita Lavelle, a conservative protégé of Edwin Meese, in charge of the toxic waste cleanup program as a way of not complying with this congressional mandate from the Carter era. Both Burford and Lavelle left the agency under clouds of suspicion, with accusations that dozens of EPA officials failed to regulate the industries they were charged with overseeing. The Department of Energy, likewise, did not enforce safety regulations at power plants. At the Department of the Interior, James Watt personally oversaw the dismissal of career civil servants who he felt did not support his pro-growth agenda.

Reaganites wanted to close the Department of Education. First set up under Jimmy Carter, the department was a lightning rod for the conservative movement, which fought against its creation and sought to abolish it as another expansion of government involvement. The White House put pressure on Secretary of Education Terrel Bell to call for cuts in aid to public schools and not to enforce antidiscrimination laws. When it turned out that Bell did not plan on going along with that agenda, Reagan fired him and replaced him with the conservative William Bennett, who supported school vouchers and teaching religion in schools.

Bennett used his post to champion what conservatives saw as the culture wars, warning of the nation's moral disintegration, which had coincided with the liberalization and secularization of American culture. Many conservatives believed that cultural arguments attracted the support of voters who had traditionally been Democratic on economic grounds. Bennett not only celebrated prayer in school but also saw education as a vehicle for shoring up traditional family values and combating drug use. If he could not dismantle the Department of Education, he could use it to lead a moral crusade on behalf of the White House (Document 22).

An institutionally strong president could subvert or at least challenge the will of Congress. Under Meese, for instance, the Department of Justice started to call for the use of signing statements in a new way. Signing statements are the letters the executive office attaches to legislation. Traditionally, they tend to be insignificant, more like press releases than policy statements. But Meese and a cohort of young lawyers, including Samuel Alito, the future Supreme Court justice appointed by George W. Bush, believed that signing statements should be used more aggressively—as weapons in the arsenal of the president against Congress. The president could proclaim that he would not follow parts of the bill Congress had passed.

In addition to enhancing presidential powers and reducing regulation, Reagan and his supporters turned to judicial activism as another strategy of conservative governance. In his years in office, Reagan appointed nearly four hundred federal judges—more than half of all sitting judges by 1989—all of whom had been carefully screened for their conservative views. That kind of ideological profiling of candidates accelerated the politicization of the nomination process that had begun in the 1960s. With a more conservative judiciary, court rulings resulted in greater police power and less protection for defendants. That, combined with the Reagan administration's "war on drugs," to which the administration committed nearly $2 billion in federal funds, fueled the rapid growth of the prison population (Document 23).[74]

The Reagan White House also hoped to influence social policy, especially on abortion, through its appointments to the Supreme Court. When the first vacancy opened up in 1981, Reagan appointed Sandra Day O'Connor, who, as the first woman to be named, was readily confirmed by Congress. When Reagan promoted William Rehnquist to chief justice in 1986, he named Antonin Scalia to the resulting vacancy. Although Congress refused to confirm Robert Bork as a Supreme Court justice in 1987 because of his outspoken conservative views, Reagan successfully appointed Anthony Kennedy, who Reagan hoped would further tip the Court in a conservative direction (Document 24).

Overall, Reagan had mixed results on domestic policy. The biggest success came with tax reduction and deregulation. The tax cut of 1981 was a crowning achievement. So, too, was the deregulation of the savings and loan industry in the early 1980s, which triggered a boom in real estate and banking. The costs would become apparent when the failure of more than seven hundred savings and loan banks resulted in the largest financial debacle since the Great Depression and contributed to a recession in 1990–1991. But throughout the 1980s, the economy grew and the stock market soared in value. Even after the crash of October 19, 1987, when the Dow Jones fell more than five hundred points, the market rebounded (Document 25). One onlooker, who was watching the chaos unfold at the New York Stock Exchange, proclaimed, "It's all over for the yuppies! Down with MBAs! It's all over! The Reagan Revolution is over!" But another group shouted in rebuttal, "Whoever dies with the most toys wins!"[75] (Document 26). Reagan had done much to rehabilitate the popular notion that opportunity comes from the workings of the free market.

Those victories did not tell the whole story. As historian James Patterson found, federal spending was higher than in the 1970s, reaching 23.5 percent of gross domestic product (GDP) in 1983, falling only to 21.2 percent in 1989. At the same time, the number of federal employees increased from 2.9 million to 3.1 million while Reagan was in office.[76] Social Security and Medicare survived the conservative onslaught, as did most other components of the welfare state, including welfare itself. When the Reagan Revolution ran up against obstacles, especially on Capitol Hill, conservatives had to devise other strategies that attempted to circumvent the legislative process (Document 27). They would have a similar experience in foreign policy.

NATIONAL SECURITY

Just as it had in the domestic sphere, the Reagan administration encountered challenges of governance in dealing with national security. The 1980 election did not remake American politics, and Democrats were much stronger in Congress than conservatives anticipated. In foreign policy, the administration's hawkish approach to communism directly clashed with the ideological and institutional inheritances from the Vietnam era, a legacy that made Americans cautious about the use of military power, even as they wanted to project a powerful national image. Reagan and his allies in Congress struggled to work their way through this complex political environment, at one point finding themselves ensnared in a potentially devastating scandal.

Peace through Strength

The Reagan presidency began on a positive note. The outcome of the Iran hostage crisis enabled Reagan to make Republican strength on national security a central theme from the start. Right after being sworn in on January 20, 1981, Reagan announced that the American hostages in Iran would be released after 444 days in captivity. Carter had literally been working into the night on a deal that fell apart in the early-morning hours. To Carter's great frustration, the Iranian leadership refused to let the hostages go while he was still president. Instead, Reagan had the privilege of announcing that the hostages were being released just after taking the oath of office. (There were charges that Reagan had orchestrated the delay so that he could claim credit for the release, although those charges were never proved.) The announcement fit comfortably within the narrative that conservatives had promoted in the campaign: Conservatives could do what liberals could not; they could assert U.S. strength and protect national security.

Conservatives had assured voters that they would promote a military buildup to fight the cold war. Like tax cuts, a tough stance toward the Soviet Union was one of the central promises that conservatives were making in the early 1980s. Reagan retained the commitment to peace through strength that he had embraced since the 1950s (Document 28). He broke with Nixon and Ford in his willingness to use inflammatory rhetoric and his steadfast refusal to engage in substantive arms negotiations. He was genuinely determined to achieve nuclear abolition whenever possible.[77] But until the United States gained an advantage in military strength, Reagan said, the Soviet Union would never agree to serious concessions. The objectives of Democratic doves, he added, could be achieved only through the methods of the Republican hawk.

Reagan appointed officials to his administration who had been at the forefront of the fight against détente in the 1970s. For example, Reagan nominated the neoconservative Richard Perle to be assistant secretary of defense for international security policy. Eugene Rostow, another prominent neoconservative, took over the Arms Control and Disarmament Agency. Paul Nitze became the top negotiator with the Soviets for arms control. Richard Allen, who had resigned from Nixon's NSC in protest of détente and was Reagan's main conduit to neoconservatives throughout the 1980 campaign, served as the national security advisor through 1981. William Clark, who agreed with Allen's views, succeeded him. Reagan nominated Jeane Kirkpatrick, a leading neoconservative critic of Democratic foreign policy, to serve as UN ambassador.

Under the leadership of Caspar Weinberger, who served as secretary of defense, the defense budget was presented as a symbol to gauge the willingness of Congress to defend the nation. If spending was high, according to Weinberger and Reagan, the United States could show that the ghosts of Vietnam no longer dictated American policy. While discretionary spending for domestic programs declined from 5.7 percent of gross national product (GNP) in 1981 to 3.7 percent in 1987, defense spending increased from 5.3 percent to 6.4 percent.[78] The military budget, combined with domestic entitlement programs, was pushing deficits higher and higher. Upon hearing a proposal by Georgia congressman Newt Gingrich to freeze the budget in response to rising deficits, Reagan refused, noting, "It's a tempting idea except that it would cripple our defense program. And if we make an exception on that every special interest group will be asking for the same."[79] The moderate voices in the administration were likewise committed to a defense buildup and insisted on higher military spending as a precondition for negotiations with the Soviets.

During his first years as president, Reagan promised Americans that the United States would not tolerate Soviet aggression (Document 29). He took a tough rhetorical stance toward the Soviets and rejected arms negotiations. Resurrecting arguments about rolling back communism that the Republican Right had promoted in the early 1950s, Reagan proclaimed that "the West won't contain Communism, it will transcend communism."[80]

To be sure, Reagan was not all fire and brimstone. Privately, he was genuinely searching for evidence of changes in the Soviet Union and relied on third-party channels to keep the lines of communication open (Document 32).[81] Following the resignation of his first secretary of state, Alexander Haig, Reagan appointed George Shultz in 1982. Shultz, a former University of Chicago economist and Nixon administration official, was a cofounder of the neoconservative Committee on the Present Danger. But Shultz also advocated negotiations with the Soviets whenever possible and a less adversarial posture in the cold war.[82] To that end, Reagan proposed the zero option, which would end the deployment of Pershing II and ground-launched cruise missiles in Western Europe on the condition that the Soviets disband every intermediate-range weapon that threatened the continent (the SS-20, SS-4, and SS-5). Confident the Soviets would not accept, Reagan used the offer to give the appearance that he was not a warmonger.

Reagan strove to achieve a delicate balance between intensifying military tensions with the Soviets while at the same time leaving open the possibility of future negotiations. The two components of this strategy, Reagan argued, went hand in hand.[83] Central to his argument was that the bar for negotiations would remain high. This was how Reagan and other conservatives distinguished themselves from Republican practitioners of détente in the 1970s, who had been more flexible and open to engaging the Soviets.

In Central America, where the administration argued that the Soviets were attempting to gain a stronghold next door to American territory, the White House sought to craft an interventionist policy (Document 30). To sell the program, Reagan reminded Congress that "El Salvador is nearer to Texas than Texas is to Massachusetts. Nicaragua is just as close to Miami, San Antonio, San Diego, and Tucson as those cities are to Washington, where we're gathered tonight."[84]

Notwithstanding Reagan's warnings, polls showed that American intervention in Central America did not command strong support in the early 1980s.[85] Beginning in 1982 and culminating in 1984, Congress passed a series of amendments to defense appropriations bills that restricted the use of funds in Central America and tried to tie the hands of the administration. These were called the Boland Amendments, after their sponsor, Massachusetts representative Edward Boland. Sensitive to the limited support for military operations among citizens, Reagan chose a more subtle strategy for expanding America's military presence. Instead of sending troops to overthrow the left-wing Sandinista regime in Nicaragua, the White House focused on the provision of financial and arms support to the Sandinistas' opponents, the contras, through the CIA.[86] In neighboring El Salvador, Reagan sent assistance to the authoritarian government to fight Communist insurgents.

The 1982 midterm elections added to the challenges Reagan faced with his national security strategy. Economics was the main issue in the election, as Democrats did well in areas such as the Midwest where the recession had hit hardest. But one consequence of the election was an increase in the number of legislators committed to a nuclear freeze (Document 31). A nuclear freeze would stipulate that the United States and the Soviet Union would freeze the production of nuclear arms at existing levels. Two-thirds of the nation supported a nuclear freeze, and following the midterm elections, 67 percent of the new House members announced that they endorsed nuclear freeze legislation.[87]

Political pressure did not dissuade Reagan from taking positions that infuriated large portions of the public domestically and internationally. In Western Europe, for example, Reagan moved forward with the deployment of 572 intermediate-range nuclear force (INF) missiles pursuant to a NATO agreement finalized in 1979. This had been a response to the Soviet decision to deploy SS-20 intermediate-range missiles in the late 1970s. For neoconservatives, the SS-20s were concrete evidence that the Soviets were not interested in détente. Many Democrats, including Carter, had been equally frustrated. While Margaret Thatcher of England, Helmut Kohl of West Germany, and François Mitterrand of France supported the U.S. deployment, tens of thousands of moderate and left-wing Europeans staged protests in 1982 on the grounds that these new weapons would escalate the potential for nuclear war.[88] Despite the opposition, Reagan deployed the missiles.

The Most Dangerous Year

Beyond worrying over the new electoral landscape in 1983, the president started genuinely to fear that the world was becoming a more dangerous place. There was a rapid turnover of leaders in the Soviet Union. When Leonid Brezhnev died on November 10, 1982, his successor, Yuri Andropov, got off to a poor start with Reagan. Fears about the possibility of nuclear war were running high. Reagan contributed to the climate of fear when, in a speech to evangelical Christians, he called the Soviets the "focus of evil" (Document 33).

At the same time, Reagan attempted to calm growing fears by proposing that the United States develop a shield against a Soviet missile attack. The centerpiece of this promise was unveiled on March 23, when Reagan introduced the Strategic Defense Initiative (SDI) (Document 34). The program proposed creating an X-ray or laser-based shield in space that would protect the country from the destructive impact of intercontinental ballistic missiles and submarine-launched ballistic missiles. SDI abandoned the policy of mutual assured destruction. If both sides developed the missile defense technology, Reagan said, there would be the opposite situation in that there would no longer be a need for nuclear weapons. Reagan was the driving force behind SDI. He worked outside the defense bureaucracy and most of his cabinet by convening an informal group of advisers to devise the plan.[89]

Most respected scientists believed that the shield would be impossible to construct with existing technology. Critics borrowed the title of the popular science fiction film *Star Wars* to ridicule the program. Former UN ambassador and undersecretary of state George Ball castigated Reagan for having engaged in one of the "most irresponsible acts by any head of state in modern times."[90] NATO leaders warned that SDI would diminish the incentive for the United States to defend the European continent.[91] The Soviets said that SDI would result in a race to create ground-based missiles, which would violate the existing agreement to limit antiballistic missile systems. If the technology ever worked, which the Soviets doubted it would, there would be no incentive for the United States to refrain from launching a first strike. Given that the United States was not reducing its offensive power, expanding its system of defense constituted an aggressive action from the Soviet perspective. The demands to invest in a comparable program, Soviet officials realized, would push up already high levels of defense spending, further weakening their shaky economy. Unwilling to be deterred, Reagan dismissed the critics and defended the legitimacy of the project. "I wonder," he liked to ask, "why some of our own carping critics who claim SDI is an impractical wasted effort don't ask themselves, if it's no good how come the Russians are so upset about it?"[92]

In addition to SDI, Reagan engaged in secret negotiations and covert military operations. He pursued both at the same time as a way to achieve his policy goals in spite of congressional opposition to his hawkish agenda and his secretive tactics (Document 35). For example, in June 1983, Secretary of State Shultz convinced the Kremlin to allow a family of Pentecostals, who had hidden in an American embassy, to depart the country on the promise that the president would not boast of the deal.[93] By this time, deputy national security advisor Robert McFarlane explained, the president felt that his administration had "restored enough momentum to our defense programs" that it could earnestly begin to start negotiations with the Soviets from a position of strength.[94] In pursuing military objectives, Reagan employed covert CIA activities. The agency cooperated with a bipartisan coalition of congressional allies, headed by Texas Democrat Charlie Wilson, to direct funds and stinger missiles to the Muslim rebels who were fighting the Soviet army in Afghanistan.[95]

Public fears intensified as international tensions escalated. On September 1, the Soviets shot down a Korean airliner (KAL 007) when the plane entered Soviet airspace, killing 269 passengers. Sixty-one Americans, including a congressman, were on board. The Soviets insisted that their pilot made a mistake. Many conservatives called for swift retaliation. Reagan condemned the strike as "murder" but resisted pressure for military action. This incident, combined with several other moments of tension, persuaded Reagan that the cold war rivalry with the Soviets had entered into a dangerous phase and that the United States needed to calm relations to avoid war.

At the same time, Reagan suffered a humiliating military defeat in Lebanon. The American crisis in Lebanon began in June 1982, when Secretary of State Haig gave Israel the green light to invade Lebanon to destroy the military bases of the Palestine Liberation Organization and diminish the power of Syria, which posed an ongoing threat to Israel. After the attack, Lebanon continued to slide into civil war. Reagan responded by sending in American troops. The president made this decision over the opposition of the Joint Chiefs of Staff, who feared the operation would be a disaster.[96] On October 23, 1983, a Muslim suicide bomber killed 241 Marines stationed in U.S. barracks in Beirut. Although the president initially warned that terrorists would see the withdrawal of troops as a sign of weakness,[97] Reagan agreed, under immense congressional pressure, to bring the troops home in eighteen months and did not order any military retaliation.[98]

Two days after the bombing in Lebanon, Reagan scored a morale-boosting victory by authorizing the U.S. invasion of the small island of Grenada. Since 1979, this tiny Caribbean island had been ruled by Marxists. In October 1983, an even more militant group seized power. Reagan claimed that this coup endangered five hundred American students living on the island and sent in troops to defeat what he saw as a Soviet plan to establish a Communist regime close to the United States. Involving only a small number of soldiers, this small-scale operation proved to be a political success for Reagan (Document 36).

There were other moments of tension that year. In the fall, ABC's airing of the movie *The Day After*, depicting a nuclear holocaust, aroused public fears of a possible nuclear war (Document 37). Days earlier, in fact, one of the worst moments of tension between the Soviets and Americans involved Able Archer 83, a NATO military exercise. Soviet military officials believed that the United States was about to attack the Soviet Union. The tensions ended when the Soviets learned the truth, but only after they had placed their forces on the highest alert. Years later, the president recalled, "Three years had taught me something surprising about the Russians: Many people at the top of the Soviet hierarchy were genuinely afraid of America and Americans. . . . I was even more anxious to get a top leader in a room alone and try to convince him we had no designs on the Soviet Union and the Russians had nothing to fear from us."[99]

As the 1984 presidential election approached, Reagan took steps to improve relations with the Soviets. On January 16, he delivered an address from the White House in which he told a story about two Americans named Jim and Sally and their Russian counterparts, Ivan and Anya. In the story, Reagan said that if the two couples were brought together unexpectedly, they would not discuss the virtues of their governments but instead talk about their daily lives and their children. Through this conversation, the couples would discover just how much they had in common. "Before they parted company," Reagan continued, "they would probably have touched on ambitions and hobbies and what they wanted for their children and problems of making ends meet. And as they went their separate ways, maybe Anya would be saying to Ivan, 'Wasn't she nice? She also teaches music.' . . . People want to raise their children in a world without fear and without war. . . . Their common interests cross all borders."[100] The president noted in his diary, "The speech was carefully crafted by all of us to counter Soviet propaganda that we are not sincere in wanting arms reductions or peace. It was low key & held the door open to the Soviets if they mean what they say about having peace to walk in."[101] On September 24, just before the election, Reagan made another conciliatory speech toward the Soviets at the United Nations.

National defense was an important theme for Reagan in his 1984 reelection bid. The president's campaign played it both ways. On the one hand, he continued to boast of his commitment to higher defense spending and appealed to the nationalistic pride of the nation. He delivered one of his most memorable speeches on the fortieth anniversary of the D-Day invasion of Normandy, celebrating the patriotism of the World War II generation (Document 38). Reagan also masterfully turned the 1984 summer Olympic Games in Los Angeles into a rallying point for the nation. ABC, which broadcast the games, joined in. The games' theme was "Rebirth of the Nation." Commercials used nationalistic rhetoric, including the McDonald's ads, which announced that when "the U.S. wins, you win."[102] During his acceptance speech at the Republican National Convention in Dallas in August, Reagan boasted that the Olympic Games "began defining the promise of this season." The delegates burst out chanting, "U.S.A.! U.S.A.! U.S.A.!" At the same time, Reagan stressed his conciliatory messages toward the Soviet Union. These latter moves were important because his words about peace and patriotism undercut Democratic candidate Walter Mondale, who devoted much of his campaign to warning that Reagan would bring the arms race into outer space and threaten world safety (Document 39).

Reagan's second term got off to a rough start. Former Treasury secretary Donald Regan, who switched places with James Baker as chief of staff, was responsible for one of the biggest public relations fiascoes of Reagan's presidency. In 1985, the president accepted an invitation from German chancellor Helmut Kohl to speak at a memorial to mark the fortieth anniversary of the end of World War II. Regan signed off on the choice of the Bitburg cemetery without further investigation. But the media soon revealed that dozens of Nazis were buried in clearly marked graves where Reagan was to lay a wreath. The president made things worse when he became defensive and stated that there was nothing wrong with honoring German soldiers who were "victims" of Nazism. "Another backbreaker," Reagan wrote in his diary. "The press continues to chew away on the German trip & my supposed insensitivity in visiting a W.W. II Germany mil. cemetery in spite of the fact I'm going to visit a Concentration camp. They are really sucking blood & finding every person of Jewish faith they can who will denounce me."[103] Still, he refused to cancel the visit, because he believed that it would look bad to go back on his word.

By this time, Reagan faced critics on his left and his right. Many conservatives were disappointed with the president's national security record. There was a growing conservative perception that Reagan's experience in Lebanon had scared him about using military force.[104] Democrats in Congress were also capitalizing on a scandal in 1985 involving extravagant and unneeded spending by the Pentagon. "Congress gave Reagan most of the military buildup he asked for in his first term," noted *Time* magazine reporter Evan Thomas, "but it will be less accommodating in his second. Scandals over vastly overpriced parts and weapons that do not work have drained the Pentagon's goodwill on Capitol Hill: even Congressmen willing to spend more for defense fear that money is being squandered."[105]

Iran-Contra

The Reagan administration's reliance on executive power as a way around congressional opposition to his national security policies resulted in a major national security scandal in 1986 that brought his presidency to a standstill. The previous year, the CIA had begun a covert program to sell weapons to Iran in exchange for assistance with the release of hostages in Lebanon.[106] Although there is still no solid evidence that Reagan knew about the final piece of the puzzle, NSC officials diverted the profits from the sale of the weapons to finance the Nicaraguan contras. This strategy was designed to circumvent the 1984 Boland Amendment, which prohibited the CIA and other intelligence agencies in helping groups seeking to overthrow the government of Nicaragua. Technically, some members of the administration felt that the NSC did not fall under this ban (Documents 41 and 43). Marine lieutenant colonel Oliver North was the NSC staffer who took on the responsibility for diverting the funds to Central America. North had been a popular figure on the Council for National Policy, a right-wing group that included

conservative activists such as the preacher Pat Robertson, beer magnate Joseph Coors, and the president of the Heritage Foundation,
Edwin Feulner.[107] When Robert McFarlane resigned from the Reagan
administration in December 1985, North gained an even bigger role and
more power. As North worked behind the scenes, Reagan sought to
change public opinion on the question of intervention in Latin America
(Document 44).

The administration soon found itself in the midst of an unfolding
scandal. On November 3, 1986, the U.S. media picked up a story from
a Lebanese newspaper, *Al-Shiraa*, which reported that McFarlane had
been in Iran the previous summer to work on a deal to exchange arms
for hostages. Given the memories of most voting-age Americans, Reagan's potential wrongdoing was immediately seen through the lens of
Watergate, the political scandal that brought down President Richard
Nixon.[108] Reagan's team scrambled to contain the damage (Document 45). Attorney General Meese reported that NSC officials had
transferred funds from weapons sales to Iran to the contras. Reagan
then publicly announced that North had been fired, and he accepted
John Poindexter's resignation as national security advisor.

On December 1, Reagan established the White House Special Review
Board to investigate the allegations and appointed former Republican
senator John Tower of Texas as its chair. What came to be known as the
Tower Commission blamed the president's management style for allowing poor decisions to be made. Reagan apologized without acknowledging any other wrongdoing.[109] In response to political pressure, Meese
launched a new inquiry through the Office of the Independent Counsel
under prosecutor Lawrence Walsh. Through these and other steps, Reagan believed that he had "cooled some of the savage beasts."[110]

But the investigation only intensified. Congress formed a joint committee to look into the scandal. Congressional hearings were widely
publicized and extensively covered by the U.S. and international media.
The committee was cochaired by Senator Daniel Inouye (D-Hawaii)
and Representative Lee Hamilton (D-Ind.). Chief committee counsel
Arthur Liman argued that the president was a driving force behind the
exchange.[111] During the summer of 1987, millions of Americans watched
the hearings on television. Through dramatic televised addresses,
Reagan sought unsuccessfully to regain the initiative and portray the
administration's actions in a sympathetic light (Documents 46 and
48). The majority report published by the committee concluded that
the president had not been sufficiently cautious when he allowed over-
zealous officials to take control of administration policies. The minority

report dismissed the charges as merely partisan politics and defended the right of the executive branch to act forcefully when congressional intransigence hamstrings national security efforts (Documents 49 and 50).[112]

Reagan's popularity plunged as a result of the investigations and the attendant media coverage. His approval rating fell to 46 percent. The administration realized that the scandal would continue as the independent counsel moved forward, and there were upcoming indictments of administration officials.[113] Reagan's team would have to chart a way out of this crisis.

Back toward Détente

The president's continued willingness to soften his national security agenda enabled Reagan to rebound politically from the scandal. In 1986 and 1987, he undertook a dramatic initiative that focused international attention on arms negotiations with the Soviet Union. The path toward a treaty with the Soviets began seriously in 1985, when Mikhail Gorbachev became premier. Recognizing that the old Soviet system was bankrupt, Gorbachev promoted economic liberalization (perestroika) and political reform (glasnost) to solve his country's problems. His plan included efforts to ease tensions with the West.

Gorbachev and Reagan began to explore possibilities for a comprehensive agreement on nuclear weapons (Document 40). Their initial encounters were difficult, although the two men clearly had an affinity for each other. Gorbachev and Reagan first met to discuss arms control in November 1985 (Document 42). One of the biggest stumbling blocks proved to be SDI. Reagan refused to abandon his nuclear shield in space. Gorbachev insisted that the United States needed to stop the project. When Gorbachev cited a scientist who said that SDI was a fantasy, the president reminded him of the scientist who had told President Eisenhower that intercontinental ballistic missiles would never work.[114]

The next summit took place in Reykjavik, Iceland, in October 1986. As the summit approached, conservatives were worried that Reagan would agree to unfavorable terms. Senator Malcolm Wallop wrote that "by focusing the summit on arms control we will have abandoned basic issues that divide us from the Soviets—issues that go to the very heart of our effort to improve our relationship. Preeminent among these issues is human rights."[115] Gorbachev, seeking to regain momentum for the negotiations, made a dramatic offer by accepting the zero-zero option of no further buildup of nuclear weapons by either side and agreeing to

implement a 50 percent reduction in strategic weapons. Gorbachev even called for the elimination of all nuclear weapons within ten years.

But the discussions came to a standstill when Gorbachev refused to accept SDI. Reagan was committed to the program, both for its potential as a defensive weapon and as part of the bargaining process. He was also feeling immense political pressure from conservatives to stand his ground. "I can't give in," Reagan told his Soviet counterpart. "The people who were the most outspoken critics of the Soviet Union over the years . . . the so-called right wing, and esteemed journalists . . . they're kicking my brains out."[116]

After Reykjavik, Reagan's will weakened. Moreover, as a result of personnel changes during Reagan's second term, many leading neoconservatives were no longer in the administration. Reagan appointed the former moderate Republican senator Howard Baker as his chief of staff when he fired Donald Regan. Colin Powell replaced Frank Carlucci as national security advisor, and Assistant Defense Secretary Richard Perle stepped down. Together with George Shultz, the new national security team pushed Reagan toward negotiations with the Soviets in 1987. Importantly, Reagan continued to take a firm public position, which he believed essential to keeping the Soviets on track and maintaining his own support at home. In a speech in June at the Brandenburg Gate dividing East and West Germany, Reagan defied many of his advisers by proclaiming, "General Secretary Gorbachev, if you seek peace, if you seek prosperity for the Soviet Union and Eastern Europe, if you seek liberalization: Come here to this gate! Mr. Gorbachev, open this gate! Mr. Gorbachev, tear down this wall!" (Document 47).

On December 8, Reagan welcomed Gorbachev to Washington for another summit. For the first time, Gorbachev accepted that arms reductions and SDI could be handled separately, which constituted a

---

(Opposite) *President Reagan Delivers a Speech at the Berlin Wall, June 12, 1987.* As Reagan entered into negotiations with Mikhail Gorbachev between 1985 and 1987, he worked to maintain his support among conservatives, who opposed negotiating with the Soviets. Reagan insisted on sending signals to the Soviets that he would remain tough even as the countries negotiated. Over the advice of many on his staff, Reagan delivered a forceful speech on June 12, 1987, at the Brandenburg Gate, where he called on Gorbachev to tear down the Berlin Wall.

Courtesy Ronald Reagan Library.

watershed. The two leaders agreed to a historic arms agreement. The INF Treaty enacted the kind of steep arms reductions that Reagan had previously warned would endanger America (Document 51). The press praised Reagan for making the agreement. Public opinion polls in his final year showed strong support for what the administration had accomplished.

Conservatives, however, were furious. They criticized the president for having sold America out to the Soviets and having accepted a dangerous treaty that would undermine U.S. power. Although conservative senators tried unsuccessfully to block ratification of the INF Treaty, the Senate ratified it by a vote of 93–5 on May 27, 1988, and Reagan ended his presidency with many in the conservative movement fuming about his policies. "For conservatives," George Will explained, "Ronald Reagan's foreign policy has produced much surprise but little delight."[117] Only in hindsight, after the collapse of the Soviet Union, would many conservatives attempt to credit Reagan with ending the cold war (Document 52).

CONSERVATISM SINCE 1988

When Reagan left Washington, he proclaimed that his presidency had been a success. In his farewell address, he said that he had been thinking about John Winthrop's 1630 description of America as the "shining city upon a hill." "And how stands the city on this winter night?" Reagan asked on January 11, 1989. "More prosperous, more secure, and happier than it was eight years ago. . . . We've done our part. And as I walk off into the city streets, a final word to the men and women of the Reagan revolution, the men and women across America who for eight years did the work that brought America back. My friends: We did it. We weren't just marking time. We made a difference. We made the city stronger. We made the city freer, and we left her in good hands."[118] Just as Reagan's supporters had first described their coming to power as a "revolution," Reagan sought to secure his legacy as a conservative president who had permanently transformed American politics.

But throughout Reagan's time in office, he and his conservative allies had to come to terms with the limits of what they could achieve. From the start, his advisers were aware that there had been no decisive electoral realignment, much less a revolution. The election did lead to an important change in power and shift in the direction of policy, but the changes were less dramatic and complete than supporters had hoped for. It turned out that Richard Nixon had been partially right with his somber forecasts in 1981: As he predicted, and as Reagan and his conservative allies discovered, it was hard to undo half a century of liberal governance or overcome the impact of the Vietnam War. Reagan's presidency and the conservative movement pushed the country in a rightward direction, but they did not produce an age of small government. Reagan, like Nixon before him, struggled with the conservative dilemma: how to square their ideology with the demands of being in office, a puzzle made all the more difficult to solve in the absence of a clear and overwhelming conservative popular mandate. Reagan, as historian Gil Troy has argued, was personally able to reconcile this dilemma given his background as both an "ideologue" and a "showman." As an ideologue, he was able to convey his devotion to a clear philosophy and set of values. But as a showman, he understood that the audience mattered, and he adjusted his script as he watched the public's reaction.[119]

Reagan's presidency left two main legacies that conservatives would build upon. First, the Reagan team came up with new tactics. When conservatives ran into obstacles once they were in office and discovered that there had not been a wholesale shift to the right in the electorate, they devised new strategies for conservative governance. As insiders, they learned how to work within the system to shift policy to the right and reassert American international strength. By expanding executive power, relying on bureaucratic warfare, pushing the judiciary to the right, and promoting conservative social values, Reagan offered a template for governance that set the terms of political rule for the generations that followed. Conservatives also reconfigured their goals—their second main legacy—so that they could still seek a reduction in certain types of government (social welfare) and an expansion in others (national security), while seeing outcomes that were realistic given the limitations they encountered.

The challenges that conservatives faced continued after Reagan left office. In 1988, Reagan's vice president, George H. W. Bush, defeated Michael Dukakis, the governor of Massachusetts, to become president (Document 53). Bush beat Dukakis in the West and South, and he ran especially well in the high-tech suburbs, where Republicans continued to fare better nationally. But Bush's presidency was a disappointment to many conservatives, as he was pressured to compromise with a Democratic-controlled Congress. Breaking his 1988 campaign pledge, "Read my lips: no new taxes!" Bush acceded to Democratic demands for a tax hike in 1990 as part of a deficit reduction plan. Dick Armey, a representative from Texas, denounced Bush, saying that he should have spent his political capital "finishing off liberalism" rather than enabling a "reversal of the Reagan Revolution."[120] Bush disappointed conservatives again by agreeing to vast expansions of government with the Civil Rights Act of 1989 and the Americans with Disabilities Act of 1990. In foreign policy, Bush fared better with the military success of the Gulf War, in which U.S. forces expelled Iraqi forces from Kuwait. This achievement, coupled with the end of the cold war, led Bush to proclaim "a new world order" (Document 54). But the disastrous aftermath of the Gulf War—as Bush's resistance toward extending the war into Baghdad allowed for Saddam Hussein to remain in power and brutally crack down on dissidents—raised doubts on the right as to the military acumen of the administration.

Conservatives faced even greater challenges after Republicans lost the White House in 1992 with the election of five-term Arkansas governor Bill Clinton. Even though he received only 43 percent of the vote, Clinton seemed like a real threat to conservatives. He was a new kind of Democrat, a favorite of the Democratic Leadership Council, which he helped found to move the party to the center after Walter Mondale's massive defeat by Reagan in 1984. Clinton ran as more of a centrist than Mondale or Dukakis. He selected Al Gore, senator from Tennessee, as his running mate in an attempt to reclaim the South for the Democrats and to appeal to moderates. To win back Democrats who had left the party in the 1980s, Clinton was willing to question basic Democratic commitments such as welfare, while retaining a progressive agenda on other issues, such as health care and entitlement programs for the elderly.

The Republicans fought back. Reagan's eight years in office had enabled the training and election of a new phalanx of conservative activists in government who continued to push politics to the right. Frustration encouraged conservatives in Congress, led by Newt Gingrich, to sharpen their political message and embrace more aggressive partisan warfare. As Republican whip in the House, Gingrich enforced party discipline and received help from rising Republican stars such as Mississippi senator Trent Lott. Gingrich was uncompromising, and although it would prove to be his downfall, his revolutionary zeal advanced the conservative cause. With the help of other recently elected southern conservatives such as Dick Armey and Tom DeLay of Texas, Gingrich fought an ideological war. As Grover Norquist, a conservative activist, explained, "Newt's argument was that you go out and fight all the time, you wake up every morning and say, 'What can I do to move things forward?'"[121]

In 1994, led by Gingrich, congressional Republicans signed the Contract with America, a campaign document that promised an "end of government that is too big, too intrusive, and too easy with the public's money" (Document 55). The contract promised to reduce the size of government, reform the political process, and enact policies such as capital gains tax cuts, a ban on having U.S. troops under UN command, and an end to Aid to Families with Dependent Children (AFDC). The biggest Republican victory was to defeat Clinton's health care proposal in 1994. In the 1994 midterm elections, Republicans gained control of both houses of Congress for the first time since 1954 and scored major victories in the South. Gingrich became Speaker of the House and led a Republican party that had become much more conservative, including seventy-three freshman congressmen.

Yet congressional conservatives confronted frustrations similar to those Reagan had when he was in the White House. A permanent realignment remained elusive for the Republican Right. In the wake of the 1994 election, Clinton moved farther to the center to outflank his opponents and steal their political thunder. The public again proved tepid about Republican proposals for radically cutting many federal programs. In 1995, Republicans proposed more than $1 trillion in spending cuts over seven years. The package included $353 billion in tax cuts and increased spending on defense. Clinton claimed that the GOP intended to take money from the elderly and the poor to benefit the wealthy. Clinton also focused public attention on specific programs that would be affected, such as food stamps.

Clinton outmaneuvered the Republicans by offering his own budget package, with $1.1 trillion in spending cuts over ten years and a smaller tax cut that would target the middle class. When a standoff on the federal budget resulted in a three-week shutdown of the government in 1995, polls showed that Americans were coming to perceive Republicans as extremists and incapable of holding power. Clinton went further, though. After he won the budget battle and Republicans tempered their demands, Clinton proposed a balanced budget by 2002 and claimed this issue as an accomplishment, both for himself and the Democratic party. In the summer of 1996, Clinton further undercut Republicans when he signed the Personal Responsibility and Work Opportunity Reconciliation Act. This measure ended the public welfare program (AFDC) that had existed for sixty-one years by limiting the number of years citizens could receive welfare and delegating power to the states (Document 56). In his 1996 reelection bid, Clinton soundly defeated Senate Majority Leader Bob Dole of Kansas.

With a political stalemate, congressional conservatives escalated their partisan attacks. Scandal warfare became a central tool for Republicans in their effort to undermine Clinton's popularity. In January 1998, rumors of an alleged affair between the president and a White House intern, Monica Lewinsky, began to circulate. Kenneth Starr, the independent counsel who had served as solicitor general under Bush, was investigating the first lady, Hillary Clinton, for her involvement in an Arkansas land deal known as Whitewater. Starr found no wrongdoing on the part of the Clintons, but upon learning about the relationship with Lewinsky, he expanded his investigation to include sexual misconduct of the president. Later in the year, the House Judiciary Committee conducted nationally televised impeachment hearings and voted for four articles of impeachment. In December, the Republican-controlled House approved two of them, charging Clinton with perjuring himself by lying about the affair before a grand jury and obstructing justice to conceal the truth. Republican party leaders, led by House whip Tom DeLay, maintained tight partisan discipline and pushed for impeachment instead of censure. Conservatives seized on the president's affair as a chance to shore up their position as keepers of "family values," though they miscalculated the support Clinton had as a popular president.

In the 1998 midterm elections, the Democrats made inroads into the Republican majorities in both houses, causing moderate Republicans to think twice about attacking a president who, in spite of his wrongdoings, remained popular. Many Senate Republicans who needed support beyond narrow districts knew their history; it was the first time since 1934 that the party of the president made gains in the midterm elections, and exit polls revealed that most voters felt that the House, under Gingrich's leadership, had gone too far by pressing for impeachment. When Republicans broke ranks in the Senate, the impeachment effort failed.

The electoral divisions of the 1990s continued unabated. That became abundantly clear in the 2000 election, when Clinton's vice president, Al Gore, ran against the former president Bush's son George W. Bush, governor of Texas (Document 57). When the polls closed, the election was too close to call. Gore, who had won the popular vote but lost in the Electoral College, demanded a recount of votes in the closely contested Florida race. Bush became president only when the Supreme Court ordered Florida to stop the recount.

Jubilant in victory, the right pinned its hopes on Bush. Indeed, he revealed himself to be to the ideological right of his father. And he surrounded himself with advisers, such as Vice President Dick Cheney and

Secretary of Defense Donald Rumsfeld, who had served in Republican administrations dating back to Nixon and knew how to advance a conservative agenda, even in the absence of a clear electoral mandate. In 2001 and again in 2003, the Republicans pushed through Congress two huge tax cuts, which continued to weaken the fiscal strength of the government. The Reagan-era precedent of nonenforcement as a conservative policy strategy also proved effective. Under the Bush administration, administrators in agencies such as the Environmental Protection Agency and the Department of Energy failed to fulfill their legislative mandates, they lobbied for trimming their own budgets, and they turned to the private sector to outsource government responsibilities.

Executive power also remained a potent tool of conservatives. In the summer of 2002, Vice President Cheney cited executive privilege as justification for refusing to reveal the minutes of the meetings he had had in his office with energy executives who, as part of Cheney's Energy Task Force, helped write a new energy bill favorable to industry. After the terrorist attacks on September 11, 2001, the president relied on executive power to legitimate a national surveillance program that ignored the Foreign Intelligence Surveillance Act of 1978. Expanding executive power undergirded the war on terrorism.[122]

As they had done in the Reagan era, conservatives continued to find considerable success in the courts. As Reagan adviser and attorney general Edwin Meese understood, getting the "right judges" appointed would ensure that the "Reagan Revolution . . . can't be set aside, no matter what happens in future elections."[123] With George H. W. Bush's appointment of Clarence Thomas, the Supreme Court continued to consolidate its conservative majority. George W. Bush's administration also filled the courts with justices on the right of the legal spectrum. The Republican Congress confirmed most appointments.

But even when they controlled the White House and Congress after the 2002 midterm elections (Democrats controlled the Senate after Senator Jim Jeffords defected from the Republican party in the summer of 2001), conservatives had trouble stopping the growth of government. The federal budget had continued to grow under all administrations since Reagan. Even by the time Reagan left office, Congress had restored the budgets for regulatory agencies that had been slashed. As in the Reagan years, government remained divided and the parties competitive. Congressional majorities were consistently slim, which gave the Senate minority significant leverage. Bush's win in the 2004 race against Senator John Kerry was followed by a Democratic victory in the 2006 midterm elections. The most potent example of the limits of the

conservative movement was the failure of George W. Bush's campaign
to privatize Social Security.

At the same time, conservatives demonstrated that they, too, had a
taste for big government, as did some of their supporters. Rhetorically,
Bush sought to link his administration to Reagan's, and upon Reagan's
death in 2004, the president delivered a sentimental eulogy praising
Reagan as one of the great conservative heroes of the century (Document 59). But just as Reagan himself discovered that he could not always
rule according to conservative principles, so, too, did Bush. The Bush
administration substantially enhanced the power of the federal government with the creation of the Department of Homeland Security and the
surveillance of American citizens in the war on terror. It extended the
reach of government into new areas of social policy, including testing
of public school students, prescription drugs for Medicare beneficiaries, and additional subsidies for the oil industry. Federal spending on
farm subsidies rose under Republican rule.

In foreign policy, the doctrine of preemptive war that Bush introduced
in response to the terrorist attacks on 9/11 vastly expanded America's
ambitions abroad by committing the United States to eliminating international threats before they strike (Document 58). With the Iraq War
beginning in 2003, the United States fully involved itself in the business
of nation building, as the construction of a democratic society in Iraq
was officially made a central component of national security. This large
commitment caused significant strains, because the U.S. government,
even while pursuing a more aggressive foreign policy, was unwilling
to devote the necessary resources to the reconstruction of Iraq. The
limits of the professional military were clear when military forces were
stretched thin. Critics and even some of Bush's allies warned that the
troop deployment in Iraq meant that the United States would not be able
to respond to other crises should they occur.

During the 2008 presidential campaign, many Republicans lamented
that the Reagan Revolution was over, as conservatives seemed to have
entered a new era of disarray. The right, according to these critics, had
been destroyed as a result of having too much power and having moved
too far away from the principles that Reagan had championed (Document 60). But even when Reagan was in office, conservatives felt frustrated, realizing the immense challenges of holding and exercising
power. In fact, conservatives grappling with the challenges of governance have been the ones fulfilling Reagan's legacy: If there was a Reagan Revolution, the revolution took place within conservatism itself, as

the movement came into power and leaders modified their strategies and goals to deal with the challenges and opportunities of governance.

Some observers saw the election of President Barack Obama in 2008, along with a Democratic Congress, as marking the end of the conservative revolution. In the wake of the ongoing war in Iraq and the collapse of the economy in 2008, the ideas of conservatism seemed discredited, and the GOP lacked any strong leadership. The presidency of George W. Bush seemed to have damaged public support for conservatism in the way that Lyndon Johnson had hurt liberalism. When Reagan left office, his popularity stood at 70 percent, the highest rating of any outgoing president since World War II. Bush's approval rating of 22 percent was the lowest.

Whether Reagan's influence on American politics is over remains unclear, and it will take decades to sort out. President Obama does not think so: "What Reagan ushered in was a skepticism toward government solutions to every problem, a suspicion of command-and-control, top-down social engineering. I don't think that has changed. I think that's a lasting legacy of the Reagan era and the conservative movement, starting with Goldwater. But I do think [what we're seeing] is an end to the knee-jerk reaction toward the New Deal and big government" (Document 61). Regardless of the political future, the Bush administration marked the culmination of the period that began in 1980, a period of conservatives in power. The failures and achievements, as well as the political tactics, of conservatives in office were a product of the challenges that started when Ronald Reagan set foot in the White House.

NOTES

[1] "Nixon Says the G.O.P. Will Need 8 Years to Undo Democrats' Work," *New York Times*, May 11, 1981.

[2] "Reagan's Revolution," *National Review*, May 15, 1981, 529.

[3] "Nixon Says the G.O.P Will Need 8 Years to Undo Democrats' Work."

[4] Hedrick Smith, "Reformer Who Would Reverse the New Deal's Legacy," *New York Times*, January 21, 1981.

[5] Kimberly Phillips-Fein, *Invisible Hands: The Making of the Conservative Movement from the New Deal to Reagan* (New York: Norton, 2009).

[6] William F. Buckley Jr., "Our Mission Statement," *National Review*, November 19, 1955; James Burnham, *The Struggle for the World* (New York: John Day, 1947), 95, 96–106.

[7] Jonathan M. Schoenwald, *A Time for Choosing: The Rise of Modern American Conservatism* (New York: Oxford University Press, 2001), 193.

[8] Ronald Reagan, *An American Life* (New York: Simon and Schuster, 1990), 119–20.

[9] Matthew Dallek, *The Right Moment: Ronald Reagan's First Victory and the Decisive Turning Point in American Politics* (New York: Free Press, 2000), 27.

[10] Kiron K. Skinner, Annelise Anderson, and Martin Anderson, "The Cold War II: Politics, Arms, and Missile Defense," in *Reagan: A Life in Letters*, ed. Kiron K. Skinner, Annelise Anderson, and Martin Anderson (New York: Free Press, 2003), 396.

[11] Paul Lettow, *Ronald Reagan and His Quest to Abolish Nuclear Weapons* (New York: Random House, 2005).

[12] Ibid., 23.

[13] Thomas J. Sugrue, *The Origins of the Urban Crisis: Race and Inequality in Postwar Detroit* (Princeton, N.J.: Princeton University Press, 1996).

[14] Godfrey Hodgson, *The World Turned Right Side Up: A History of Conservative Ascendancy in America* (Boston: Houghton Mifflin, 1996), 65.

[15] Lisa McGirr, *Suburban Warriors: The Origins of the New American Right* (Princeton, N.J.: Princeton University Press, 2001).

[16] Richard Bergholz, "Reagan Raps Democrats on State Crime," *Los Angeles Times*, September 21, 1966.

[17] Dallek, *The Right Moment*, 106.

[18] Ibid., 120–24.

[19] Robert M. Collins, *Transforming America: Politics and Culture during the Reagan Years* (New York: Columbia University Press, 2007), 40–41.

[20] Ibid., 41.

[21] Lou Cannon, *President Reagan: The Role of a Lifetime* (New York: Public Affairs, 2003), 54–55.

[22] Bruce J. Schulman and Julian E. Zelizer, eds., *Rightward Bound: Making America Conservative in the 1970s* (Cambridge, Mass.: Harvard University Press, 2008).

[23] Alice O'Connor, "Financing the Counterrevolution: The 1970s, Right-Wing Philanthropy, and the Making of a Conservative Policy Establishment," in Schulman and Zelizer, *Rightward Bound*, 148–68.

[24] James Reston, "Thunder on the Right," *New York Times*, March 5, 1975.

[25] "Fordism, Reaganism and Extremism," Editorial, *Wall Street Journal*, January 5, 1976.

[26] "Let Them Find Bread," Editorial, *New York Times*, January 20, 1976.

[27] Peter Milius, "Social Security—Election Quagmire," *Washington Post*, February 17, 1976.

[28] Edwin Diamond, "How a Media Pro Took on New Hampshire," *New York Times*, February 22, 1976.

[29] William A. Rusher, *The Rise of the Right* (New York: William Morrow, 1984), 278.

[30] William F. Buckley Jr., "Ford, in a Fast Start, Can Thank Reagan," *Los Angeles Times*, August 26, 1976.

[31] Albert R. Hunt, "Reagan: 'A Man, a Plan, a Canal . . . ,' " *Wall Street Journal*, August 26, 1977.

[32] The best analysis of the "Malaise" speech can be found in Kevin Mattson, *"What the Heck Are You Up To, Mr. President?": Jimmy Carter, America's "Malaise," and the Speech That Should Have Changed the Country* (New York: Bloomsbury, 2009).

[33] Major Garrett, *The Enduring Revolution: How the Contract with America Continues to Shape the Nation* (New York: Crown, 2005), 33–34, quotation on 34.

[34] Patrick Caddell, Untitled correspondence, 1980, Jimmy Carter Presidential Library, Office of Staff: Jordan, box 77, Campaign Strategy—Caddell file.

[35] Lou Cannon, "Reagan: Castigating the 'Betrayal' of Workers' Aspirations," *Washington Post*, September 2, 1980.

[36] Commission on Presidential Debates, "Debate Transcript: The Carter-Reagan Presidential Debate," October 28, 1980, http://www.debates.org/index.php?page=october-28-1980=debate-transcript.

[37] Earl Black and Merle Black, *The Rise of Southern Republicans* (Cambridge, Mass.: Harvard University Press, 2002), 26.

[38] E. J. Dionne Jr., *Why Americans Hate Politics*, 2nd ed. (New York: Simon and Schuster, 2004), 93.

[39] Michael Schaller, *Reckoning with Reagan: America and Its President in the 1980s* (New York: Oxford University Press, 1992), 26–27.

[40] Associated Press, "Michael K. Deaver, Longtime Adviser to President Reagan, Dies," *San Diego Union Tribune*, August 18, 2007.

[41] Peggy Noonan, *What I Saw at the Revolution: A Political Life in the Reagan Era* (New York: Ballantine, 1990), xvi.

[42] Ibid., 10–11.

[43] David A. Stockman, *The Triumph of Politics: Why the Reagan Revolution Failed* (New York: Harper and Row, 1986), 39–40, quotation on 40.

[44] William Greider, "The Education of David Stockman," *Atlantic Monthly*, December 1981, 51.

[45] Michael Schaller, *Right Turn: American Life in the Reagan-Bush Era, 1980–1992* (New York: Oxford University Press, 2007), 72.

[46] Hedrick Smith, "Taking Charge of Congress," *New York Times Magazine*, August 9, 1981.

[47] "Reagan's Revolution," *National Review*, May 15, 1981, 529.

[48] Stockman, *The Triumph of Politics*, 75, 76.

[49] Hedrick Smith, "The President Attains Mastery at the Capitol," *New York Times*, July 30, 1981; Smith, "Taking Charge of Congress."

[50] Schaller, *Reckoning with Reagan*, 51.

[51] Eric Patashnik, "Congress and the Budget since 1974," in *The American Congress: The Building of Democracy*, ed. Julian E. Zelizer (Boston: Houghton Mifflin, 2004), 680.

[52] Jeffrey M. Berry, *The New Liberalism: The Rising Power of Citizen Groups* (Washington, D.C.: Brookings Institution, 1999).

[53] Julian E. Zelizer, *On Capitol Hill: The Struggle to Reform Congress and Its Consequences, 1948–2000* (New York: Cambridge University Press, 2004); David W. Rohde, *Parties and Leaders in the Postreform House* (Chicago: University of Chicago Press, 1991).

[54] Tom W. Smith, "Liberal and Conservative Trends in the United States since World War II," *Public Opinion Quarterly* 54 (1990): 497–507.

[55] Schaller, *Reckoning with Reagan*, 33.

[56] Ibid., 18.

[57] Kevin Phillips, "Post-Conservative America," *New York Review of Books*, May 13, 1982.

[58] David Shribman, "Neoconservatives and Reagan: Uneasy Coalition," *New York Times*, September 28, 1981.

[59] Greider, "The Education of David Stockman," 44, 54.

[60] Gil Troy, *Morning in America: How Ronald Reagan Invented the 1980s* (Princeton, N.J.: Princeton University Press, 2005), 104.

[61] Ronald Reagan, diary entry, September 28, 1982, in *The Reagan Diaries*, ed. Douglas Brinkley (New York: HarperCollins, 2007), 103.

[62] Donald Critchlow, "When Republicans Become Revolutionaries," in Zelizer, *The American Congress*, 715.

[63] Tom Wicker, "The End of the Affair," *New York Times*, November 5, 1982.

[64] Judith Stein, *Running Steel, Running America: Race, Economic Policy, and the Decline of Liberalism* (Chapel Hill: University of North Carolina Press, 1998).

[65] "Here Come the Yuppies," *Time*, January 9, 1984, 66; "The Year of the Yuppie," *Newsweek*, December 31, 1984, 14–31.

[66] "Watt Calls for Christian Revolution," Eugene (Ore.) *Register-Guard*, May 10, 1983.

[67] Lou Cannon, *Governor Reagan: His Rise to Power* (New York: Public Affairs, 2003), 321.

[68] Warren B. Rudman, "A Firm Hand for the Big Bad Budget," *New York Times*, October 26, 1985.

[69] Nolan McCarty, "The Policy Effects of Political Polarization," in *The Transformation of American Politics: Activist Government and the Rise of Conservatism*, ed. Paul Pierson and Theda Skocpol (Princeton, N.J.: Princeton University Press, 2007), 223–24.

70 Schaller, *Reckoning with Reagan*, 100.

71 Sean Wilentz, *The Age of Reagan: A History, 1974–2008* (New York: HarperCollins, 2008), 140.

72 Collins, *Transforming America*, 81.

73 John Ehrman, *The Eighties: America in the Age of Reagan* (New Haven, Conn.: Yale University Press, 2005), 91.

74 Schaller, *Reckoning with Reagan*, 79.

75 Schaller, *Right Turn*, 123.

76 James T. Patterson, *Restless Giant: The United States from Watergate to Bush v. Gore* (New York: Oxford University Press, 2005), 165.

77 Martin Anderson and Annelise Anderson, *Reagan's Secret War: The Untold Story of His Fight to Save the World from Nuclear Disaster* (New York: Crown, 2009); Lettow, *Ronald Reagan and His Quest.*

78 Daniel Wirls, *Buildup: The Politics of Defense in the Reagan Era* (Ithaca, N.Y.: Cornell University Press, 1992), 54.

79 Reagan, diary entry, January 3, 1983, in Brinkley, *The Reagan Diaries*, 123.

80 Ronald Reagan, "Address at Commencement Exercises at the University of Notre Dame," in *Public Papers of the Presidents of the United States: Ronald Reagan, 1981* (Washington, D.C.: U.S. Government Printing Office, 1983), 1:434.

81 James Mann, *The Rebellion of Ronald Reagan: A History of the End of the Cold War* (New York: Viking, 2009).

82 Robert Dallek, *Ronald Reagan: The Politics of Symbolism* (Cambridge, Mass.: Harvard University Press, 1984), 137.

83 Melvyn P. Leffler, *For the Soul of Mankind: The United States, the Soviet Union, and the Cold War* (New York: Hill and Wang, 2007), 355.

84 Ronald Reagan, "Address before a Joint Session of the Congress on Central America," in *Public Papers of the Presidents of the United States: Ronald Reagan, 1983* (Washington, D.C.: U.S. Government Printing Office, 1985), 1:601.

85 Richard Sobel, *The Impact of Public Opinion on U.S. Foreign Policy since Vietnam* (New York: Oxford University Press, 2001), 40–41, 101–40.

86 John Patrick Diggins, *Ronald Reagan: Fate, Freedom, and the Making of History* (New York: Norton, 2007), 255.

87 Hedrick Smith, "New House Seems Less in Tune with Reagan," *New York Times*, November 4, 1982.

88 See, for example, Jon Nordheimer, "500,000 Join Dutch Antimissile Rally," *New York Times*, October 30, 1983.

89 George Keyworth, Interview with Donald Baucom, Ronald Reagan Library, Strategic Defense Initiative Oral History Project, George Keyworth folder.

90 Collins, *Transforming America*, 202.

91 Elizabeth Pond, "Europe Fears 'Star Wars' May Destroy, Not Defend West," *Christian Science Monitor*, April 12, 1984.

92 Collins, *Transforming America*, 204.

93 George P. Shultz, *Turmoil and Triumph: My Years as Secretary of State* (New York: Scribner, 1993), 171.

94 Collins, *Transforming America*, 222–23, quotation on 223.

95 George Crile, *Charlie Wilson's War: The Extraordinary Story of the Largest Covert Operation in History* (New York: Atlantic Monthly, 2003), 234.

96 Dale R. Herspring, *The Pentagon and the Presidency: Civil-Military Relations from FDR to George W. Bush* (Lawrence: University Press of Kansas, 2005), 279–80.

97 Ronald Reagan, "Address to the Nation on Events in Lebanon and Grenada," in *Public Papers of the Presidents of the United States: Ronald Reagan, 1983* (Washington, D.C.: U.S. Government Printing Office, 1985), 2:1517–22.

98 Timothy Naftali, *Blind Spot: The Secret History of American Counterterrorism* (New York: Basic Books, 2005), 134.

[99] Beth A. Fischer, *The Reagan Reversal: Foreign Policy and the End of the Cold War* (Columbia: University of Missouri Press, 1997), 136–37.

[100] Ronald Reagan, "Address to the Nation and Other Countries on United States–Soviet Relations," in *Public Papers of the Presidents of the United States: Ronald Reagan, 1984* (Washington, D.C.: U.S. Government Printing Office, 1986), 1:44.

[101] Reagan, diary entry, January 16, 1984, in Brinkley, *The Reagan Diaries*, 212.

[102] Troy, *Morning in America*, 151–53.

[103] Reagan, diary entry, April 18, 1985, in Brinkley, *The Reagan Diaries*, 316.

[104] Lou Cannon, "What Happened to Reagan the Gunslinger?" *Washington Post*, July 7, 1985.

[105] Evan Thomas, "A Preview of the Reagan Revolution, Part Two," *Time*, November 19, 1984.

[106] Memorandum of Conversation, November 18, 1986, National Security Online Archive (NSOA), George Washington University.

[107] Sidney Blumenthal, *Our Long National Daydream: A Political Pageant of the Reagan Era* (New York: Harper and Row, 1988), 322.

[108] Michael Schudson, *Watergate in American Memory: How We Remember, Forget, and Reconstruct the Past* (New York: Basic Books, 1992), 165–84.

[109] Ronald Reagan, "Address to the Nation on the Iran Arms and Contra Aid Controversy," in *Public Papers of the Presidents of the United States: Ronald Reagan, 1987* (Washington, D.C.: U.S. Government Printing Office, 1989), 1:209.

[110] Reagan, diary entry, December 2, 1986, in Brinkley, *The Reagan Diaries*, 455.

[111] Haynes Johnson, *Sleepwalking through History: America in the Reagan Years* (New York: Norton, 1991), 350–51.

[112] U.S. Congress, *Joint Committee Investigating the Iran-Contra Affair*, Report, November 1987 (Washington, D.C.: U.S. Government Printing Office, 1987).

[113] William B. Lytton III to Arthur Culvahouse Jr., August 19, 1987, Ronald Reagan Library, Dan Crippen Files, box 7, Legislative Strategy (I) folder.

[114] Transcript, Meeting at Geneva, November 20, 1985, Ronald Reagan Library, Robert Linhard Files, box 92178, Geneva Summit Records file.

[115] Malcolm Wallop to Ronald Reagan, August 15, 1986, Ronald Reagan Library, Presidential Handwriting File, box 16, folder 257.

[116] Richard Reeves, *President Reagan: The Triumph of Imagination* (New York: Simon and Schuster, 2005), 351–52.

[117] Sidney Blumenthal, *Pledging Allegiance: The Last Campaign of the Cold War* (New York: HarperCollins, 1990), 249.

[118] Ronald Reagan, "Farewell Address," in *Public Papers of the Presidents of the United States: Ronald Reagan, 1988–1989* (Washington, D.C.: U.S. Government Printing Office, 1991), 2:1722.

[119] Gil Troy, *The Reagan Revolution: A Very Short Introduction* (New York: Oxford University Press, 2009), 106–7.

[120] Schaller, *Right Turn*, 65.

[121] Thomas B. Edsall, "Right in the Middle of the Revolution: Activist Rises to Influence in Conservative Movement," *Washington Post*, September 4, 1995.

[122] Charlie Savage, *Takeover: The Return of the Imperial Presidency and the Subversion of American Democracy* (New York: Little, Brown, 2007).

[123] Schaller, *Right Turn*, 134.

PART TWO

The Documents

Origins, 1957–1980

1

RONALD REAGAN

Commencement Address at Eureka College
June 7, 1957

Anticommunism became central to the brand of conservatism Ronald Reagan embraced. He developed his views on anticommunism early in his adult life. He perceived the cold war as a moral struggle between two distinct systems of politics that could not coexist. In this speech, he explained to students at his alma mater the dangers that he believed Americans faced in the cold war from the Soviet Union abroad and from Communist subversion and the growth of government at home. This was one of the many speeches that Reagan made while touring the country as president of the Screen Actors Guild and a spokesman for General Electric. These speeches helped him refine his positions.

You members of the graduating class of 1957 are today coming into your inheritance. You are taking your adult places in a society unique in the history of man's tribal relations. I would like to play the role of a "legal light" in the reading of the will, and to discuss with you the terms and conditions of your legacy.

Looming large in your inheritance is this country, this land America, placed as it is between two great oceans. Those who discovered and pioneered it had to have rare qualities of courage and imagination. . . .

From Ronald Reagan Memorabilia Collection, Textual Materials, Speeches and Addresses, Eureka College Archives.

. . . This is a land of destiny, and our forefathers found their way here by some Divine system of selective service gathered here to fulfill a mission to advance man a further step in his climb from the swamps. . . .

. . . Today we find ourselves involved in . . . a cold war. This cold war between great sovereign nations isn't really a new struggle at all. It is the oldest struggle of human kind, as old as man himself. This is a simple struggle between those of us who believe that man has the dignity and sacred right and the ability to choose and shape his own destiny and those who do not so believe. This irreconcilable conflict is between those who believe in the sanctity of individual freedom and those who believe in the supremacy of the state.

In a phase of this struggle not widely known, some of us came toe to toe with this enemy, this evil force in our own community in Hollywood, and make no mistake about it, this is an evil force. Don't be deceived because you are not hearing the sound of gunfire, because even so you are fighting for your lives. And you're fighting against the best organized and the most capable enemy of freedom and of right and decency that has ever been abroad in the world. Some years ago, back in the thirties, a man who was apparently just a technician came to Hollywood to take a job in our industry, an industry whose commerce is in tinsel and colored lights and make-believe. He went to work in the studios, and there were few to know he came to our town on direct orders from the Kremlin. When he quietly left our town a few years later the cells had been formed and planted in virtually all of our organizations, our guilds and unions. The framework for the Communist front organizations had been established. . . .

Now today as you prepare to leave your Alma Mater, you go into a world in which, due to our carelessness and apathy, a great many of our freedoms have been lost. It isn't that an outside enemy has taken them. It's just that there is something inherent in government which makes it, when it isn't controlled, continue to grow. So today for every seven of us sitting here in this lovely outdoor theater, there is one public servant, and 31 cents of every dollar earned in America goes in taxes. To support the multitudinous and gigantic functions of government, taxation is levied which tends to dry up the very sources of contributions and donations to colleges like Eureka. So in this time of prosperity we find these church schools, these small independent colleges and even the larger universities, hard put to maintain themselves and to continue doing the job they have done so unselfishly and well for all these years. Observe the contrast between these small church colleges and our government, because, as I have said before, these have always given far more than was ever given to them in return.

Class of 1957, it will be part of the terms of the will for you to take stock in the days to come, because we enjoy a form of government in which mistakes can be rectified. The dictator can never admit he was wrong, but we are blessed with a form of government where we can call a halt, and say, "Back up. Let's take another look." Remember that every government service, every offer of government financed security, is paid for in the loss of personal freedom. I am not castigating government and business for those many areas of normal cooperation, for those services that we know we must have and that we do willingly support. It is very easy to give up our personal freedom to drive 90 miles an hour down a city street in return for the safety that we will get for ourselves and our loved ones. Of course, that might not be a good example; it seems sometimes that this is a thing we have paid for in advance and the merchandise hasn't yet been delivered. But in the days to come whenever a voice is raised telling you to let the government do it, analyze very carefully to see whether the suggested service is worth the personal freedom which you must forego in return for such service.

There are many well-meaning people today who work at placing an economic floor beneath all of us so that no one shall exist below a certain level or standard of living, and certainly we don't quarrel with this. But look more closely and you may find that all too often these well-meaning people are building a ceiling above which no one shall be permitted to climb and between the two are pressing us all into conformity, into a mold of standardized mediocrity. . . .

So you should resolve, here and now, that you will not only accept your heritage but abide by the terms and conditions of the will. You should firmly resolve that these schools will not just be a part of America's past, but that they will continue to be a part of America's great future. Democracy with the personal freedoms that are ours we hold literally in trust for that day when we shall have fulfilled our destiny and brought mankind a great and long step from the swamps. Can we deliver it to our children?

2

RONALD REAGAN

A Time for Choosing

October 27, 1964

Reagan's speech endorsing Republican Barry Goldwater for president made the Hollywood actor a serious political figure in the national arena. Goldwater's campaign in 1964 is seen as a turning point in the history of modern conservatism, as he was a candidate who openly and defiantly embraced the ideas of the right in his run for president. While endorsing Goldwater, Reagan outlined the case for conservatism. Although Goldwater lost the race to President Lyndon Johnson in a landslide, Reagan emerged as a favorite of conservative activists, who believed that he could win the presidency one day.

Thank you and good evening. The sponsor has been identified, but unlike most television programs, the performer hasn't been provided with a script. As a matter of fact, I have been permitted to choose my own words and discuss my own ideas regarding the choice that we face in the next few weeks. . . .

. . . I think it's time we ask ourselves if we still know the freedoms that were intended for us by the Founding Fathers. . . .

. . . This idea that government is beholden to the people, that it has no other source of power except the sovereign people, is still the newest and the most unique idea in all the long history of man's relation to man.

This is the issue of this election: Whether we believe in our capacity for self-government or whether we abandon the American revolution and confess that a little intellectual elite in a far-distant capitol can plan our lives for us better than we can plan them ourselves. . . .

. . . The Founding Fathers . . . knew that governments don't control things. A government can't control the economy without controlling people. And they knew when a government sets out to do that, it must use force and coercion to achieve its purpose. They also knew, those Founding Fathers, that outside of its legitimate functions, government does nothing as well or as economically as the private sector of the economy. . . .

From Ronald W. Reagan Speeches and Articles (1950–1964), Ronald Reagan Library.

. . . Well, now, if government planning and welfare had the answer—and they've had almost 30 years of it—shouldn't we expect government to read the score to us once in a while? Shouldn't they be telling us about the decline each year in the number of people needing help? The reduction in the need for public housing?

But the reverse is true. Each year the need grows greater. . . .

Yet anytime you and I question the schemes of the do-gooders [the Democrats], we're denounced as being against their humanitarian goals. They say we're always "against" things—we're never "for" anything.

Well, the trouble with our liberal friends is not that they're ignorant; it's just that they know so much that isn't so. . . .

No government ever voluntarily reduces itself in size. So governments' programs, once launched, never disappear.

Actually, a government bureau is the nearest thing to eternal life we'll ever see on this earth.

Federal employees—federal employees number two and a half million; and federal, state, and local, one out of six of the nation's work force employed by government. These proliferating bureaus with their thousands of regulations have cost us many of our constitutional safeguards. How many of us realize that today federal agents can invade a man's property without a warrant? They can impose a fine without a formal hearing, let alone a trial by jury? And they can seize and sell his property at auction to enforce the payment of that fine. . . .

Last February 19th at the University of Minnesota, Norman Thomas, six-times candidate for President on the Socialist Party ticket, said, "If Barry Goldwater became President, he would stop the advance of socialism in the United States." I think that's exactly what he will do. . . .

Now it doesn't require expropriation or confiscation of private property or business to impose socialism on a people. What does it mean whether you hold the deed to the—or the title to your business or property if the government holds the power of life and death over that business or property? And such machinery already exists. The government can find some charge to bring against any concern it chooses to prosecute. Every businessman has his own tale of harassment. Somewhere a perversion has taken place. Our natural, unalienable rights are now considered to be a dispensation of government, and freedom has never been so fragile, so close to slipping from our grasp as it is at this moment. . . .

Those who would trade our freedom for the soup kitchen of the welfare state have told us they have a utopian solution of peace without victory. They call their policy "accommodation." And they say if we'll only avoid any direct confrontation with the enemy, he'll forget his evil ways and learn to love us. All who oppose them are indicted as warmongers. They say we offer simple answers to complex problems. Well, perhaps there is a simple answer—not an easy answer—but simple: If you and I have the courage to tell our elected officials that we want our national policy based on what we know in our hearts is morally right.

We cannot buy our security, our freedom from the threat of the bomb, by committing an immorality so great as saying to a billion human beings now enslaved behind the Iron Curtain, "Give up your dreams of freedom because to save our own skins, we're willing to make a deal with your slave masters." . . .

You and I have the courage to say to our enemies, "There is a price we will not pay. There is a point beyond which they must not advance." And this—this is the meaning in the phrase of Barry Goldwater's "peace through strength." . . .

You and I have a rendezvous with destiny.

We'll preserve for our children this, the last best hope of man on earth, or we'll sentence them to take the last step into a thousand years of darkness.

We will keep in mind and remember that Barry Goldwater has faith in us. He has faith that you and I have the ability and the dignity and the right to make our own decisions and determine our own destiny.

Thank you very much.

3

RONALD REAGAN

Campaign Speech at the Cow Palace, San Francisco

May 12, 1966

During the 1960s, student activists protested on college campuses for free speech and civil rights and against the war in Vietnam. The protests created a sense among many middle-class Americans that order had broken down in the nation's institutions. In his bid for the governorship of California, Reagan tapped into these anxieties, calling the free-speech

From Ronald Reagan Gubernatorial Campaign Files, Box C 30, file: RR Speeches and Statements, Book 11(5), Ronald Reagan Library.

movement the filthy speech movement. He argued that campus unrest symbolized the decay of American society, and he made strong arguments against student protests to solidify his credentials as a law-and-order politician.

There is a leadership gap and a morality and decency gap in Sacramento [the state capital]. And there is no better illustration of that than what has been perpetrated on the Berkeley campus at the University of California at Berkeley, where a small minority of beatniks, radicals and filthy speech advocates have brought such shame to, and such a loss of confidence in, a great University that applications for enrollment were down 21% this year and are expected to decline even further next year.

You have read about the report of the Senate Subcommittee on Un-American Activities—its charges that the campus has become a rallying point for Communists and a center of sexual misconduct.

Now, I have not seen that report—it has not yet been made public—but I do have information that verifies at least part of that report. The incidents in this report are so bad, so contrary to our standards of decent human behavior, I cannot recite them to you in detail.

But there is clear evidence of the sort of things that should not be permitted on a University campus.

The report tells us that many of those attending [a dance] were clearly of high school age. The hall was entirely dark except for the light from two movie screens. On these screens the nude torsos of men and women were portrayed, from time to time, in suggestive positions and movements.

Three rock and roll bands played simultaneously. The smell of marijuana was thick throughout the hall. There were signs that some of those present had taken dope. There were indications of other happenings that cannot be mentioned here.

How could this happen on the campus of a great University? It happened because those responsible abdicated their responsibilities.

The dance was only called to a halt when janitors finally cut off the power in the gymnasium forcing those attending to leave.

And this certainly is not the only sign of a leadership gap on the campus.

It began a year ago when so-called "free speech advocates," who in truth have no appreciation of freedom, were allowed to assault and humiliate an officer of the law. This was the moment when the ringleaders should have been taken by the scruff of the neck and thrown off the campus permanently.

It continued through the filthy speech movement, through activities of the Vietnam Day Committee [an antiwar left-wing organization] and this has been allowed to go on in the name of academic freedom.

What in heaven's name does "academic freedom" have to do with rioting, with anarchy, with attempts to destroy the primary purpose of the University, which is to educate our young people?

This is why I know there must be some substance to the Committee's report. This is why I am also convinced that just the issuance of that report is not enough, not enough for the people of California and not enough for those involved.

The charges made by the Committee are the results of private investigations. They must now be brought out in public hearings at which those involved must be forced to testify.

Otherwise there is a real danger that the charges will be swept under the rug.

These charges must neither be swept under the rug by a timid administration or by public apologists for the University. The public has a right to know from open hearings whether the situation is as the report says.

The citizens who pay the taxes that support the University also have a right to know that, if the situation is as the report says, that those responsible will be fired, that the University will be cleaned up and restored to its position as a major institution of learning and research.

The Governor has abdicated his responsibility in this area. His only answer has been to ask the Board [of] Regents to investigate. This is a straight cover-up. What kind of political nonsense is it to ask the Board of Regents to investigate a situation in which it may be involved?

For this reason, I today have called on the State Legislature to hold public hearings into the charges of Communism and blatant sexual misconduct on the campus. I have sent personal wires to Senator Hugh Burns, the President Pro Tem of the [California] Senate, and to Assembly Speaker Jesse Unruh, urging that they hold joint public hearings.

Only in this way can we get at the facts. Only [in] this way can we find out who is responsible for the degradation of a great University.

Only in this way can we determine what steps must be taken to restore the University to its position, steps that might go even beyond what I have already suggested.

Yes, there are things that can be done at the University even if a hearing is never held. This administration could make changes. It could demand that the faculty jurisdictions be limited to academic matters. It could demand that the administrators be told that it is your job to administer the University properly and if you don't, we will find someone who will.

The faculty could also be given a code of conduct that would force them to serve as examples of good behavior and decency for the young people in their charge.

When those who advocate an open mind keep it open at both ends with no thought process in the middle, the open mind becomes a hose for any idea that comes along. If scholars are to be recognized as having a right to press their particular value judgements, perhaps the time has come also for institutions of higher learning to assert themselves as positive forces in the battles for men's minds.

This could mean they would insist upon mature, responsible conduct and respect for the individual from their faculty members and might even call on them to be proponents of those ethical and moral standards demanded by the great majority of our society.

Those things could be done and should be done. The people not only have a right to know what is going on at their universities, they have a right to expect the best from those responsible for it.

4

RONALD REAGAN

California and the Problem of Government Growth
January 5, 1967

The nation witnessed a dramatic expansion of federal government services during the 1960s as a result of President Lyndon Johnson's Great Society. Many states, including California, also provided new social services. Conservatives perceived this expansion of government to be a significant threat. Reagan faulted the Great Society for creating large deficits and sought to win political support in this inaugural address by promising to cut taxes, welfare, and deficits. In reality, as governor, Reagan had to learn to live with many of the government programs he attacked.

From Pre-Presidential Speeches, Ronald Reagan Library, http://www.reagan.utexas.edu/archives/speeches/govspeech/01051967a.htm.

Government is the people's business, and every man, woman and child becomes a shareholder with the first penny of tax paid. With all the profound wording of the Constitution, probably the most meaningful words are the first three: "We, the People." Those of us here today who have been elected to constitutional office or legislative position are in that three-word phrase. We are of the people, chosen by them to see that no permanent structure of government ever encroaches on freedom or assumes a power beyond that freely granted by the people. We stand between the taxpayer and the tax spender. . . .

Welfare is [one] of our major problems. We are a humane and generous people and we accept without reservation our obligation to help the aged, disabled, and those unfortunates who, through no fault of their own, must depend on their fellow man. But we are not going to perpetuate poverty by substituting a permanent dole for a paycheck. There is no humanity or charity in destroying self-reliance, dignity, and self-respect . . . the very substance of moral fiber.

We seek reforms that will, wherever possible, change relief check to paycheck. . . .

. . . Only private industry in the last analysis can provide jobs with a future. . . .

In the whole area of welfare, everything will be done to reduce administrative overhead, cut red tape, and return control as much as possible to the county level. And the goal will be investment in, and salvage of, human beings. . . .

Here in our own Capitol, we will seek solutions to the problems of unrealistic taxes which threaten economic ruin to our biggest industry. We will work with the farmer as we will with business, industry, and labor to provide a better business climate so that they may prosper and we all may prosper. . . .

I have put off until last what is by no means least among our problems. Our fiscal situation. . . .

If we accept the present budget as absolutely necessary and add on projected increases plus funding for property tax relief (which I believe is absolutely essential and for which we are preparing a detailed and comprehensive program), our deficit in the coming year would reach three-quarters of a billion dollars.

But Californians are already burdened with combined state and local taxes $113 per capita higher than the national average. Our property tax contributes to a slump in the real estate and building trades industries and makes it well-nigh impossible for many citizens to continue owning their own homes.

For many years now, you and I have been shushed like children and told there are no simple answers to the complex problems which are beyond our comprehension.

Well the truth is, there are simple answers; they just are not easy ones. The time has come for us to decide whether collectively we can afford everything and anything we think of simply because we think of it. The time has come to run a check to see if all the services government provides were in answer to demands or were just goodies dreamed up for our supposed betterment. The time has come to match outgo to income, instead of always doing it the other way around. . . .

. . . We are going to squeeze and cut and trim until we reduce the cost of government. It won't be easy, nor will it be pleasant, and it will involve every department of government. . . .

We will put our fiscal house in order. And as we do, we will build those things we need to make our state a better place in which to live and we will enjoy them more, knowing we can afford them and they are paid for. . . .

If this is a dream, it is a good dream, worthy of our generation and worth passing on to the next.

Let this day mark the beginning.

5

RONALD REAGAN

Speech to America

March 31, 1976

After finishing his second term as governor, Reagan remained in the political arena. Although he rejected a proposal by conservatives to head a third party, Reagan challenged Gerald Ford in the 1976 Republican primaries. In addition to his usual antigovernment themes, Reagan decided to focus much of his campaign on détente as he did in this speech, which he delivered after a crucial victory in the North Carolina primary. This was an approach to foreign policy developed by Presidents Nixon and Ford, which centered on negotiations with the Soviet Union over arms

From Ronald Reagan Subject Collection, Box 1, file: RR Speeches, 1975, 1976, Hoover Institution Archives, Stanford University.

agreements. In 1972, the Soviet Union and the United States signed the SALT I accord. Reagan criticized Ford and Secretary of State Henry Kissinger for being too willing to negotiate with the Soviets. Conservatives believed that détente posed a danger to the United States because the Soviets were not serious about abiding by these agreements.

Good evening to all of you from California. Tonight, I'd like to talk to you about issues. Issues which I think are involved—or should be involved—in this primary election season. I'm a candidate for the Republican nomination for president. But I hope that you who are Independents and Democrats will let me talk to you also tonight because the problems facing our country are problems that just don't bear any party label. . . .

An effort has been made in this campaign to suggest that there aren't any real differences between Mr. Ford and myself. Well, I believe there are, and these differences are fundamental. One of them has to do with our approach to government. Before Richard Nixon appointed him Vice President, Mr. Ford was a Congressman for 25 years. His concern, of necessity, was the welfare of his congressional district. For most of his adult life he has been a part of the Washington Establishment. Most of my adult life has been spent outside of government. My experience in government was the eight years I served as governor of California. If it were a nation, California would be the 7th-ranking economic power in the world today. . . .

I had never in my life thought of seeking or holding public office and I'm still not quite sure how it all happened. In my own mind, I was a citizen representing my fellow citizens against the institution of government. I turned to the people, not to politicians, for help. . . .

We didn't stop just with getting our administration from the ranks of the people. We also asked for help from expert people in a great many fields, and more than 250 of our citizens volunteered to form into task forces. . . . They made eighteen hundred specific recommendations. We implemented more than sixteen hundred of those recommendations.

This was government-by-the-people, proving that it works when the people work at it. When we ended our eight years, we turned over to the incoming administration a balanced budget, a $500 million surplus, and virtually the same number of employees we'd started with eight years before. . . .

I believe that what we did in California can be done in Washington if government will have faith in the people and let them bring their common sense to bear on the problems bureaucracy hasn't solved. I believe in the people. Now, Mr. Ford places his faith in the Washington Establishment. This has been evident in his appointment of former Congressmen and longtime government workers to positions in his Administration. Well, I don't believe that those who have been part of the problem are necessarily the best qualified to solve those problems.

The truth is, Washington has taken over functions that don't truly belong to it. In almost every case it has been a failure. Now, understand, I'm speaking of those programs which logically should be administered at state and local levels. Welfare is a classic example. Voices that are raised now and then urging a federalization of welfare don't realize that the failure of welfare is due to federal interference. Washington doesn't even know how many people are on welfare, how many cheaters are getting more than one check. It only knows how many checks it's sending out. Its own rules keep it from finding out how many are getting more than one check. . . .

. . . We created at the local level and administered at the local level for many years the greatest public school system in the world. Now through something called federal aid to education, we have something called federal interference, and education has been the loser. Quality has declined as federal intervention has increased. Nothing has created more bitterness, for example, than forced busing to achieve racial balance. It was born of a hope that we could increase understanding and reduce prejudice and antagonism. And I'm sure we all approved of that goal. But busing has failed to achieve the goal. Instead, it has increased the bitterness and animosity it was supposed to reduce. California's Superintendent of Public Instruction, Wilson Riles (himself a Black), says, "The concept that Black children can't learn unless they are sitting with white children is utter and complete nonsense." Well, I agree. The money now being wasted on this social experiment could be better spent to provide the kind of school facilities every child deserves. Forced busing should be ended by legislation if possible, by constitutional amendment if necessary. And, control of education should be returned to local school districts. . . .

. . . There is one problem which must be solved or everything else is meaningless. I am speaking of the problem of our national security. Our nation is in danger, and the danger grows greater with each passing day. Like an echo from the past, the voice of Winston Churchill's grandson was heard recently in Britain's House of Commons warning that the spread of totalitarianism threatens the world once again and the democracies are wandering without aim. . . .

... We are told Washington is dropping the word "detente," but keeping the policy. But whatever it's called, the policy is what's at fault. ...

Mr. Ford says detente will be replaced by "peace through strength." Well now, that slogan has a nice ring to it, but neither Mr. Ford nor his new Secretary of Defense will say that our strength is superior to all others. ...

The Soviet Army outnumbers ours more than two-to-one and in reserves four-to-one. They out-spend us on weapons by 50 percent. Their Navy outnumbers ours in surface ships and submarines two-to-one. We're outgunned in artillery three-to-one and their tanks outnumber ours four-to-one. Their strategic nuclear missiles are larger, more powerful and more numerous than ours. The evidence mounts that we are Number Two in a world where it's dangerous, if not fatal, to be second best. ...

... I believe in the peace of which Mr. Ford spoke as much as any man. But peace does not come from weakness or from retreat. It comes from the restoration of American military superiority. ...

Recently on one of my campaign trips I was doing a question-and-answer session, and suddenly I received a question from a little girl [who] couldn't have been over six or seven years old standing in the very front row. I'd heard the question before but somehow in her asking it, she threw me a little bit. She said, why do you want to be president? Well, I tried to tell her about giving government back to the people; I tried to tell her about turning authority back to the states and local communities, and so forth; winding down the bureaucracy. [It] might have been an answer for adults, but I knew that it wasn't what that little girl wanted, and I left very frustrated. It was on the way to the next stop that I turned to Nancy and I said I wish I had it to do over again because I'd like to answer her question.

Well, maybe I can answer it now. I would like to go to Washington. I would like to be president, because I would like to see this country become once again a country where a little six-year-old girl can grow up knowing the same freedom that I knew when I was six years old, growing up in America. If this is the America you want for yourself and your children; if you want to restore government not only of and for but by the people; to see the American spirit unleashed once again; to make this land a shining, golden hope God intended it to be, I'd like to hear from you. Write, or send a wire. I'd be proud to hear your thoughts and your ideas.

6

NEWT GINGRICH

Campaign Speech to College Republicans in Atlanta
June 24, 1978

In 1978, Reagan found new allies in a group of young conservative Republicans who challenged Democrats, as well as the Republican establishment, during the midterm elections. Newt Gingrich was a young southern Republican in Georgia who believed that his party had to move to the right to effectively recruit southerners away from the Democratic party and strengthen the Republicans' appeal nationally. These activist Republicans formed close connections to the grassroots conservative movement in the 1970s. Over time, Gingrich, who won his congressional race in 1978, and other southern Republicans would become central to the Republican party.

I really believe that institutions live and die based on the quality of the leaders they get out of the next generation. . . . I think that one of the great problems we have in the Republican Party is that we don't encourage you to be nasty. We encourage you to be neat, obedient, and loyal and faithful and all those Boy Scout words, which would be great around the camp fire, but are lousy in politics. . . .

Do you like the state of the Republican Party? Do you think you ought to respect Bill Brock [chairman of the Republican National Committee] because he has done such a great job? Or Richard Nixon, or Gerald Ford, the only incumbent president since Herbert Hoover to lose an election? They have done a terrible job, a pathetic job. In my lifetime, literally in my lifetime, I was born in 1943, we have not had a competent national Republican leader. Not ever! We've had some guys who weren't too embarrassed. But what's the primary purpose of a political leader, above anything else? In this system, it is to build a majority capable of sustaining itself, because if we don't do that, we don't make the laws, we don't write the taxes, we don't decide how to start a war, we don't keep the country strong, we don't do nothing except carve from these

---

From West Georgia *News*, July 5, 1978.

people's ability. And in my lifetime, we have not had a single Republican leader capable of doing that. Oh, they've had opportunities: The Korean War, rapid inflation, the racial crisis of the 50's and 60's, the Vietnam war. We've had tremendous opportunities and we've blown it, but we're all nice people.

One of the great weaknesses of the Republican party is we recruit middle-class people. Middle-class people, as a group, are told you should not shout at the table, you should be nice, you should have respect for other people, which usually means giving way to them. You want to go to the beach, they want to go to the movie, well, you ought to go to the movie, cause otherwise they'll get mad at you. So what do you do? We ended up going to Watergate because we didn't want to offend Richard Nixon. We ended up allowing Gerald Ford to do some things that were incredibly dumb, just unbelievably dumb. Gerald Ford personally cost me a Congressional seat. . . . He pardoned Richard Nixon. Which, if now I don't care if he pardoned Nixon or not, in terms of politics, I wish he'd done it the day after the election, just utterly stupid. No Democratic politician would ever have done that, because he would have known better. No Republican politician before World War I would have done that, because they understood that their business was to build a majority. Theodore Roosevelt would have thought he was an idiot for doing it. . . .

Now the reason I am being harshly critical is because I want you all to learn a lesson. When you see somebody doing something dumb, say it. You don't help your party any by neatly sitting off to one side and saying, "God I wish you weren't so stupid." You weaken your party. And when you say it, say it in the press, say it loud, fight, scrap, issue a press release, go make a speech. Take yourself seriously, because many of us that are there are in this state right now I think this is an accurate figure that there are about 127,000 college students. College students of this state if they were mobilized, which is probably impossible theoretically, but if they were mobilized, the college students of this state could elect the government. But to do that we've got to take them seriously. . . .

. . . Find a job in politics that's real. If you decide that your job is building a CR (College Republicans) club, build a huge club. That means you got to go to listen to the people on your campus and find out what they care about. If they care about parking lots, then talk about parking lots. If they care about student activity fees, talk about student activity fees. If they care about tuition grants, talk about tuition grants. But the first rule of politics is you got to listen to them enough for them to be able to understand you when you talk to them. Don't try to educate them, that is not your job. You're in the politics business, and you can measure your results very simply. How big is your club? If your club isn't very big, then go back and listen some more, because you haven't figured out the magic solution yet. . . . Raise hell. Raise hell all the time. Make speeches, pass out leaflets, be in the newspaper, find issues that you can deal with. Accept your mistakes and learn from them, don't stop and say, "I made a mistake and I'm not going to do anything else this quarter." Just smile and say, "Yeah, isn't it great we're out there pitching?" So you occasionally walk somebody, at least you know you're on your own pitcher's mound. . . .

This party does not need another generation of cautious, prudent, careful, bland, irrelevant, quasi-leaders who are willing as people to drift into positions because nobody else is available. What we really need are people who are tough, hard-working, energetic, willing to take risks, willing to stand up in a . . . slug fest and match it out with their opponent, and people who take themselves and saving the country so seriously that when they have to choose between a week on the lake and a week saving the country they never worry about which choice they make, because they know that next spring when there are no campaigns, they can go to the lake. But the only time you get to try to save the country is between June and November of every other year. It does take time, it takes a lot of hard work. . . .

All of you should know that by now you're old enough to know that all human beings are weak and frail and occasionally tempted, probably even one or two of you have been tempted. So you don't want to trust politicians, you want to hold them accountable. You want to be able to say to them, "We have a contractual relationship, based on that I am a stockholder for you in your campaign, and if you do not listen to me and do something," I don't mean that they're going to obey you like a puppet, but at least understand where your problems are, "If you're not going to listen to me and honor me, then I'm going to sell my stock in you and I'm going to invest in somebody else and we're going to beat you." Now that's the basis of a healthy, free society and I hope all of you will consider getting involved.

7

RONALD REAGAN

Speech at Neshoba County Fair

August 3, 1980

In his 1980 campaign for the presidency, Reagan went to the Neshoba County fair in Mississippi, near the site of a gruesome civil rights murder in 1964. In this speech to a crowd of white southerners, Reagan pointed to President Carter's failure to improve the economy. He also included a defense of states' rights, explaining that states and localities should have a say over regional matters. This led to accusations that Reagan was using race to win support from southern white Democratic voters, who were unhappy with their party's active support of federal policies, such as school integration, to promote civil rights. Reagan's campaign rejected the charge, but the defection of southern Democrats to the Republican party would become one of the most important accomplishments of Reagan's campaign and would continue throughout the 1980s and 1990s.

I know that in speaking to this crowd, that I'm speaking to what has to be about 90 percent Democrat. [Shouts of "No" from the crowd.] I just meant by party affiliation. I didn't mean how you feel now. I was a Democrat most of my life myself, but then decided that there were things that needed to be changed.

I know, people have been telling me, that Jimmy Carter has been doing his best. And that's our problem.

The President lately has been saying that I am irresponsible. And you know, I'll admit to that if he'll confess he's responsible.

We've had the New Deal, and then Harry Truman gave us the Fair Deal, and now we have a misdeal.

They're having quite a fight in that convention that's coming up. Teddy Kennedy—I know why he's so interested in poverty: He never had any when he was a kid.

From Ronald Reagan 1980 Presidential Campaign Papers, 1964–1980, Ronald Reagan Library.

All of us in this race, of course—you know, there's talk now about getting our commercials together, and our television ads and so forth. I heard the other day they have one for Jimmy Carter. It's called, "The Best of the Carter Years." It's a 3-second station break.

But I don't know—do you feel as I do, when they talk in Washington of balancing the budget? That makes me think of a fellow sitting in a restaurant. He's ordered dinner. He knows he doesn't have any money in his pocket to pay for it, but he's hoping maybe he'll find a pearl in his oysters.

Seriously, and I'm not going to take a great deal of time talking about the particular troubles—we know what confronts us in this country. We know that an administration for three and a half years, that told us when they took office that it was going to reduce inflation to less than four percent and reduce unemployment to less than four percent, has betrayed the people with an inflation rate that they hope that they might get back down to 10 percent after it having reached 18 at the beginning of the year.

The unemployment in the months of April and May alone—1,700,000 American working people lost their jobs. I don't know how many since.

But probably the worst thing is what had been done to this country on the international scene. This once proud country, this country that all the world turned to and looked to as the shelter, as the safety and as the anchor to windward. Today, our friends don't know whether they can trust us, and certainly our enemies have no respect for us. . . .

Sure, it's right that we should say we want to do something about unemployment, and about inflation, about the value of our money and to get this country moving again. But I think even more important on a broader scale [is] in doing that, what we will have to do is to bring back to this country what is so evident here: Bring back the recognition that the people of this country can solve the problems, that we don't have anything to be afraid of as long as we have the people of America.

[In] more recent years with the best intention, they have created a vast bureaucracy, or a bureaucratic structure—bureaus and departments and agencies—to try and solve all the problems and eliminate all the things of human misery that they can. They have forgotten that when you create a government bureaucracy, no matter how well intentioned it is, almost instantly its top priority becomes preservation of the bureaucracy.

Today, and I know from our own experience in California when we reformed welfare, I know that one of the great tragedies of welfare in America today are people in need who are there simply because they prefer to be there. We found the overwhelming majority would like nothing better than to be out, with jobs for the future, and out here in the society with the rest of us. The trouble is, again, that bureaucracy has them so economically trapped that there is no way they can get away. And they're trapped because that bureaucracy needs them as a clientele to preserve the jobs of the bureaucrats themselves.

I believe that there are programs like that, programs like education and others, that should be turned back to the states and the local communities with the tax sources to fund them, and let the people [applause drowns out end of statement].

I believe in states' rights: I believe in people doing as much as they can for themselves at the community level and at the private level. And I believe that we've distorted the balance of our government today by giving powers that were never intended in the Constitution to that federal establishment. And if I do get the job I'm looking for, I'm going to devote myself to trying to reorder those priorities and to restore to the states and local communities those functions which properly belong there.

I'm going to try also to change federal regulations in the tax structure that has made this once powerful industrial giant in this land and in the world now with a lower rate of productivity than any of the other industrial nations, with a lower rate of savings and investment on the part of our people, and put us back where we belong. . . .

Thank you all very much.

Reaganomics, 1981

8

RONALD REAGAN

Inaugural Address
January 20, 1981

In his first inaugural address, Ronald Reagan articulated the basic differences between conservatism and liberalism and set the stage for the policies he would attempt to implement during his presidency. Most important, he argued that government would have to have a reduced role in America. He believed that tax cuts should be a centerpiece of his domestic agenda because they signaled a commitment to the free market over government intervention. Reagan's words resonated with conservative activists, who believed that they finally had an ally in the White House.

These United States are confronted with an economic affliction of great proportions. We suffer from the longest and one of the worst sustained inflations in our national history. It distorts our economic decisions, penalizes thrift, and crushes the struggling young and the fixed-income elderly alike. It threatens to shatter the lives of millions of our people.

Idle industries have cast workers into unemployment, human misery, and personal indignity. Those who do work are denied a fair return for their labor by a tax system which penalizes successful achievement and keeps us from maintaining full productivity.

From Ronald Reagan, "Inaugural Address," in *Public Papers of the Presidents of the United States: Ronald Reagan, 1981* (Washington, D.C.: U.S. Government Printing Office, 1982), 1:1–4.

But great as our tax burden is, it has not kept pace with public spending. For decades we have piled deficit upon deficit, mortgaging our future and our children's future for the temporary convenience of the present. To continue this long trend is to guarantee tremendous social, cultural, political, and economic upheavals.

You and I, as individuals, can, by borrowing, live beyond our means, but for only a limited period of time. Why, then, should we think that collectively, as a nation, we're not bound by that same limitation? We must act today in order to preserve tomorrow. And let there be no misunderstanding: We are going to begin to act, beginning today.

The economic ills we suffer have come upon us over several decades. They will not go away in days, weeks, or months, but they will go away. They will go away because we as Americans have the capacity now, as we've had in the past, to do whatever needs to be done to preserve this last and greatest bastion of freedom.

In this present crisis, government is not the solution to our problem; government is the problem. From time to time we've been tempted to believe that society has become too complex to be managed by self-rule, that government by an elite group is superior to government for, by, and of the people. But, if no one among us is capable of governing himself, then who among us has the capacity to govern someone else? All of us together, in and out of government, must bear the burden. The solutions we seek must be equitable, with no one group singled out to pay a higher price.

We hear much of special interest groups. Well, our concern must be for a special interest group that has been too long neglected. It knows no sectional boundaries or ethnic and racial divisions, and it crosses political party lines. It is made up of men and women who raise our food, patrol our streets, man our mines and factories, teach our children, keep our homes, and heal us when we're sick—professionals, industrialists, shopkeepers, clerks, cabbies, and truck drivers. They are, in short, "We the people," this breed called Americans.

Well, this administration's objective will be a healthy, vigorous, growing economy that provides equal opportunities for all Americans, with no barriers born of bigotry or discrimination. Putting America back to work means putting all Americans back to work. Ending inflation means freeing all Americans from the terror of runaway living costs. All must share in the productive work of this "new beginning," and all must share in the bounty of a revived economy. With the idealism and fair play which are the core of our system and our strength, we can have a strong and prosperous America, at peace with itself and the world.

So, as we begin, let us take inventory. We are a nation that has a government—not the other way around. And this makes us special among the nations of the Earth. Our government has no power except that granted it by the people. It is time to check and reverse the growth of government, which shows signs of having grown beyond the consent of the governed.

It is my intention to curb the size and influence of the Federal establishment and to demand recognition of the distinction between the powers granted to the Federal Government and those reserved to the States or to the people. All of us need to be reminded that the Federal Government did not create the States; the States created the Federal Government.

Now, so there will be no misunderstanding, it's not my intention to do away with government. It is rather to make it work—work with us, not over us; to stand by our side, not ride on our back. Government can and must provide opportunity, not smother it; foster productivity, not stifle it. . . .

It is no coincidence that our present troubles parallel and are proportionate to the intervention and intrusion in our lives that result from unnecessary and excessive growth of government. It is time for us to realize that we're too great a nation to limit ourselves to small dreams. We're not, as some would have us believe, doomed to an inevitable decline. I do not believe in a fate that will fall on us no matter what we do. I do believe in a fate that will fall on us if we do nothing. So, with all the creative energy at our command, let us begin an era of national renewal. Let us renew our determination, our courage, and our strength. And let us renew our faith and our hope.

9

RONALD REAGAN

Address to the Nation on the Economy
February 5, 1981

Tax cuts and deregulation were central to Reagan's agenda. In this speech just weeks after his inauguration, Reagan explained his plan to cut spending and reduce the role of government in the economy. Reagan played a major role in selling his tax bill directly to Americans as a way of putting pressure on the Democratic-controlled House of Representatives. From the beginning of his administration, Reagan had high popularity ratings. His ability to charm, convince, and soothe the public in speeches like this one contributed to his reputation as "the Great Communicator."

Good evening.

I'm speaking to you tonight to give you a report on the state of our Nation's economy. I regret to say that we're in the worst economic mess since the Great Depression. . . .

. . . One way out would be to raise taxes so that government need not borrow or print money. But in all these years of government growth, we've reached, indeed surpassed, the limit of our people's tolerance or ability to bear an increase in the tax burden. Prior to World War II, taxes were such that on the average we only had to work just a little over 1 month each year to pay our total Federal, State, and local tax bill. Today we have to work 4 months to pay that bill.

Some say shift the tax burden to business and industry, but business doesn't pay taxes. Oh, don't get the wrong idea. Business is being taxed, so much so that we're being priced out of the world market. But business must pass its costs of operations — and that includes taxes — on to the customer in the price of the product. Only people pay taxes, all the taxes. Government just uses business in a kind of sneaky way to help

From Ronald Reagan, "Address to the Nation on the Economy," in *Public Papers of the Presidents of the United States: Ronald Reagan, 1981* (Washington, D.C.: U.S. Government Printing Office, 1982), 1:79–83.

collect the taxes. They're hidden in the price; we aren't aware of how much tax we actually pay.

Today this once great industrial giant of ours has the lowest rate of gain in productivity of virtually all the industrial nations with whom we must compete in the world market. We can't even hold our own market here in America against foreign automobiles, steel, and a number of other products. Japanese production of automobiles is almost twice as great per worker as it is in America. Japanese steelworkers outproduce their American counterparts by about 25 percent.

Now, this isn't because they're better workers. I'll match the American working man or woman against anyone in the world. But we have to give them the tools and equipment that workers in the other industrial nations have.

We invented the assembly line and mass production, but punitive tax policies and excessive and unnecessary regulations plus government borrowing have stifled our ability to update plant and equipment. When capital investment is made, it's too often for some unproductive alterations demanded by government to meet various of its regulations. Excessive taxation of individuals has robbed us of incentive and made overtime unprofitable. . . .

All of you who are working know that even with cost-of-living pay raises, you can't keep up with inflation. In our progressive tax system, as you increase the number of dollars you earn, you find yourself moved up into higher tax brackets, paying a higher tax rate just for trying to hold your own. The result? Your standard of living is going down.

Over the past decades we've talked of curtailing government spending so that we can then lower the tax burden. Sometimes we've even taken a run at doing that. But there were always those who told us that taxes couldn't be cut until spending was reduced. Well, you know, we can lecture our children about extravagance until we run out of voice and breath. Or we can cure their extravagance by simply reducing their allowance.

It's time to recognize that we've come to a turning point. We're threatened with an economic calamity of tremendous proportions, and the old business-as-usual treatment can't save us. Together, we must chart a different course.

We must increase productivity. That means making it possible for industry to modernize and make use of the technology which we ourselves invented. That means putting Americans back to work. And that means above all bringing government spending back within government revenues, which is the only way, together with increased productivity, that we can reduce and, yes, eliminate inflation. . . .

On February 18th, I will present in detail an economic program to Congress embodying the features I've just stated. It will propose budget cuts in virtually every department of government. It is my belief that these actual budget cuts will only be part of the savings. As our Cabinet Secretaries take charge of their departments, they will search out areas of waste, extravagance, and costly administrative overhead which could yield additional and substantial reductions.

Now, at the same time we're doing this, we must go forward with a tax relief package. I shall ask for a 10-percent reduction across the board in personal income tax rates for each of the next 3 years. Proposals will also be submitted for accelerated depreciation allowances for business to provide necessary capital so as to create jobs.

Now, here again, in saying this, I know that language, as I said earlier, can get in the way of a clear understanding of what our program is intended to do. Budget cuts can sound as if we're going to reduce total government spending to a lower level than was spent the year before. Well, this is not the case. The budgets will increase as our population increases, and each year we'll see spending increases to match that growth. Government revenues will increase as the economy grows, but the burden will be lighter for each individual, because the economic base will have been expanded by reason of the reduced rates. . . .

Our aim is to increase our national wealth so all will have more, not just redistribute what we already have which is just a sharing of scarcity. We can begin to reward hard work and risk-taking, by forcing this Government to live within its means.

Over the years we've let negative economic forces run out of control. We stalled the judgment day, but we no longer have that luxury. We're out of time.

And to you, my fellow citizens, let us join in a new determination to rebuild the foundation of our society, to work together, to act responsibly. Let us do so with the most profound respect for that which must be preserved as well as with sensitive understanding and compassion for those who must be protected.

We can leave our children with an unrepayable massive debt and a shattered economy, or we can leave them liberty in a land where every individual has the opportunity to be whatever God intended us to be. All it takes is a little common sense and recognition of our own ability. Together we can forge a new beginning for America.

Thank you, and good night.

10

ROBERT MICHEL

Letter to Republican Colleagues

May 29, 1981

As Reagan's tax bill worked its way through Congress, Republicans com-
plained about Democrats' heavy-handed use of procedural rules to stifle
the GOP minority. Younger Republicans such as Newt Gingrich worried
that senior members of the GOP, such as House Minority Leader Robert
Michel, were too willing to compromise with Democrats and feared using
hardball political tactics to achieve their objectives. But the Republican
leadership in the House realized that they would have to work with the
Democratic majority on issues such as spending in order to pass their
tax cuts. The debate over compromise would continue to intensify within
the GOP over the next few years. In this letter to all House Republicans,
Michel balanced the need for party members to stand strong behind
Reagan's agenda with the need to work with the Democratic majority. In
the end, Republicans were able to achieve much of what they wanted, and
Reagan signed the Economic Recovery Tax Act on August 13, 1981.

Dear Republican Colleagues:

I was very disheartened by the posture of Democratic leaders this
week on working out a compromise tax bill in the House. I do not believe
their take-it-or-leave-it attitude expressed Thursday reflects the senti-
ments of a good many of our colleagues on the other side and I do not
believe it is at all consistent with what the general public wants out of
the Congress.

We have tried to walk that extra mile in our efforts to accommodate
the Speaker, but he has not budged. His attitude remains unchanged.
His defiance of the President and what he seeks to accomplish is remi-
niscent of the old-fashioned iron-fisted Democratic rule we have had in
the House for the past 25 years. Tip [O'Neill] is clearly still on top, but
Tip is more clearly out of touch with the times.

From Lee Atwater Files, Box 2, file: Economic Recovery Program, Ronald Reagan
Library.

Make no mistake about it, there is a reason behind the hard-line approach taken by the Speaker. The House that Tip built will topple without an ever escalating flow of tax revenues into the Treasury. He knows full well that tax reduction will force spending reduction just as spending reduction will force tax reduction. The Speaker cannot accept either without abandoning the big government philosophy he has adhered to for so many years. I have seen in my years in Congress times when the American people supported the massive expanse of federal programs we have today. Yet today I see the public repudiate those programs and demand change. The Speaker truly believes that public attitudes have not changed. He considers public opinion polls to be only a temporary phenomenon that his kind of Democrats can ride out if they hold firm to their Great Society principles, while we wrestle with the critical tax and spending issues. Such a position in my opinion is antique politics from a bygone era. It must not and will not prevail.

Our fundamental position must not change. We must continue to strive for multi-year, across the board tax rate reductions this year. We must not accept anything less. We can compromise, but we must not capitulate. I believe that if we continue to keep the door open, continue to express our willingness to cooperate and to negotiate, we can adopt a tax bill in the House that will meet the principle [sic] goals of the President's program. I hope all Republicans will continue to press hard for these goals and remind their constituents that economic recovery cannot be achieved without the dual implementation of spending and tax reductions.

ROBERT H. MICHEL

11

RONALD REAGAN

Air Traffic Controllers Strike

August 3, 1981

Ronald Reagan took a tough stand against PATCO, one of the few unions that had supported him in the 1980 election, when these workers went on strike. The union sought improved safety, pay, and working conditions. Unions had been a target of conservatives ever since the New Deal. In this case, Reagan fired the workers rather than negotiate with them. Although Reagan sought the political support of working Americans, with this action he signaled the pro-business stance of his administration.

This morning at 7 A.M. the union representing those who man America's air traffic control facilities called a strike. This was the culmination of 7 months of negotiations between the Federal Aviation Administration and the union. At one point in these negotiations agreement was reached and signed by both sides, granting a $40 million increase in salaries and benefits. This is twice what other government employees can expect. It was granted in recognition of the difficulties inherent in the work these people perform. Now, however, the union demands are 17 times what had been agreed to—$681 million. This would impose a tax burden on their fellow citizens which is unacceptable.

I would like to thank the supervisors and controllers who are on the job today, helping to get the nation's air system operating safely. In the New York area, for example, four supervisors were scheduled to report for work, and 17 additionally volunteered. At National Airport a traffic controller told a newsperson he had resigned from the union and reported to work because, "How can I ask my kids to obey the law if I don't?" This is a great tribute to America.

Let me make one thing plain. I respect the right of workers in the private sector to strike. Indeed, as president of my own union, I led the

From Ronald Reagan, "Statement and a Question-and-Answer Session with Reporters on the Air Traffic Controllers Strike," in *Public Papers of the Presidents of the United States: Ronald Reagan, 1981* (Washington, D.C.: U.S. Government Printing Office, 1982), 1:687–90.

first strike ever called by that union. I guess I'm maybe the first one to ever hold this office who is a lifetime member of an AFL-CIO union. But we cannot compare labor-management relations in the private sector with government. Government cannot close down the assembly line. It has to provide without interruption the protective services which are government's reason for being.

It was in recognition of this that the Congress passed a law forbidding strikes by government employees against the public safety. Let me read the solemn oath taken by each of these employees, a sworn affidavit, when they accepted their jobs: "I am not participating in any strike against the Government of the United States or any agency thereof, and I will not so participate while an employee of the Government of the United States or any agency thereof."

It is for this reason that I must tell those who fail to report for duty this morning they are in violation of the law, and if they do not report for work within 48 hours, they have forfeited their jobs and will be terminated. . . .

Q: Mr. President, why have you taken such strong action as your first action? Why not some lesser action at this point?

The President: What lesser action can there be? The law is very explicit. They are violating the law. . . . We called this to the attention of their leadership. Whether this was conveyed to the membership before they voted to strike, I don't know. But this is one of the reasons why there can be no further negotiation while this situation continues. You can't sit and negotiate with a union that's in violation of the law and their oath.

12

WILLIAM GREIDER

The Education of David Stockman

December 1981

Journalist William Greider conducted a series of interviews with David Stockman, director of the Office of Management and Budget (OMB), for a featured story in the Atlantic Monthly. *Stockman was one of the architects of Reagan's first budget. In these interviews, Stockman acknowledged the difficulties that the administration faced in reducing spending. As much as Stockman succeeded in pushing through Reagan's agenda, he recognized the enduring legacy of New Deal programs and the reluctance of many Americans to have them significantly altered. Many in the Reagan White House felt that Stockman had betrayed them by admitting that tax cuts in the absence of significant budget cuts would likely lead to a deficit—in spite of what supply-side theory predicted.*

During four years in Congress, Stockman had made himself a leading conservative gadfly, attacking Democratic budgets and proposing leaner alternatives. Now the President-elect was inviting him to do the same thing from within. Stockman had lobbied for the OMB job and was probably better prepared for it, despite his youthfulness, than most of his predecessors. . . .

While David Stockman would speak passionately against the government in Washington and its self-aggrandizing habits, there was this small irony about his siblings and himself: Most of them worked for government in one way or another—protected from the dynamic risk-taking of the private economy. Stockman himself had never had any employer other than the federal government, but the adventure in his career lay in challenging it. Or, more precisely, in challenging the "permanent government" that modern liberalism had spawned.

By that phrase, Stockman and other conservatives meant not only the layers and layers of federal bureaucrats and liberal politicians who

---

From William Greider, "The Education of David Stockman," *Atlantic Monthly*, December 1981, 27–54.

sustained open-ended growth of the central government but also the less visible infrastructure of private interests that fed off of it and prospered. . . .

While ideology would guide Stockman in his new job, he would be confronted with a large and tangible political problem: how to resolve the three-sided dilemma created by Ronald Reagan's contradictory campaign promises. In private, Stockman agreed that his former congressional mentor, John Anderson, running as an independent candidate for President in 1980, had asked the right question: How is it possible to raise defense spending, cut income taxes, and balance the budget, all at the same time? . . .

But Stockman was confident, even cocky, that he and some of his fellow conservatives had the answer. It was a theory of economics—the supply-side theory—that promised an end to the twin aggravations of the 1970s: high inflation and stagnant growth in America's productivity. . . .

The supply-side approach, which Stockman had only lately embraced, assumed, first of all, that dramatic action by the new President, especially the commitment to a three-year reduction of the income tax, coupled with tight monetary control, would signal investors that a new era was dawning, that the growth of government would be displaced by the robust growth of the private sector. If economic behavior in a climate of high inflation is primarily based on expectations about the future value of money, then swift and dramatic action by the President could reverse the gloomy assumptions in the disordered financial markets. As inflation abated, interest rates dropped, and productive employment grew, those marketplace developments would, in turn, help Stockman balance the federal budget.

"The whole thing is premised on faith," Stockman explained. "On a belief about how the world works." . . .

How the world works. It was a favorite phrase of Stockman's, frequently invoked in conversation to indicate a coherent view of things, an ideology that was whole and consistent. Stockman took ideology seriously, and this distinguished him from other bright, ambitious politicians who were content to deal with public questions one at a time, without imposing a consistent philosophical framework upon them. . . .

Stockman was impressed by the ease with which the President-elect accepted the broad objective: find $40 billion in cuts in a federal budget running well beyond $700 billion. But, despite the multitude of expenditures, the proliferation of programs and grants, Stockman knew the exercise was not as easy as it might sound. . . .

No president had balanced the budget in the past twelve years. Still, Stockman thought it could be done, by 1984, if the Reagan Administration adhered to the principle of equity, cutting weak claims, not merely weak clients, and if it shocked the system sufficiently to create a new political climate. He still believed that it was not a question of numbers. "It boils down to a political question, not of budget policy or economic policy, but whether we can change the habits of the political system." . . .

Stockman proposed to White House counselor Edwin Meese an alternative approach—a budget working group, in which each Cabinet secretary could review the proposed cuts and argue against them. As the group evolved, however, with Meese, chief of staff James Baker, Treasury Secretary Donald Regan, and policy director Martin Anderson, among others, it was stacked in Stockman's favor. "Each meeting will involve only the relevant Cabinet member and his aides with four or five strong keepers of the central agenda," Stockman explained at one point. . . .

In general, the system worked. Stockman's agency did in a few weeks what normally consumes months; the process was made easier because the normal opposition forces had no time to marshal either their arguments or their constituents and because the President was fully in tune with Stockman. After the budget working group reached a decision, it would be taken to Reagan in the form of a memorandum, on which he could register his approval by checking a little box. "Once he checks it," Stockman said, "I put that in my safe and I go ahead and I don't let it come back up again." . . .

By March, . . . Stockman could see the status quo yielding to the shock of the Reagan agenda. In dozens of meetings and hearings, public and private, Stockman perceived that it was now inappropriate for a senator or a congressman to plead for his special interests, at least in front of other members with other interests. . . .

. . . He began to believe that the Reagan budget package, despite its scale, perhaps because of its scale, could survive in Congress. With skillful tactics by political managers, with appropriate public drama provided by the President, the relentless growth rate of the federal budget, a permanent reality of Washington for twenty years, could actually be contained. . . .

In political terms, Stockman's analysis was sound. The Reagan program was moving toward a series of dramatic victories in Congress. Beyond the brilliant tactical maneuvering, however, and concealed by the public victories, Stockman was privately staring at another reality—a gloomy portent that the economic theory behind the President's program wasn't working. While it was winning in the political arena, the plan was losing on Wall Street. The financial markets, which Stockman had thought would be reassured by the new President's bold actions, and which were supposed to launch a historic "bull market" in April, failed to respond in accordance with Stockman's script. The markets not only failed to rally, they went into a new decline. Interest rates started up again; the bond market slumped. The annual inflation rate, it was true, was declining, dropping below double digits, but even Stockman acknowledged that this was owing to "good luck" with grain harvest and world oil supplies, not to Reaganomics. . . .

Reagan's policy-makers knew that their plan was wrong, or at least inadequate to its promised effects, but the President went ahead and conveyed the opposite impression to the American public. With the cool sincerity of an experienced television actor, Reagan appeared on network TV to rally the nation in support of [his program], promising a new era of fiscal control and balanced budgets, when Stockman knew they still had not found the solution. . . .

Indeed, Stockman began in May to plot what he called the "recalibration" of Reagan policy, which he hoped could be executed discreetly over the coming months to eliminate the out-year deficits for 1983 and 1984 that alarmed Wall Street—without alarming political Washington and losing control in the congressional arena. . . .

Stockman saw three main areas of opportunity for closing the gap: defense, Social Security, and health costs, meaning Medicare and Medicaid. And there was a fourth: the Reagan tax cut; if it could be modified in the course of the congressional negotiations already under way, this would make for additional savings on the revenue side. The public alarm over the deficits was, to some extent, "fortuitous," from Stockman's viewpoint, because the Wall Street message supported the sermon that he was delivering to his fellow policy-makers at the White House: the agonies of budget reduction were only beginning, and, more to the point, the Reagan Administration could not keep its promise of balanced budgets unless it was willing to back away from its promised defense spending, its 10-10-10 tax-cut plan, and the President's pledge to exempt from cutbacks the so-called "safety-net" programs. . . .

. . . Without recognizing it at the time, the budget director was headed into a summer in which not only financial markets but life itself seemed to be absolutely perverse. The Reagan program kept winning in public, a series of well-celebrated political victories in Congress—yet privately Stockman was losing his struggle.

Stockman was changing, in a manner that perhaps he himself did not recognize. His conversations began to reflect a new sense of fatalism, a brittle edge of uncertainty.

"There was a certain dimension of our theory that was unrealistic . . ."

"The system has an enormous amount of inertia . . ."

"I don't believe too much in the momentum theory any more . . ."

"I have a new theory—there are no *real* conservatives in Congress..."

The turning point, which Stockman did not grasp at the time, came in May, shortly after the first House victory. Buoyed by the momentum, the White House put forward, with inadequate political soundings, the Stockman plan for Social Security reform. Among other things, it proposed a drastic reduction in the benefits for early retirement at age sixty-two. Stockman thought this was a privilege that older citizens could comfortably yield, but 64 percent of those eligible for Social Security were now taking early retirement, and the "reform" plan set off a sudden tempest on Capitol Hill. Democrats accused Reagan of reneging on his promise to exempt Social Security from the budget cuts and accused Stockman of trying to balance his budget at the expense of Social Security recipients, which, of course, he was. . . .

There was less "courage" among politicians than Stockman assumed. Indeed, one politician who scurried away from the President's proposed cuts in Social Security was the President. Stockman wanted him to go on television again, address the nation on Social Security's impending bankruptcy, and build a popular constituency for the changes. But White House advisers did not. . . .

. . . Ronald Reagan kept his distance from the controversy, but it would not go away. In September, Reagan did finally address the issue in a televised chat with the nation: he disowned Stockman's reform plan. . . . It was a retreat, and, for David Stockman, a fundamental defeat. He lost one major source of potential budget savings. . . .

Stockman's interest was made clear to the others: he wanted a compromise on the tax bill which would substantially reduce its drain on the federal treasury and thus moderate the fiscal damage of Reaganomics. . . .

The final [congressional bill] authorized budget reductions of $35.1 billion, about $6 billion less than the President's original proposal. . . .

In political terms, it was a great victory. Ronald Reagan became the first President since Lyndon Johnson to demonstrate both the tactical skill and the popular strength to stare down the natural institutional opposition of Congress. . . .

Yet, in the glow of victory, why was David Stockman so downcast? . . . Because he knew that much more traumatic budget decisions still confronted them." . . .

All in all, Stockman gave a modest summary of what had been wrought by the budget victory: "It has really slowed down the momentum, but it hasn't stopped what you would call the excessive growth of the budget." . . .

But Stockman was buoyant about the political implications of the tax legislation: first, because it put a tightening noose around the size of the government; second, because it gave millions of middle-class voters tangible relief from inflation, even if the stimulative effects on the economy were mild or delayed. Stockman imagined the tax cutting as perhaps the beginning of a large-scale realignment of political loyalties, away from old-line liberalism and toward Reaganism.

And where did principle hide? Stockman, with his characteristic mixture of tactical cynicism and intellectual honesty, was unwilling to defend the moral premises of what had occurred. The "idea-based" policies that he had espoused at the outset were, in the final event, greatly compromised by the "constituency-based" politics that he abhorred. What had changed, fundamentally, was the list of winning clients, not the nature of the game. . . .

. . . What was new about the Reagan revolution, in which oil-royalty owners win and welfare mothers lose? Was the new philosophy so different from old Republicanism when the federal subsidies for Boeing and Westinghouse and General Electric were protected, while federal subsidies for unemployed black teenagers were "zeroed out"? One could go on, at great length, searching for balance and equity in the outcome of the Reagan program without satisfying the question; the argument will continue as a central theme of electoral politics for the next few years. For now, Stockman would concede this much: that "weak clients" suffered for their weakness. . . .

. . . The administration had prevailed brilliantly as politicians. And yet, it also seemed that the status quo, in an intangible sense that most politicians would not even recognize, much less worry over, had prevailed over David Stockman. . . .

Still, things might work out, Stockman said. They might find an answer. The President's popularity might carry them through. The tax cuts would make people happy. The economy might start to respond, eventually, to the stimulation of the tax cuts. "Who knows?" Stockman said. From David Stockman, it was a startling remark.

Mobilizing on the Political Left and Right, 1982

13

ELIZABETH H. DOLE

Black Strategy
February 24, 1982

The White House was aware that African Americans were not enthusiastic about the Reagan presidency. Notwithstanding his charismatic appeal and charm, much of Reagan's domestic agenda targeted programs that had been crucial to the black community, a population hard hit by the recession that began in the fall of 1981. Yet Reagan and his advisers were not willing to abandon these voters, as they sought to achieve a landslide victory in 1984 and to build a durable majority like the one Franklin Roosevelt had enjoyed during the Great Depression. To do that, they hoped to secure constituencies that were formerly loyal Democrats. In this memo, Elizabeth Dole, director of the White House Office of Public Liaison, mapped out a strategy to reach out to African Americans. She formulated similar strategies to appeal to Jewish, Hispanic, and female voters, who were also seen as unenthusiastic but potentially viable as a voter base.

MEMORANDUM FOR JAMES A. BAKER III

The development of this strategy was based on three factors which distinguish Blacks from other groups, such as small business and labor, for whom similar strategies have recently been developed:

From Elizabeth H. Dole Files, Box 5, file: Black Strategy 1982, Ronald Reagan Library.

- Blacks are a group which provided little support for the President in 1980.
- The Black community is at odds with this Administration on a wide range of key policy issues.
- Significant numbers of moderates and independents gauge treatment of Blacks and minorities as an important barometer of the fairness and commitment to equality of this Administration. . . .

Black Strategy

BACKGROUND: BLACK UNREST AND CONCERNS

Ronald Reagan won the 1980 election with strong support from virtually every segment of America. One of the few exceptions was the Black community which supported Jimmy Carter with 90% of their vote. Given these political circumstances, it was anticipated that Blacks would greet the Reagan Administration with at least some measure of uneasiness and that a transition period would be necessary to build bridges and determine where our potential strength with this group might be.

Today, after one year, the original uneasiness among Blacks has hardened into outright opposition, even among some former supporters. This opposition threatens to grow stronger and more activist. The policies and programs of the Reagan Administration are consistently criticized and attacked by prominent Black leaders, Black organizations and Black press. Many of the more recent attacks have been aimed personally at the President. A November 1981 WASHINGTON POST/ABC poll revealed that Black approval of the President's job performance was only 19%–34% lower than the rating from the general population. A NEW YORK TIMES/CBS poll released January 19, 1982, put Black approval of the President at a "rock-bottom" 8%.

The increase in Black opposition is obviously not the result of a single statement, policy or action on the part of the President or his Administration. Rather, as we all know, it is the result of a series of events over a period of time. Some of the major examples follow:

a. A series of "stops and starts" in the policy area have communicated the impression that the President lacks a sincere commitment to the advancement of civil rights. Notable examples are:

— The delay in advocating an extension of the Voting Rights Act.

— Confusion and inconsistency over the Administration's affirmative action policies.

— The racial overtones of the issue of tax exemptions for segregated schools, which was highlighted by the press.

b. The combined impact of the budget cuts, growing unemployment and government RIFs [reductions in forces] has had a demoralizing effect on Blacks. Continual accusations are made that these actions impact disproportionately on minorities, and especially Blacks. The Administration's efforts to reverse this negative perception have been both insufficient and inefficient to date.

c. The relatively low number of Black appointments compared with the previous administration is perceived as a lack of interest in Black involvement in this Administration.

As a result of these factors, we are now grappling with the larger issue of the President's image, reputation and public esteem. We are confronted by the erroneous and dangerous stereotype of a President who is unsympathetic to the plight of the poor and needy, and a threat to the gains in civil rights over the past twenty years.

These perceptual issues impact most negatively on Black Americans, but have serious ramifications for other groups as well. In particular, the "lack of compassion" label is one which has harmful long-term implications for women, the elderly, and moderates of all parties.

The following recommendations attack both the substantive and perceptual problems through four major initiatives:

a. *Policy Actions*: Identifying those issues which require immediate clarification, and those which require future policy development.

b. *Liaison Activities*: Communicating with Black organizations and leadership to develop trust and a continuing dialogue.

c. *Media Activity*: Assuring that the Black press is aware of this Administration's accomplishments on behalf of Blacks.

d. *Ceremonial Activities*: Development of events and activities which signal the President's interest [in] and involvement with Black people and issues.

Policy Actions

This Administration has not communicated the President's policies regarding Black concerns in a clear, concise and definitive manner. On several issues of specific concern to Blacks, there is no identifiable policy in place. In other areas, the Administration's positions are confusing, conflicting or viewed as "waffling."

In many cases, the time and *clarity* of a policy needs to be given the same level of professional attention as the *substance*. It is harmful for the President to be viewed as vacillating or backpeddling [*sic*], particularly on civil rights matters.

14

WILLIAM F. SITTMANN

Summer Alternatives

May 5, 1982

By 1982, Republicans started to worry about a liberal mobilization against their domestic and international policies. Liberals faulted Republican economic policy for generating unemployment, and the nuclear freeze movement warned that Reagan's policies could lead to nuclear war. William Sittmann, special assistant to the president and special assistant to Michael Deaver, the president's deputy chief of staff, outlined the problems Republicans were facing as the midterm elections approached and how to address them.

MEMORANDUM FOR MICHAEL K. DEAVER

In [Deputy Assistant to the President] Red Cavaney's memorandum to you, a presentation is made to you of the possible types of demonstrations that may occur this summer. In this regard, Red's memo raises points concerning why demonstrations may occur, what kinds of people will be involved, and alternatives that could be employed to deter or limit the affects [*sic*] of such uprisings.

Types of demonstrations:

1. *Urban disadvantaged*, a group most susceptible to "abandoning" hope for a better life. This group includes black teenages [*sic*] and the cronically [*sic*] unemployed. Recent media

From Michael K. Deaver Files, Box 15, file: Miscellaneous Memos—1982 (January through June), Ronald Reagan Library.

attention of these people, as well as the media's attempt to discredit the President's economic program, heightens the prospects of demonstrations in major cities. This group has vast numbers on its side to increase the impact—and possible violence—of a demonstration.

2. *Displaced workers*, those people who have been recently dislocated from employment. This is a much more tolerant[,] i.e., more peaceful, group since they have a deep commitment to and investment in the system. People who have been unemployed for less than a year . . . still have hope that the employment situation will improve. It is important to note that displaced workers don't usually live in pockets as do the urban disadvantaged.

3. *Self-determinists*, these are people who are usually employed inside or outside of the home, or are students who stand behind issues; including, gay rights, right to life, equal rights, etc. This is advocacy at its best and there is little we can do to prevent such demonstrations. The impact of self-determinists' demonstrations comes from the intensity of their issues.

4. *Nuclear freeze*, made up of all types of people and cuts across traditional party lines. The vast assortment of new printed materials distributed this spring as well as the very real threat of war intensifies the impact of a demonstration by this group. In Red's analysis of this group, he makes a very strong point of the two-pronged war arising from the nuclear freeze issue which includes those oriented to a strong national security versus the anti-war (made up [of] an entire generation of young professionals who haven't had to grapple with a world-wide war) people who include churches and the clergy who are especially concerned with the quality of life and the distruction [*sic*] of mankind.

Recommendations that Red has made include focusing a White House group on the Urban disadvantaged and the Nuclear freeze groups. He feels that it would be wise to develop a list of undertakings that would be aimed at relieving tensions and create hope before an opportunity for a demonstration develops. Included in his list are entertainment extravaganzas, self-improvement projects, and quasi-community improvement programs. . . .

With regards to the nuclear freeze groups, Red advises that the President continue to discuss the arms reduction debate with the Soviets. He suggests using this issue as an educational exercise through debate and media in order to present both sides of the nuclear issue. A Preparedness Working Group is suggested to work on keeping this group at a low roar.

15

ELIZABETH H. DOLE

Conservative Social Agenda
March 9, 1982

Even as Reagan was trying to broaden the Republican coalition, he had to worry about his conservative base. The tensions between conservative activists and the administration emerged early in Reagan's presidency. In this memo, Dole warned of the need to improve relations with conservatives before the 1982 midterm elections. Many of her strategies would not be sufficient, as the economic recession helped Democrats vastly expand their majority in the House.

MEMORANDUM FOR EDWIN MEESE III [and]
JAMES A. BAKER, III

For better than a year, the President has marshalled the forces of his conservative supporters behind his efforts to revitalize the economy and restructure government which, in turn, relegated the conservative social agenda to the back burner. As you are aware, the Senate is already moving forward on several of the issues, and we can expect a few more during the year. Our conservative supporters are raising the question "Where is the President when it's our turn at bat?" As elements of public support waver, the President's core group needs assurance that its agenda is important to him in order to keep the group unified.

Rather than be forced to deal with social issues on an *ad hoc* basis and/or on someone else's timetable, I recommend we undertake an analysis of key components of the social agenda with an eye towards

From Elizabeth H. Dole Files, Box 18, file: Conservatives—General 1982 (2 of 6), Ronald Reagan Library.

deciding which ones we are willing to support and under what terms and conditions. This includes voluntary prayer in school, busing, Family Protection Act, tuition tax credits, etc. By moving to the forefront on one or two of these issues, the President's social link can be reforged, and the conservative grassroots can be rejuvenated for the upcoming legislative battles. To do little or nothing will lead to greater conservative dissatisfaction and diminished active support for the economic battles.

16

JOHN T. (TERRY) DOLAN

Letter to James Baker

August 12, 1982

Conservative activists believed that Reagan made a mistake by accepting a tax increase in 1982. The administration worked with Republican fiscal conservatives such as Senator Bob Dole in passing the tax increase, based on the argument that large deficits were going to unsettle Wall Street and undermine economic growth. The tax increase was one instance where Reagan publicly broke with his campaign agenda. Reagan would continue to feel pressure from the right on economic issues as well as on social issues, as this letter from the chairman of the National Conservative Political Action Committee shows.

Dear Jim:

I thought you should see the latest survey data from Montana. In all our polls we regularly ask "Do you have a favorable or unfavorable opinion of Ronald Reagan?" The results among self-identified conservatives from February to August show:

	February '82	*August '82*
Favorable	79.6	71.1
Unfavorable	13.0	24.6

From Edwin Meese Files, Box 19, file: Conservative Issues—General, Ronald Reagan Library.

As you can see Reagan's favorable/unfavorable rating has dropped an incredible 20 percent. Unfortunately this is precisely what I predicted might happen if the White House continued to push this foolish tax increase.

It is not fair to presume one poll in Montana conclusively proves anything. But conservatives nationwide tend to act in similar ways. We will continue to poll and will keep you advised. You also have access to information from all Republican pollsters. I strongly urge you to corraborate [sic] the information we are getting, and determine why it is happening.

It is my belief that conservatives and Republicans are becoming increasingly aware that the king has no clothes: that Reagan is not the same as Reaganism, and that it really does not mean anything to vote Republican.

Unless you stop this erosion immediately, Republican and conservative candidates could be facing another 1974 election, where sympathetic voters will stay home because of the signals being sent from Washington.

These tax increases will do incredible harm to our country economically. Now they are destroying the conservative coalition Ronald Reagan was so instrumental in building. If political stupidity were a criminal offense, whoever thought of this should get the death penalty.

There are actions I think you can take to mitigate this incredibly unnecessary disaster, beginning with doing what the people of America elected you to do: oppose tax increases and cut spending. There are other cosmetic actions you can undertake, but they are symptomatic, not causative of your problems today. I support the balanced budget rallies and other "symbols." But all the symbols in the world can't overcome the increasing media barrage of "Reagan raising your taxes."

Sincerely,
JOHN T. (TERRY) DOLAN

17

RONALD REAGAN

Letter to Barry Goldwater
September 7, 1982

Reagan gave minimal attention to social issues in the first year of his presidency. He came under fire from religious conservatives who had worked for his campaign and who felt that issues such as restrictions on abortion were essential. Reagan never had a strong attachment to these positions, though he had courted the religious Right in his 1980 campaign. By 1982, with the midterm elections approaching, Reagan lent support to legislation that would demonstrate his support for pro-life activists.

Dear Barry:

A broad spectrum of concerned Americans are joining with me in calling upon the Senate to bring to an end its debate on Senator [Jesse] Helms' anti-abortion amendment to the debt ceiling bill. Senator [Orrin] Hatch, whose Constitutional Abortion Amendment I continue to support, has generously joined in the call for a vote on the amendment now before the Senate.

This amendment is a responsible statutory approach to one of the most sensitive problems our society faces—the taking of the life of an unborn child. Specifically, the Senate is debating an amendment which:

1. Affirms the humanity of the unborn child in our society;

2. Bans permanently Federal funding and support for the taking of the life of an unborn child except to save the life of the mother; and

3. Provides opportunity for the Supreme Court to reconsider its usurpation of the role of legislatures and State courts in this area.

I realize that this amendment reflects a moderate approach. My purpose is not to impede any other anti-abortion measures, including Senator Hatch's amendment, that may come before you. But this is the first

---

From Elizabeth H. Dole Files, Box 1, file: Abortion 1982 (1 of 6), Ronald Reagan Library.

clear-cut vote in this Congress on the humanity of the unborn, and it is crucial that a filibuster not prevent the representatives of our citizens from expressing their judgment on so vital a matter.

It is time to stand and be counted on this issue. I urge you to lend your support to Senator [Howard] Baker's petition to invoke cloture [60 votes needed to end Senate filibuster] on this measure.

Beyond the matter of cloture, it is vitally important for the Congress to affirm, as this amendment does, the fundamental principle that all human life has intrinsic value. We must never become a society in which an individual has the right to do away with inconvenient life. I ask that you keep these thoughts in mind when you vote your conscience on the amendment.

I hope that you will be able to join me on this issue. If not, please give me a call.

Sincerely,
RON

18

LEE ATWATER

"The Gender Gap": A Postelection Assessment

November 23, 1982

The 1982 midterm elections were a blow to the Reagan administration. The Democrats enjoyed large gains in the House of Representatives, expanding their majority from 242 to 269. During their campaigns, Democrats stressed the "Reagan Recession," which had left more than 10 percent of the workforce unemployed. Speaker Tip O'Neill led a national campaign that highlighted "fairness" in domestic policy. Some Democrats came out in support of a nuclear freeze, taking a stand against Reagan's aggressive rhetoric about the Soviet Union. Contemporaries also asserted that Reagan and the Republican party suffered from an emerging "gender gap" in which women were tilting more toward the left. In this memo, Reagan political strategist Lee Atwater assessed the problem. Atwater

From Elizabeth H. Dole Files, Box 35, file: Women—Gender Gap (1 of 2), Ronald Reagan Library.

said that both female and male voters might be attracted to the GOP by a platform stressing family values.

Executive Summary

One of the most severe challenges facing the Administration in the next two years is the "gender gap." Some observers speculate that a new sex-based political realignment is occurring; one that could lock the GOP into permanent minority status. Clearly we will have to take some action.

Whereas women formerly were barely distinguishable from men in terms of ideology and partisanship, they are now emerging as considerably more liberal and Democratic than men.

Administration efforts to close the gender gap have proven so far to be inadequate. One complicating factor is that new data are emerging that suggests women are so different from men that a message men receive positively could cause a negative reaction in women. Another complicating factor is the enormous surge of women into the work force, which has changed forever the outlook of women on many issues, including political issues.

Attempts to analyze the "cause" of the gender gap are frustrated by a paucity of good data and a multiplicity of possible explanations. It is clear that we have to be very careful in our public expressions on three major issue clusters that concern women: economic issues, the "war and peace" issue and social issues. . . .

The Republican Opportunity

1. *Long Term.* The only way that we can get working women out of the Democratic Party and keep them out is by proving that our strategy for growth is correct.

    Recall that the Republican boom of the 1920's kept not only working class men but also newly enfranchised women in the GOP column. It was not until the Depression that we lost substantial parts of both groups.

2. *Short Term.* In the meantime, we must show working women that we are sensitive to their needs. There is no reason why we should be seen as lagging behind on important issues such as child care, sexual discrimination and harrassment [*sic*], and equal

pay for equal work. Surely there are creative solutions to these problems that don't require a lot of government interference. . . .

The Four Issues in Perspective

OVERKILL

[Earlier parts of] this piece discussed issues which allegedly are creating and/or widening the gender gap. Each issue—economics, social, war and peace, and rhetoric and sensitivity—has at one time or another been depicted as the cause of the gender gap.

Taken together, these alleged causes prove too much. If all of these issues were hurting us with women, the gender gap would be 50 points, not the 10 or so points that it actually is. Either some of these issues aren't hurting us, or else there are counterfactors which the pollsters and pundits are neglecting. Maybe women are "put off" by President Reagan's stands on some issues but are "put back on" by the fact that he and his wife have such a good relationship.

The point is, nobody knows.

THE MASCULINE SURPLUS?

It is not even clear that the phenomenon we are witnessing is a shortfall in our support among women. Maybe what we have here is a "masculine surplus": extraordinarily strong support among men.

After all, Ronald Reagan is a man's man. The November issue of *Psychology Today* cites reasons why men would be particularly attracted to the President: his image as an outdoorsman, his articulation of the benefits of freedom, his expansive view of human potential. . . .

The Reagan Administration and Women

1. We should start by acknowledging that we have a problem, and that we have not been particularly successful in dealing with it in the last two years. . . .

2. We should somehow make it resoundingly and decisively clear that we accept the new role of women, especially working women. Women should know that they will have their place in the sun under either party. . . .

3. . . . We should avoid splashy pronouncements and instead work to integrate competent women into non-token positions in policy-making areas [of the administration]. . . .

4. The President might consider a Trumanesque public call for advice on women's issues from the general public. . . .

5. The President could issue a direct personal challenge to business at an appropriate forum to hire and promote more women. . . . Otherwise, voluntary self-regulation could turn into mandatory government at the hands of another administration. . . .

6. We need to go back to the 1980 Republican Platform, which offered up a whole panoply of issues and themes which offer a sharp contrast to the business-national security groups of issues that have dominated the public discourse in the last two years.

A simple perusal of the five main headings on the cover of the platform document arouses a different perception of the Republican Party than many have come to expect:

Family
Neighborhood
Work
Peace
Freedom

There is a strong strand of thought in the Republican tradition which emphasizes voluntarism, community, neighborhoods, small towns, self-help, self-reliance, home ownership, decentralization, etc.

We have pretty much ignored these "soft" issues for the last two years and one result is the gender gap. These issues have no "negatives." They also don't have any "positives," because they exist below the level of mass consciousness. However, a proper focus on them, along with a proper follow through, from the top of the Administration to the bottom, would broaden and humanize the image of the Administration and the Republican Party. This would help us with women and men.

Morning in America: Reagan's Reelection, 1983–1985

19

THOMAS P. O'NEILL JR.

Campaign to Save Medicare/Medicaid

1984

Democrats started to regain their strength as they realized that many of the programs that Republicans were trying to cut remained enormously popular. When Reagan directly attacked domestic programs, Democrats found that public opinion often turned against the administration. House Democrats capitalized on this by mounting campaigns to save popular social programs from conservative attack. In this fund-raising letter to Democrats, Speaker Tip O'Neill began to energize the Democratic coalition through a defense of Medicare and Medicaid.

Dear Friend,

Hardly an American could have missed the enormous battle waged here in Washington earlier this year to save the Social Security system. And when Congress placed this all-important program on a sound financial foundation for future generations, headlines and TV reports proclaimed "Social Security Saved!"

Well, sad to say, the battle is not yet over.

What millions of Americans do not realize is that our battle to ensure the *health and economic security of older Americans is only half-won.*

From Edwin Meese Files, Box 19, file: Campaign '84—Democratic, Ronald Reagan Library.

Because *without adequate health care insurance*, the economic protection that Social Security provides to millions of elderly people is hollow and meaningless.

And right this moment, my Democratic colleagues and I are in the midst of a crucial fight to block the Reagan Administration and New Right Republicans from callously slashing the benefits and services of what is literally the life's blood of our elderly — *Medicare and Medicaid*.

We are vehemently opposed to their vicious proposed cuts. And I am personally appealing to you to enlist your immediate help in preventing Medicare and Medicaid from being gutted. Just as the Democratic-controlled House prevented the Reagan Administration from destroying Social Security, we must now save Medicare and Medicaid. And I urge you to help us right now, by making a contribution to the Democratic Congressional Campaign Committee's *CAMPAIGN TO SAVE MEDICARE/MEDICAID*.

If you could see some of the letters I receive from older Americans throughout the country, I am sure you would be as appalled as I am with the stories all too many of them tell.

Here are honest, upstanding citizens, who have worked hard — many even fought hard in our nation's wars — to keep America strong. They have given this great country their entire lives. Their only crime is that they have gotten old and sick. . . .

. . . Ronald Reagan and the New Right Republicans advocate a utopian kind of self-responsibility. In their country-club mentality, they seem to think that every American can somehow find the money to pay for enormous medical bills, hospitalization, and physicians' services. And in their ruthless attempt to cut to the bare bones domestic services, they totally ignore the real facts. The average American over age 65 has a total gross yearly income of *only* $9,700! The Republicans could not care less that low-income, elderly Americans are already spending at least 16% of their annual income on medical care!

If passed, *the Republican plan would substantially increase the financial burden of medical care for older citizens*. Reagan has proposed over $1.9 billion in cuts to Medicare in the 1984 budget. More than 50% would come out of the pockets of the elderly.

I, for one, am not going to stand by silently and let the Republicans add intolerable medical expenses to the budgets of millions of older Americans already struggling just to get by. And I don't think you will stand by either.

That's why I'm writing to ask you to join with me and the Democrats in our CAMPAIGN TO SAVE MEDICARE/MEDICAID.

MEDICARE was first instituted under *Democrat* Lyndon Johnson in 1967. Medicare fulfilled the earlier commitment of Franklin Delano Roosevelt, who founded Social Security, to provide the security of guaranteed medical health care. . . .

Over the years it has been *the Democratic Party* that has guarded Social Security, Medicare, Medicaid, and other critically needed programs.

With the health and economic security of millions of older Americans under attack by the Reagan Administration, we Democrats have set as our number one priority the goal of saving Medicare/Medicaid. . . .

You and I must not turn our backs on millions of older Americans who have planned their retirement and their monthly budgets on their trust in the good faith and commitment of our federal government.

Just as Americans have a legitimate right to expect their monthly Social Security checks, so they have an equally legitimate right to expect that their government will continue to protect against the high costs of hospitalization, surgery, and the long-term care required after a devastating illness.

Growing old and getting sick is a natural part of life. Citizens should *not* be penalized and burdened with medical bills beyond their ability to pay.

But unless we act now, the Republicans following President Reagan's lead will penalize and burden older Americans for the natural and inevitable results of aging and illness.

The only way you and I can make sure that insensitive politicians do not undermine or dismantle Medicare and Medicaid is to elect Democrats who will stand for, work for, and fight for a strong, secure health program for older Americans. . . .

Sincerely,

THOMAS P. O'NEILL, JR.

20

RONALD REAGAN

Radio Address to the Nation on the Presidential Campaign

October 13, 1984

The economic recovery that was under way by the summer of 1984 provided Reagan with significant political capital. He had come into office after a decade of stagflation, the devastating combination of inflation and recession. As indicators finally moved in the right direction, Reagan boasted that the economic recovery was evidence that conservative policies such as tax cuts were working. Reagan's 1984 campaign against Democratic former vice president Walter Mondale revolved around the theme of "morning in America," arguing that America had finally escaped from the malaise of the 1970s.

My fellow Americans:

The 1984 campaign is in full swing. And no matter who you are — student, construction worker, farmer, nurse, or high-tech entrepreneur — this election offers you the clearest choice for your future in many years.

The central economic issue in this campaign is growth. Will we have policies that give each of you opportunities to climb higher and push America to challenge the limits of growth, policies like those that in the [last] 22 months have given this nation the strongest economic expansion in 30 years, or will we go back to those failed policies of the Carter-Mondale administration that inflicted unprecedented hardship on our people?

Our vision of strong economic growth is not a pipe dream; it's a living accomplishment. And it can continue to get better, offering new hope for everyone, including all of you who have not yet recovered from the Carter-Mondale past.

From Ronald Reagan, "Radio Address to the Nation on the Presidential Campaign," in *Public Papers of the Presidents of the United States: Ronald Reagan, 1984* (Washington, D.C.: U.S. Government Printing Office, 1987), 2:1528–29.

We came to Washington with a pledge to make a new beginning by putting more power, earnings, and decisions back in your hands. That's why we passed the first tax rate reduction for everyone since President John Kennedy's program 20 years ago. And it's no coincidence that once those tax cuts took hold, the American economy woke up with a roar from years of economic slumber.

Think about this success, because you're the ones who made it happen and who can and must keep it going. Twenty-two straight months of economic expansion and yet inflation is only one-third what it was when my opponent was in office. Six hundred thousand new business incorporations last year—an all-time record. Over 6 million new jobs created; in fact, more jobs created on average each month than were created in all the Common Market countries combined during the last 10 years.

But we can't and won't be satisfied until every American who wants a job can find a job, until inflation is down to 0.0 and interest rates have been brought down more, until the farm community has fully recovered from the legacy of record interest rates, inflation, and the grain embargo—and until we modernize and make our older industries more competitive with new technologies. In other words, all of us have made great progress, but even greater challenges lie ahead.

We want to go forward with exciting new opportunities to help America challenge the limits of growth—for example, an historic simplification of our tax system, making the entire system more fair and easier to understand so we can bring yours and everybody's personal tax rates further down, not up.

My opponent has a very different vision—a gloomy vision of weakness that doesn't look to you with confidence or challenge you to dream great dreams and make America grow, but that places its trust in bigger government. We must ask ourselves one question: What has he ever done or said to suggest, let alone convince us, that his vision can do anything but fail? . . .

My opponent puts government first, which is why his policies fail and his predictions are wrong. We trust in you, and that spells success through economic growth. Nor has he learned from his mistakes. He has proposed to raise taxes by $85 billion. In fact, he would have to raise taxes the equivalent of $1,890 per household to pay for his promises. . . .

Asking you to buy his failed policies is a little like someone expecting you to go to a used-car lot to buy back the lemon you got rid of 4 years ago. But you don't have to. You can stick with leadership that's working; leadership that trusts in you and offers growth and opportunity so all of us can go forward together to build a better American future.

21

RONALD REAGAN

*Remarks of the President to the Twelfth Annual
Conservative Political Action Conference*
March 1, 1985

---

*There were many commentators who credited Reagan's 1980 victory to
the problems of the Carter administration and questioned whether voters had really sent a message. But the 1984 landslide victory seemed to
confirm the notion that there had been some kind of realignment. Reagan
was aware of the opportunity afforded to him by the election, and in this
talk to right-wing political activists, he claimed that his victory in 1984
was proof that a conservative revolution was changing American politics.*

When you work in the White House you don't get to see your old friends
as much as you'd like. And I always see [this speech] as my opportunity
to "dance with the one that brung you.". . .

In 1964 came a voice in the wilderness—Barry Goldwater. . . .

A new movement was stirring. And in the 1960's, Young Americans
for Freedom is born. *National Review* gains readership and prestige in
the intellectual community. *Human Events* [a conservative magazine]
becomes a major voice on the cutting edge. In the seventies, the anti-tax
movement begins. . . . In the late seventies, Proposition 13. . . . In 1980,
for the first time in 28 years, a Republican Senate is elected. So, may I
say, is a conservative President.

In 1984, that conservative administration is reelected in a 49-state
sweep. And the day the votes came in, I thought of Walt Whitman, "I
hear America singing."

This great turn from left to right was not just a case of the pendulum
swinging—first, the left hold sway and then the right, and here comes
the left again. The truth is, conservative thought is no longer over here
on the right. It's the mainstream now.

And the tide of history is moving irresistibly in our direction. Why?
Because the other side is virtually bankrupt of ideas. It has nothing

From Strategic Defense Initiative Open Collection, Box 1, file: Strategic Defense Initiative, January–June 1985, Ronald Reagan Library.

more to say, nothing to add to the debate. It has spent its intellectual capital—such as it was—and it has done its deeds. . . .

But along with that, perhaps the greatest triumph of modern conservatism has been to stop allowing the left to put the average American on the moral defensive. By average American, I mean the good, decent, rambunctious and creative people who raise the families, go to church, and help out when the local library holds a fundraiser. People who have a stake in the community because they are the community.

These people had held true to certain beliefs and principles that for 20 years the intelligentsia were telling us we're hopelessly out of date, utterly trite and reactionary. You want prayer in the schools? How primitive, they said. You oppose abortion? How oppressive, how anti-modern. The normal was portrayed as eccentric, and only the abnormal was worthy of emulation. The irreverent was celebrated—but only irreverence about certain things. Irreverence toward, say, organized religion, yes. Irreverence toward establishment liberalism—not too much of that. They celebrated their courage in taking on safe targets, and patted each other on the back for slinging stones at a confused Goliath, who was too demoralized, and really too good, to fight back.

But now one simply senses it. The American people are no longer on the defensive. I believe the conservative movement deserves some credit for this. You spoke for the permanent against the merely prevalent, and ultimately you prevailed.

I believe we conservatives have captured the moment, captured the imagination of the American people. And what now? What are we to do with our success? Well, right now, with conservative thought accepted as mainstream thought, and with the people of our country leading the fight to freedom—now we must move. . . .

I spoke in the State of the Union of a "second American revolution," and now is the time to launch that revolution and see that it takes hold. If we move decisively, these years will not be just a passing era of good feeling—not just a few good years—but a true golden age of freedom.

The moment is ours, and we must seize it. There's work to do. We must prolong and protect our growing prosperity so that it doesn't become just a passing phase, a natural adjustment between periods of recession. We must move further to provide incentive and make America the investment capital of the world.

We must institute a fair tax system and turn the current one on its ear. I believe there is natural support in our country for a simplified tax system with still lower tax rates, but a broader base, with everyone paying their fair share and no more. We must eliminate unproductive tax shelters. Again, there is natural support among Americans, because Americans are a fair-minded people.

We must institute enterprise zones and a lower youth minimum wage so we can revitalize—revitalize distressed areas and teenagers can get obs. We're going to take our revolution to the people—all of the people. We're going to go to black Americans, and members of all minority groups, and we're going to make our case.

Part of being a revolutionary is knowing that you don't have to acquiesce to the tired, old ideas of the past. One such idea is that the opposition party has black America and minority America locked up—that they own black America. Well, let me tell you, they own nothing but the past. The old alignments are no longer legitimate, if they ever were. . . .

Once during the campaign, I said, "This is a wonderful time to be alive," and I meant that. I meant that we're lucky not to live in pale and timid times. We've been blessed with the opportunity to stand for something—for liberty, and freedom and fairness. And these are things worth fighting for, worth devoting our lives to. And we have good reason to be hopeful and optimistic.

We've made much progress already. So let us go forth with good cheer and stout hearts—happy warriors out to seize back a country and a world to freedom.

22

WILLIAM J. BENNETT

Completing the Reagan Revolution

July 8, 1986

Many conservatives argued that cultural and social issues needed to move to the forefront of the movement, especially after Reagan's reelection. Conservative activists argued that America's moral values had decayed in the post–World War II period, especially during the 1960s, with the secularization and liberalization of popular culture and American education. Some Republicans felt that cultural issues appealed to working- and middle-class voters, who had traditionally supported Democrats but who were feeling alienated from the social values of the party. In this speech, former education secretary William Bennett, who emerged as one of the leading figures in the debate, talked to conservatives at the Heritage Foundation about the centrality of what came to be called the "culture wars" in American politics. At the time, Bennett was acting as the nation's drug czar in the war against drugs, a campaign that Reagan launched to restore what conservatives called "family values."

It may be that nothing the president has done is more important than his achievement [on the moral and cultural front]. In his evocation of our national memory and symbols of pride, in his summoning us to our

From William J. Bennett, "Completing the Reagan Revolution" (Speech at Heritage Foundation, Washington, D.C., July 8, 1986), http://www.heritage.org/Research/PolicyReview/PR0189revolution.cfm.

national purpose, he has performed the crucial task of political leadership. Moreover, he has done this precisely when many were wondering whether such presidential leadership was still possible. If, as the president has said, "In recent years, Americans' values almost seemed in exile," no public act has been more significant than his welcoming them home. The American people have renewed their commitment to our common principles; the task of cultural reformation and reconstruction has begun.

But the task has only just begun; the triumph is nowhere near complete. Far too many decent Americans remain, in effect, on the moral defensive before their own social and cultural institutions. Can Americans be confident that our children are likely to inherit the habits and values our parents honor? Are we confident they will learn enough about our history and our heritage? Are we confident they will be raised in an environment that properly nurtures their moral and intellectual qualities? Can we be confident in the cultural signals our children receive from our educational institutions, from the media, from the world of the arts, even from our churches? Are we confident that our society transmits to our young the right messages—teaches them the right lessons—about the family, about drug use, about respect for religious beliefs, about our meaning as a nation and our responsibilities as individuals? Is the public air conducive to moral and intellectual health, or do we have cause for worry as we contemplate the future well-being of our families, of our children, of our fellow citizens? . . .

About 15 years ago, Harvard professor Nathan Glazer entitled a book of essays *Remembering the Answers*. His point was that in the 1960s we forgot—many willfully rejected—the most basic and sensible answers to the first questions, to the questions about what contributes to social well-being and prosperity, about what makes for individual character and responsibility.

Well, thanks to the president and many others, we have begun to remember the answers, and we are no longer too timid to speak them out loud. On fundamental issues of individual character and responsibility, on the role of social institutions like religion and the family, on the common purposes of our national life, we have come a long way in the last few years. But it is the work of more than a few years to reinvigorate and renew and restore our common culture. . . .

Let me give three brief examples of the failure of our institutions to fulfill our hopes as individuals, as parents, as citizens.

First, our children need to learn about our nation, about our history, our heroes, our heritage, our national memories. . . .

A second example is the family. This is our most important social institution. It is perfectly clear that its decline has been disastrous for many of our youth. . . .

Now there may be no simple answer to the question of how to strengthen the family. But prior to any discussion of ways and means must come the simple unapologetic public affirmation that the family is an absolute value, and that heroic measures are justified in preserving and strengthening it. As a polity, as a society, as a culture, we now send, at best, mixed signals about this—and we get mixed results. In the rates of youth drug use and crime and lesser forms of irresponsibility and waste of talents and opportunities, we see the human cost of those mixed signals and mixed results. It is a cost we should resolve to bear no longer.

A third and final example is drugs. The Department of Education is releasing a book and announcing other initiatives that will help parents and school personnel to get drugs out of our schools. Here, once again, government has a definite role to play, and individuals and families have an even greater role to play. But, with the recent deaths of young athletes in mind, let me also ask this: what of the role of our cultural institutions? Our colleges and universities often, and sometimes quite properly, call to task the rest of society for failing to live up to its stated ideals. They set themselves the role of moral gadfly, moral conscience. But what of them? Surely when parents send their children to college they have a right to expect the colleges to take some measures to protect their sons and daughters from drugs. . . .

. . . A reinvigoration of our institutions and a resumption of responsibilities has, I believe, begun in America. The meaning of the Reagan Revolution extends beyond tax reform and a stronger defense to a recovery of our national purpose, a strengthening of our social bonds, a reaffirmation of our common cultural beliefs.

23

RONALD REAGAN

Address to the Nation on the Campaign against Drug Abuse
September 14, 1986

The "war on drugs" was one of the most prominent social issues that Reagan dealt with in his second term. Increasing drug use, according to the president and his wife, Nancy Reagan, signaled a breakdown in social values. The Reagan administration treated this problem by using the rhetoric of a military conflict rather than a social crisis. The administration focused on policing, tougher sentencing, and imprisonment as the solutions to the use of drugs. At the same time, the first lady urged middle-class suburban youths to "just say no" and implored parents and schools to play a bigger role in setting moral standards.

The President: Good evening. Usually, I talk with you from my office in the West Wing of the White House. But tonight there's something special to talk about, and I've asked someone very special to join me. Nancy and I are here in the West Hall of the White House, and around us are the rooms in which we live. It's the home you've provided for us, of which we merely have temporary custody.

Nancy's joining me because the message this evening is not my message but ours. And we speak to you not simply as fellow citizens but as fellow parents and grandparents and as concerned neighbors. It's back-to-school time for America's children. And while drug and alcohol abuse cuts across all generations, it's especially damaging to the young people on whom our future depends. So tonight, from our family to yours, from our home to yours, thank you for joining us.

America has accomplished so much in these last few years, whether it's been rebuilding our economy or serving the cause of freedom in the world. What we've been able to achieve has been done with your

From Ronald Reagan, "Address to the Nation on the Campaign against Drug Abuse," in *Public Papers of the Presidents of the United States: Ronald Reagan, 1986* (Washington, D.C.: U.S. Government Printing Office, 1989), 2:1178–82.

help—with us working together as a nation united. Now, we need your support again. Drugs are menacing our society. They're threatening our values and undercutting our institutions. They're killing our children.

From the beginning of our administration, we've taken strong steps to do something about this horror. Tonight I can report to you that we've made much progress. Thirty-seven Federal agencies are working together in a vigorous national effort, and by next year our spending for drug law enforcement will have more than tripled from its 1981 levels. We have increased seizures of illegal drugs. Shortages of marijuana are now being reported. Last year alone over 10,000 drug criminals were convicted and nearly $250 million of their assets were seized by the DEA, the Drug Enforcement Administration.

And in the most important area, individual use, we see progress. In 4 years the number of high school seniors using marijuana on a daily basis has dropped from 1 in 14 to 1 in 20. The U.S. military has cut the use of illegal drugs among its personnel by 67 percent since 1980. These are a measure of our commitment and emerging signs that we can defeat this enemy. But we still have much to do.

Despite our best efforts, illegal cocaine is coming into our country at alarming levels, and 4 to 5 million people regularly use it. Five hundred thousand Americans are hooked on heroin. One in twelve persons smokes marijuana regularly. Regular drug use is even higher among the age group 18 to 25—most likely just entering the workforce. Today there's a new epidemic: smokable cocaine, otherwise known as crack. It is an explosively destructive and often lethal substance which is crushing its users. It is an uncontrolled fire. . . .

Mrs. Reagan: . . . As a mother, I've always thought of September as a special month, a time when we bundled our children off to school, to the warmth of an environment in which they could fulfill the promise and hope in those restless minds. But so much has happened over these last years, so much to shake the foundations of all that we know and all that we believe in. Today there's a drug and alcohol abuse epidemic in this country, and no one is safe from it—not you, not me, and certainly not our children, because this epidemic has their names written on it. Many of you may be thinking: "Well, drugs don't concern me." But it does concern you. It concerns us all because of the way it tears at our lives and because it's aimed at destroying the brightness and life of the sons and daughters of the United States. . . .

Our young people are helping us lead the way. Not long ago, in Oakland, California, I was asked by a group of children what to do if they were offered drugs, and I answered, "Just say no." Soon after that, those children in Oakland formed a Just Say No club, and now there are over 10,000 such clubs all over the country. Well, their participation and their courage in saying no needs our encouragement. We can help by using every opportunity to force the issue of not using drugs to the point of making others uncomfortable, even if it means making ourselves unpopular. . . .

The President: . . . Last month I announced six initiatives. . . .

First, we seek a drug-free workplace at all levels of government and in the private sector. Second, we'll work toward drug-free schools. Third, we want to ensure that the public is protected and that treatment is available to substance abusers and the chemically dependent. Our fourth goal is to expand international cooperation while treating drug trafficking as a threat to our national security. In October I will be meeting with key U.S. Ambassadors to discuss what can be done to support our friends abroad. Fifth, we must move to strengthen law enforcement activities such as those initiated by Vice President Bush and Attorney General Meese. And finally, we seek to expand public awareness and prevention. . . .

As we mobilize for this national crusade, I'm mindful that drugs are a constant temptation for millions. Please remember this when your courage is tested: You are Americans. You're the product of the freest society mankind has ever known. No one, ever, has the right to destroy your dreams and shatter your life.

24

EDWARD M. KENNEDY

Robert Bork's America

July 1, 1987

Democrats scored several victories over the Reagan administration during the second term. One area in which congressional Democrats enjoyed success was in the judicial confirmation process, which had become increasingly partisan since the 1960s. In 1987, President Reagan nominated Yale professor Robert Bork to fill a vacancy on the Supreme Court.

From 100th Cong., 1st sess., *Congressional Record* (July 1, 1987): S 9188–89.

Bork was a controversial figure because of his outspoken conservative views on the law and because, while serving as U.S. solicitor general under Richard Nixon, he fired special prosecutor Archibald Cox in the middle of the Watergate investigation. With this political speech, made forty-five minutes after Reagan's nomination of Bork, Senator Edward Kennedy launched a successful campaign against Bork by painting him as a threat to the civil rights advances of the past few decades. Bork's confirmation was defeated in a bitter and partisan battle that left bruises for decades to come.

I oppose the nomination of Robert Bork to the Supreme Court, and I urge the Senate to reject it.

In the Watergate scandal of 1973, two distinguished Republicans—Attorney General Elliot Richardson and Deputy Attorney General William Ruckelshaus—put integrity and the Constitution ahead of loyalty to a corrupt President. They refused to do Richard Nixon's dirty work, and they refused to obey his order to fire Special Prosecutor Archibald Cox. The deed devolved on Solicitor General Robert Bork, who executed the unconscionable assignment that has become one of the darkest chapters for the rule of law in American history.

That act—later ruled illegal by a Federal court—is sufficient, by itself, to disqualify Mr. Bork from this new position to which he has been nominated. The man who fired Archibald Cox does not deserve to sit on the Supreme Court of the United States.

Mr. Bork should also be rejected by the Senate because he stands for an extremist view of the Constitution and the role of the Supreme Court that would have placed him outside the mainstream of American constitutional jurisprudence in the 1960s, let alone the 1980s. He opposed the Public Accommodations Civil Rights Act of 1964. He opposed the one-man one-vote decision of the Supreme Court the same year. He has said that the First Amendment applies only to political speech, not literature or works of art or scientific expression.

Under the twin pressures of academic rejection and the prospect of Senate rejection, Mr. Bork subsequently retracted the most neanderthal of these views on civil rights and the first amendment. But his mind-set is no less ominous today.

Robert Bork's America is a land in which women would be forced into back-alley abortions, blacks would sit at segregated lunch counters, rogue police could break down citizens' doors in midnight raids, and schoolchildren could not be taught about evolution, writers and artists would be censored at the whim of government, and the doors of the federal courts would be shut on the fingers of millions of citizens for whom the judiciary is often the only protector of the individual rights that are the heart of our democracy.

America is a better and freer nation than Robert Bork thinks. Yet in the current delicate balance of the Supreme Court, his rigid ideology will tip the scales of justice against the kind of country America is and ought to be.

The damage that President Reagan will do through this nomination, if it is not rejected by the Senate, could live on far beyond the end of his presidential term. President Reagan is still our President. But he should not be able to reach out from the muck of Irangate, reach into the muck of Watergate, and impose his reactionary vision of the Constitution on the Supreme Court and on the next generation of Americans. No justice would be better than this injustice.

25

GARY L. BAUER

Issues Update — Taxes and the Budget
October 23, 1987

In 1987, conservatives were becoming increasingly defensive as Democrats blamed Republican policies for the stock market crash that October. With an election on the horizon and the Reagan administration bogged down in the Iran-contra scandal, many in the GOP feared that the crash would undercut the claims that Republicans had been making about the contribution of their 1981 tax cuts to economic growth. Gary Bauer, a Reagan adviser, addressed this problem in this memo.

MEMORANDUM FOR THE PRESIDENT

In the wake of Monday's stock market collapse a number of pundits and politicians, defying logic, stepped forward to blame your failure to raise taxes as an explanation for the 500 point drop in the Dow Jones

From Howard Baker Files, Box 1, file: Budget Negotiations (2), Ronald Reagan Library.

Industrial Average. Democrats in Congress quickly called for a "summit" between you and congressional leaders to work out a deal on cutting the deficit. What liberals futilely hope for, of course, is that such a summit would result in your adoption of Walter Mondale's view that the American people are undertaxed. While we should be willing to talk about everything, we should not agree to sign onto the tax and spending policies that the American people so soundly rejected in 1980 and 1984—as you so well expressed in last night's press conference.

The fact is that higher taxes would not ultimately reduce the deficit, in any case, but would instead fuel increased spending.

Many of us in the White House well remember the "deal" we cut with congressional leaders in 1982, in which we were promised $3 of spending cuts for every $1 of new taxes. . . .

We all know what happened, however. Like Lucy, who pulls the football out from under Charlie Brown, the Congress reneged on its end of the deal and not only failed to deliver the spending cuts but actually increased spending. . . .

. . . Only spending restraint produces lower deficits. Nevertheless, there are those on the Left who would attempt to exploit the current situation to press their cherished goal of higher taxes.

The causes of the stock market collapse are many and complicated, and we may never understand all of them. But one thing we do know is that the market did not fall because it suddenly decided that taxes are too low. Indeed, there is some evidence that the tax bill working its way through Congress, with its irresponsible tax on corporate takeovers, may have been a major culprit. Nor does it make sense to blame the budget deficit, which has been around for years and is dramatically improving. Those who would make this argument, therefore, ought to be seen for what they are; not as people genuinely concerned about the budget deficit and the health of financial markets, but as liberal opportunists willing to use any crisis, any opportunity to expand government's share of the national wealth and income.

26

FRANK J. DONATELLI

"Selfishness" as a 1988 Campaign Issue
January 6, 1988

As Reagan's presidency reached its conclusion, Democrats argued that the White House had been at the center of a Me Decade in which greed, profit, and markets took precedence over equity and social justice. The collapse of the stock market in October 1987 had fueled economic anxiety. Democrats sensed that even with all the gains conservatives had made, they had an opportunity to champion some of the core themes that had been central to the party since the New Deal. As the 1988 election approached, Democrats and Republicans would square off over the issue of who had benefited the most from the yuppie culture, as well as from the tax cuts and deregulation of the 1980s. In this memo, Frank Donatelli, the White House political director, addressed how the Democrats might use "selfishness" as an issue in the 1988 presidential campaign.

MEMORANDUM FOR SENATOR HOWARD H. BAKER, JR.
          KEN DUBERSTEIN [Deputy Chief of Staff]
          TOM GRISCOM [Director of White House Communications and Planning]

There is at least one recurrent Democratic theme this year that we can anticipate. Our opponents will allege that the 1980's have been the decade when public purpose and civic responsibility were shunted aside in favor of personal profit. They will also allege that we have stopped asking what we can do for our country, and rather what can we do for ourselves. In addition, they will maintain that Republicans have contributed to and encouraged this attitude, which has made our people poorer spiritually (this from the same people who accuse the party of being in the grip of the religious right). In short, they will claim greed has been the big winner in the 1980's.

From Ken Duberstein Files, Box 3, file: 1988 Political Campaign (2), Ronald Reagan Library.

135

The media is cooperating fully in the campaign. Note the *Newsweek* cover story last week.

(The 80's were) . . . a time when avarice got respectable, poverty expanded and wealth became a kind of state religion . . . when insider trading was winked at, greedy young money changers were seen as pop heroes and nothing was more fascinating than the lifestyle of the rich and famous. . . .

The brilliance of this theme is that it turns the administration's greatest accomplishment, economic growth and opportunity, into a negative legacy of greed and selfishness. It also gives rise to apologies for the excesses of the 1960's (which continue to haunt the national Democratic Party) when, it is alleged at least, idealism and good intentions were the motivating factors in people's lives.

What specifically will the opposition point to as evidence of this revival of the virtue of selfishness?

Ethics

Our critics will make generous references to the scandals on Wall Street and in the U.S. government executive branch. . . . The insider trading scandals have also made suspect legitimate takeover and arbitrage activities. Liberals now seek to draw a distinction between "wealth creating" activities and "those which merely manipulate existing wealth." This makes them allies of heads of major corporations, who, not surprisingly, are also opposed to takeovers. . . .

Wealth

The Democrats are refining their 1984 message that there was no economic recovery, which no one believed, to there's a recovery, but only for the wealthy. They will argue that our policies have not had much positive impact on most Americans and that the very rich have derived most of the benefits.

Consider this from Senator George Mitchell of Maine:

. . . The past decade has been marked by a significant shift toward greater income inequality in America that has been aggravated by changes in the federal tax system over the same period.

We should look for a major campaign designed to stir resentment and envy against "high income" individuals and an attempt to gloss over the "insignificant" economic gains of the average American.

What should our response be? I would suggest that we emphasize several themes as we move into 1988.

1. Stress issues with a non-economic component. The emphasis on children and education championed by Secretary Bennett is so important in this regard. It allows us to talk about altruism and concern for the next generation, not about disposable income. This should be a major theme in the State of the Union address.

2. Emphasize the central role of values (work, neighborhood, family, peace, freedom) in American life and the President's central role in restoring a sense of optimism about the future for the American people.

3. Emphasize the broad based nature of the recovery. This decade has seen real advances for *all* Americans that should be emphasized again and again.

27

RONALD REAGAN

1988 Legislative and Administrative Message: A Union of Individuals

January 25, 1988

Even at the very end of his presidency, with all the political compromises that he had made, Reagan still believed in the conservative ideology that had animated his political career since the 1950s. In this message, Reagan emphasized a defense of individualism as being at the heart of his political legacy. From personal welfare to education to AIDS, Reagan stressed the need for individual responsibility instead of government intervention. The language of self-help resonated with many Americans, even though the expansion of government that took place under Reagan's watch contradicted some of this rhetoric.

From Ronald Reagan, "1988 Legislative and Administrative Message: A Union of Individuals," in *Public Papers of the Presidents of the United States: Ronald Reagan, 1988* (Washington, D.C.: U.S. Government Printing Office, 1990), 1:91–121.

This Administration is deeply committed to decreasing the power of the Federal government to its intended scope and to increasing the power of individuals. These policies establish conditions most conducive to individual initiative and enterprise and, consequently, to the creation of wealth and public well-being. The preservation of freedom, the highest value in our Republic, requires placing the rights of individuals above the power of government. The great challenge of our national government is to use only its carefully enumerated powers in promoting the general welfare by empowering individuals to help themselves. . . .

It is a fact of American life that many Federal programs, while attempting to help the poor, have made them more dependent on the government. Much is within our reach to help dependent citizens lift themselves to self-sufficiency.

. . . The current welfare system has trapped too many Americans in a dependency on welfare that is hard to break and easy to pass on to succeeding generations. In recent years, a consensus has emerged that it is through work and the acceptance of responsibility that people develop the self-esteem to pull themselves up from dependency.

Last year I launched a major effort to encourage the States, working with established community self-help groups, to undertake a wide range of "workfare" and other responsibility-building reform experiments. Experience has clearly shown that it is in the States that real welfare reform will occur. This was true back in the 1970s in California when we started this movement; it is increasingly the case today. The States' and my objective is to make work and self-sufficiency more attractive than welfare. However, because the current welfare system is so complex and restrictive in its endless rules and restrictions, we need legislation to give the States added flexibility and encouragement to undertake truly innovative and individualized reform experiments. . . .

Improving choice in education continues to be an important goal of this Administration. Study after study has found that when parents have a say and are involved in their children's education, the children do better in school. For example, the Congress should authorize a program of giving parents a choice of schools when providing Federal funds to benefit students. . . .

. . . Polls show that millions of Americans would like, but do not have, the ability of choosing the education program and institution that is best for their children. A voucher system at the State level would empower parents. I will ask the Department of Education to develop model voucher legislation and make it available to the 50 States, so that they can implement programs that promote choice in education. . . .

We must continue to take preventive measures against AIDS while at the same time treating AIDS victims with compassion and care. Although increased Federal funding is not the only solution, I am proposing $1.5 billion in fiscal 1989 for research, treatment, testing, counseling, and education, up ten-fold since 1985. Administration scientists were centrally involved in the discovery of the Human Immuno-deficiency Virus (HIV), developing the HIV blood antibody test and the anti-AIDS drug AZT. And testing has been initiated in human volunteers for two experimental AIDS vaccines.

However, the primary responsibility for avoiding AIDS lies with the individual. As the Surgeon General, the Secretary of Health and Human Services, and the Secretary of Education have been reminding us all, the best way to prevent AIDS is to abstain from sex until marriage and then to maintain a faithful relationship, as well as to avoid illicit drugs altogether. If the American people follow this wise and timeless counsel, if our schools and families and media communicate it effectively, the spread of AIDS can be greatly diminished. . . .

It was the need to secure inalienable, God-given rights from oppression that moved our forefathers to institute a new government in America. . . .

. . . I am leading my Administration in efforts to shore up the moral foundations of our individual freedom. . . .

None are more powerless than the unborn. Since the legalization of abortion-on-demand in 1973, there have been an estimated 21 million abortions in this country. I am committed to reducing the number of abortions in this country and reaffirming life's sacred position in our Nation.

The Congress should pass expeditiously my Human Life Bill. The first section of the bill contains a finding that abortion takes the life of a human being and that *Roe v. Wade* was wrong not to recognize the humanity of the unborn child. The second section would enact, on a permanent and government-wide basis, the Hyde Amendment restriction prohibiting Federal dollars from going for abortion unless a mother's life is endangered. In addition, the Congress should pass the Human Life Amendment [to overturn *Roe* and prohibit abortions].

At my direction, the Department of Health and Human Services is about to issue regulations prohibiting the use of Title X [family planning] funds (approximately $140 million) for any program that performs abortion, counsels for abortion, or promotes abortion through lawsuits, lobbying, or other such activities. . . .

The First Amendment protects the right of Americans to freely exercise their religious beliefs in an atmosphere of toleration and accommodation. As I have noted in the past, certain court decisions have in my view interpreted the First Amendment so as to restrict, rather than protect, individual rights of conscience. I have repeatedly affirmed my belief that school prayer on a voluntary basis is permissible, indeed desirable, in the public school. In my State of the Union addresses in 1986 and 1987, I expressed my support for a constitutional amendment that would make it clear that the Constitution does not prohibit voluntary prayer in public schools. . . .

. . . Thanks in large measure to [the Founding Fathers'] wisdom, America has enjoyed the blessings of liberty for 2 centuries. It is my belief that the policies presented in this message will contribute to the continuing restoration of the Federal government to a sound constitutional footing and thus preserve these same blessings for our posterity in the 21st century.

Reagan's Foreign Policy: Peace through Strength, 1980–1983

28

RONALD REAGAN

A Strategy for Peace in the Eighties
October 19, 1980

Reagan's national security theme in the election of 1980 was "peace through strength." This was a position that he had espoused for several decades. Reagan had come to support nuclear abolition in the 1940s and 1950s, and he had privately accepted the need for negotiation with the Soviet Union. Yet negotiation, in his mind, was impossible if the Soviets thought that America was weak. Reagan argued that diminishing tensions with the Soviet Union required strengthening America's military. As a candidate, Reagan criticized President Carter's foreign policy as inadequate, especially in light of the Iran hostage crisis. In this televised address, Reagan promised to build up the country's defense if voters elected him to office.

Good Evening.

Three months ago, in accepting the nomination of my party to be its presidential candidate, I said: "Of all the objectives we seek, first and foremost is the establishment of lasting world peace." . . .

Whatever else history may say about my candidacy, I hope it will be recorded that I appealed to our best hopes, not our worst fears, to our confidence rather than our doubts, to the facts, and not to fantasies.

From Ronald Reagan 1980 Campaign Speeches, October 10, 1980–October 31, 1980, Ronald Reagan Library.

And these three—hope, confidence, and facts—are at the heart of my vision of peace.

We have heard the phrase "peace through strength" so often, its meaning has become blurred through overuse.

The time has come for America to recall once more the basic truths behind the familiar words.

Peace is made by the fact of strength—economic, military, and strategic.

Peace is lost when such strength disappears or—just as bad—is seen by an adversary as disappearing.

We must build peace upon strength. There is no other way. And the cold, hard fact of the matter is that our economic, military, and strategic strength under President Carter is eroding.

Only if we are strong will peace be strong. . . .

With effective machinery in place, we must first address the conduct of our relations with our allies, with the Soviet Union, and with the People's Republic of China.

Confidence and trust in the United States has fallen to an all-time low. This must be reversed. The United States has an important leadership role, and this role can be effective only if our alliances are cemented by unity of purpose and mutual respect.

Worldwide, our allies are stronger, most are robust and healthy. But the challenge of the 1980s is to assemble that strength in a manner which allows us to pursue the objective of peace together. If our alliances are divided, only our adversaries benefit.

With our allies, we can conduct a realistic and balanced policy toward the Soviet Union. I am convinced that the careful management of our relationship with the Soviet Union depends on a principled, consistent American foreign policy. We seek neither confrontation nor conflict, but to avoid both, we must remain strong and determined to protect our interests.

Our relationship with the People's Republic of China is in its beginning stages. It is one that can and will grow, and I repeat my intention to assist its rapid growth. There is an historic bond of friendship between the American and Chinese peoples, and I will work to amplify it wherever possible. Expanded trade, cultural contact and other arrangements will all serve the cause of preserving and extending the ties between our two countries. . . .

My task as President will be to strengthen our defenses and to lead our allies in a sustained and prudent effort to keep us, and the entire world, secure from confrontation. The preservation of peace will require the best resources we can marshal in this precarious decade. We can marshal them by reaffirming our national purpose, by reasserting our will and determination, and by regaining our economic vitality.

29

ALEXANDER M. HAIG JR.

Letter to Brezhnev

September 18, 1981

In their first term, Reagan officials sent a tough message to the Soviet Union. Reagan filled key positions in his administration with neoconservatives who were opposed to negotiations with the Soviet Union. He also used tough rhetoric when talking about the Soviet Union, which created a hostile atmosphere between the leadership of the two countries. While privately creating an opening for potential dialogue, Reagan generally followed the advice of hard-liners by insisting that he would not give ground on arms agreements or Soviet influence in Central America and Africa. The letter crafted by Haig, Reagan's secretary of state, to Soviet premier Leonid Brezhnev spelled out the administration's position. The final version of the letter, sent four days later, mentioned the need for constructive dialogue but maintained Haig's strong emphasis on the Soviets as the source of international tensions.

MEMORANDUM FOR THE PRESIDENT

As you know, we have now embarked on a public campaign within the Alliance to take the political offensive away from the Soviets. The purpose is to demonstrate to Western publics that it is the Soviets, not the United States, who are blocking the path to a more stable East West relationship, and that for our part we are ready for better relations if Moscow is ready to show greater restraint.

To get this campaign off the ground, I believe that you should send a letter to Brezhnev timed with the start of the fall session of the U.N. General Assembly describing your views on the future direction of US-

From Presidential Handwriting Files, Box 1, File 4, Ronald Reagan Library.

Soviet relations. Although we would not release the text of the letter, we envisage briefing the press on its main themes in order to create the maximum possible impact on Western opinion.

The proposed letter (attached) makes some of the same points that I plan to use with [Soviet foreign minister Andrei] Gromyko in my talks next week. The basic message is that the U.S. is prepared to defend its interests by whatever means necessary, but that a more constructive relationship is possible if the Soviets exercise restraint.

RECOMMENDATION

That you sign the attached letter to Brezhnev.

Dear President Brezhnev:

. . . Let me say at the outset that the United States is deeply interested in the peaceful resolution of international tensions and in a more constructive and stable relationship with your country. We have repeatedly demonstrated our willingness to settle disagreements by negotiations and to observe scrupulously our international commitments.

I believe, however, that a great deal of the present tension in the world is due to actions by the Soviet government. As we and our allies have frequently stated, two aspects of Soviet behavior are of particular concern to us:

— First, the Soviet Union's pursuit of unilateral advantage in various parts of the globe and its repeated resort to the direct and indirect use of force in regional conflicts. The role of Cuba in Africa and Latin America is particularly disturbing and unacceptable to us.

— Second, the USSR's unremitting and comprehensive military build-up over the past 15 years, a buildup which in our view far exceeds purely defensive requirements and carries disturbing implications of a search for military superiority.

Despite these trends, we are committed to a dialogue with the Soviet Union. We are gravely concerned over the threat to mankind in the age of nuclear weapons. I have stated publicity [*sic*] that the United States is ready to engage in discussions with the USSR that would lead to genuine arms reductions. The existing stockpiles of these weapons and ongoing programs are such that only a serious effort at arms reductions would contribute to the objective which we both share, namely, lifting the threat of nuclear annihilation which hangs over mankind.

While the United States is committed to a stable and peaceful world, it will never accept a position of strategic disadvantage. Because the

Soviet Union has, over the past years, embarked on a major program to improve its strategic forces, the United States must also upgrade its forces. We have no desire to tax our society with a costly and burdensome build-up of armaments. The United States, however, will invest whatever is needed to maintain a secure strategic posture. . . .

In sum, the United States is more interested in actions which further the cause of world peace than in words. We are fully committed to solving outstanding differences by peaceful means, but we are not willing to accept double standards of international behavior. Words and public statements are, however, important. A major contribution to the reduction of world tensions would be for your country to curb the escalating campaign of anti-Americanism and disinformation both inside the Soviet Union and abroad, a campaign which only serves to poison the political atmosphere.

Mr. President, my country stands ready to begin the search for a better U.S.-Soviet relationship. We are prepared to discuss with the Soviet Union the full range of issues which divide us, to seek significant, verifiable reductions in nuclear weapons, and to increase contacts between our nations. I am hopeful that the meetings between Secretary of State Haig and Foreign Minister Gromyko will start a process leading toward such a relationship.

For such a process to bear fruit, your country must understand the need for restraint in the international arena. At the same time, let me add that the United States is fully prepared to take legitimate Soviet interests into account. If we succeed in establishing a framework of mutual respect for each other's interests and mutual restraint in the resolution of international crises, I think we will create a sound and enduring basis for U.S.-Soviet relations.

RONALD REAGAN

30

Minutes of National Security Council Meeting on Strategy toward Cuba and Central America

November 10, 1981

The Reagan administration believed that Central America was a principal arena in the cold war of the 1980s. The president feared that the Soviets were trying to establish a military foothold close to U.S. borders and believed that liberals, especially those in Congress, did not take the threat seriously. Administration officials designed a plan to offer assistance to anti-Communist forces in Nicaragua and El Salvador, even as they anticipated domestic opposition to these plans.

Mr. [Richard] Allen opened the meeting by pointing out the two papers in front of us: the State Department paper and a DOD [Department of Defense] submission. . . .

Secretary [of State Alexander M.] Haig explained the State paper was an interdepartmental effort over an extended period, and it faces up to the fundamental issue: namely, a deteriorating situation in Central America. If we wait much longer to act, then the price will be much higher. . . .

Secretary [of Defense Caspar W.] Weinberger then made his presentation. He opened by saying he believed that there was agreement on the nature and seriousness of the problem. There is a narrow point of difference between DOD and State. DOD cannot accept the decision to use unilateral force now. We must go step by step. We must prepare public opinion, and we must work on getting a coalition of Latin American countries to work with us. The Secretary emphasized that we should not make the commitment without doing the above first. . . .

[United Nations] Ambassador [Jeane] Kirkpatrick argued that the situation was deteriorating and action must be taken. What to do? Some decisions are more urgent than others. Decisions should have been taken months ago—but clearly El Salvador is the first priority. The

From National Security Council Meeting Files, Executive Secretariat, NSC24, Ronald Reagan Library.

present government will collapse if the guerrillas continue to destroy the economy. Weak governments cannot survive that kind of action indefinitely. We do not have time to build coalitions. We can cooperate with individual countries, but they will never work together in time. We cannot wait for public opinion either to form. . . .

Secretary Haig observed . . . that any plan we adopt will leak[,] therefore, we must not get onto any track unless we are ready to do something. If we do not and instead have a set of actions that merely do some damage—they will leak too and [Cuban president Fidel] Castro will use that against us. We cannot start another Vietnam in our hemisphere. . . .

Secretary Haig said the President can stop at any point. But if you are not prepared to move right up to the threshhold [*sic*], then don't start down the path in the first place. We should go back and look at it again and do only the easy actions.

Mr. [William J.] Casey [CIA director] then reiterated the principal target is Nicaragua.

Ambassador Kirkpartick [*sic*] disagreed. She argued that El Salvador had to be stabilized first. Then we should move [into] Nicaragua and let others do the work for us. . . .

Secretary Haig agreed. But he warned against creating an insurgency in Nicaragua unless you are prepared to go all the way.

Mr. Allen observed that Cubans in Nicaragua do create opportunities for us. That's very different than going directly to Cuba with warlike actions.

Mr. [Edwin] Meese [White House adviser] then summarized the situation. The key element is whether U.S. land forces and naval actions are to be contemplated. Would we use them?

The President then asked should everyone—Americans, Cubans, Nicaraguans—feel that the U.S. will commit its forces?

The President then observed that what worries him most is this: if the people won't support the leader and the cause, then there will be failure. The President then said it was clear the press would like to accuse us of getting into another Vietnam. How can we solve this problem with Congress and public opinion being what they are? We are talking about an impossible option. Are there other things we can do? Can covert actions be traced back to us[?] How do we deal with the image in Latin America of the Yankee collossus [*sic*]? . . .

Ambassador Kirkpatrick . . . rejected the Vietnam analogy. The Vietnam war did not involve direct national security interests. The loss of Central America does.

The President said but then what. People will want to know, what are you going to do?

Mr. Meese then said it seems agreed that we do those things already listed to help El Salvador. As for Nicaragua, we can do political, military, propaganda/covert actions that do not require U.S. forces.

The Vice President asked if we could mine Nicaraguan east coast ports. . . .

The President then asked to hear more (at the next meeting) about various alternatives including mining. He added I don't want to back down. I don't want to accept defeat.

Mr. Meese then said we must continue the meeting on Thursday. He suggested we take each item short of the ultimatum to Nicaragua and the employment of U.S. forces against Nicaragua and find out what it takes to implement each action in terms of money and bureaucratic follow-up. He then said we should discuss what other steps could also be contemplated. Then finally we can go and discuss further the most serious actions both pros and cons.

The President then asked what other covert actions could be taken that would be truly disabling and not just flea bites? . . .

The President asked can we take more training exercises? Can we introduce a few battalions into Panama or Honduras? Have we ever done that in Central America?

General [Paul F.] Gorman [of the Joint Chiefs of Staff] said no, we have never done that.

31

A Public Affairs Program to Support the Administration's Nuclear Policy

May 5, 1982

The White House recognized public anxiety about Reagan's tough stance toward the Soviet Union. The international nuclear freeze movement was generating widespread support for curtailing nuclear weapons, including strong support in the U.S. Congress. Polls revealed that there was great concern about the possibility of nuclear war in the early 1980s. Support for a nuclear freeze created a check on Reagan's hawkish foreign policies. Reagan and his team would develop a strategy to counteract these fears to show that they were genuinely committed to achieving peace. In this memo, the administration outlines its response to this pressure.

Objective: To rally public backing for the Administration's approach to negotiating with the Soviet Union on the reduction of strategic and tactical nuclear weapons.

Negotiating nuclear questions with the Soviet Union is a domestic political issue as well as a foreign policy issue. Current public and press opinion on this issue can be summarized as follows:

Public Opinion (based on polls taken over the past five months)

1. The American public is concerned about the possibility of the U.S. and the Soviet Union stumbling into a nuclear war. Only about 30% are confident that a nuclear war between the super-powers will not occur within the next decade.

2. The public is more fearful of nuclear war happening by accident than premeditation. Few expect a carefully calculated Soviet first strike. Only 7% believe it "very likely" and 20% think it

From Sven Kraemer Files, Box 90100, file: Nuclear Freeze, April 28, 1982 (2 of 3), Ronald Reagan Library.

"somewhat likely." On the other hand, 67% believe it "not likely at all."

3. The public is divided quite evenly on whether the U.S. needs to strengthen its present nuclear arsenal in order to deter a Soviet attack. When a *Washington Post* poll asked if the "U.S. should continue developing nuclear weapons because the ones we have now are not enough to make the Russians afraid to attack," 43% agreed but 49% disagreed.

4. Public concern about the likelihood of nuclear war co-exists with public approval of the President's "tough" stance against the Soviet Union. (In January 1980, 56% thought President Carter was "not tough enough." In December 1981, only 17% thought President Reagan "not tough enough.") The explanation for this seeming contradiction is that the confrontational policy the public has wanted has heightened concern that nuclear war could be the unintended outcome.

5. The public is now substantially more confident than during the previous administration that U.S. officials will protect U.S. security interests when negotiating with the Soviet Union. (60% expressed confidence in October 1981, compared to 48% in October 1979).

6. The public is increasingly concerned that the President does not genuinely desire to negotiate with the Soviet Union on nuclear arms. There was overwhelming approval of the President's zero-option speech. Yet, according to a *Time* magazine poll taken early in December, a larger percentage of the public thought he made the proposal "for political or propaganda reasons" than thought it a "serious attempt to reduce nuclear weapons" (50% vs. 39%). Between December and March, an increased percentage of the public believed that "President Reagan is putting more emphasis on expanding our nuclear arsenal["] (up from 42% in December to 56% in March) rather than on "negotiating on nuclear disarmament" (down from 40% in December to 27% in March). . . .

Premises for a Public Affairs Campaign

1. The public believes that the President is a sufficiently tough negotiator, but that he is not sufficiently interested in negotiating.

2. This public affairs campaign can be effective only if it persuasively addresses the public's deep-seated concerns (outlined above).

3. The public—and the press—want persuasive evidence that the Administration will soon undertake a sincere effort to negotiate arms control measures that would halt the development of nuclear weapons, reduce the number of weapons on both sides, and lessen the possibility of a nuclear exchange.

4. Overcoming public skepticism about Administration intentions will require that a comprehensive, explicit negotiating position be put forward—by the President—and then that it be promoted forcefully by a united Administration.

5. Until such a policy is articulated, we lack a firm foundation for building a public affairs campaign. The policy will provide the essential "talking points" on which to base the public affairs campaign.

6. Until such time, however, our public affairs efforts must: stress that we share the public's concern over the prospect of nuclear war and that we all have the same goal—peace; highlight that the U.S., not the Soviet Union, has been a leader in arms control initiatives, and that START [Strategic arms reduction talks], by offering reductions instead of growth limitations, continues that leadership tradition; point out that we do have a coherent, credible, and moral nuclear policy which has kept the peace for more than 35 years; and sketch to the extent possible our desired outcome for arms control steps.

32

NATIONAL SECURITY COUNCIL

Directive No. 75 on U.S. Relations with the USSR

January 17, 1983

Reagan was critical of the containment policy that had guided American policymakers since the 1950s. He felt that containment accepted the permanence of Communist rule and ignored the possibility of creating democracy in Eastern Europe. Rather than just checking Soviet expansion, Reagan's goal was to undermine the strength of the Soviet Union and create pressure for its demise. He supported the concept of "rollback," promoted by conservatives since the 1950s, which stipulated that the goal of U.S. policy should be to eliminate, rather than to contain, communism. Yet as this National Security Council memo illustrates, by 1983 Reagan began to open the door to secret negotiations with Soviet officials.

U.S. policy toward the Soviet Union will consist of three elements: external resistance to Soviet imperialism; internal pressure on the USSR to weaken the sources of Soviet imperialism; and negotiations to eliminate, on the basis of strict reciprocity, outstanding disagreements. Specifically, U.S. tasks are:

1. To contain and over time reverse Soviet expansionism by competing effectively on a sustained basis with the Soviet Union in all international arenas—particularly in the overall military balance and in geographical regions of priority concern to the United States. This will remain the primary focus of U.S. policy toward the USSR.

2. To promote, within the narrow limits available to us, the process of change in the Soviet Union toward a more pluralistic political and economic system in which the power of the

---

From William Clark Files, Box 8, file: U.S.–Soviet Relations Paper (2), Ronald Reagan Library.

privileged ruling elite is gradually reduced. The U.S. recognizes that Soviet aggressiveness has deep roots in the internal system, and that relations with the USSR should therefore take into account whether or not they help to strengthen this system and its capacity to engage in aggression.

3. To engage the Soviet Union in negotiations to attempt to reach agreements which protect and enhance U.S. interests and which are consistent with the principle of strict reciprocity and mutual interest. This is important when the Soviet Union is in the midst of a process of political succession.

In order to implement this threefold strategy, the U.S. must convey clearly to Moscow that unacceptable behavior will incur costs that would outweigh any gains. At the same time, the U.S. must make clear to the Soviets that genuine restraint in their behavior would create the possibility of an East-West relationship that might bring important benefits for the Soviet Union. It is particularly important that this message be conveyed clearly during the succession period, since this may be a particularly opportune time for external forces to affect the policies of Brezhnev's successors.

Shaping the Soviet Environment: Arenas of Engagement

Implementation of U.S. policy must focus on shaping the environment in which Soviet decisions are made both in a wide variety of functional and geopolitical arenas and in the U.S.-Soviet bilateral relationship.

FUNCTIONAL

1. *Military Strategy*: The U.S. must modernize its military forces — both nuclear and conventional — so that Soviet leaders perceive that the U.S. is determined never to accept a second place or a deteriorating military posture. Soviet calculations of possible war outcomes under any contingency must always result in outcomes so unfavorable to the USSR that there would be no incentive for Soviet leaders to initiate an attack. The future strength of U.S. military capabilities must be assured. U.S. military technology advances must be exploited, while controls over transfer of military related/dual-use technology, products, and services must be tightened.

In Europe, the Soviets must be faced with a reinvigorated NATO. In the Far East we must ensure that the Soviets cannot count on a secure flank in a global war. Worldwide, U.S. general purpose forces must be strong and flexible enough to affect Soviet calculations in a wide variety of contingencies. In the Third World, Moscow must know that areas of interest to the U.S. cannot be attacked or threatened without risk of serious U.S. military countermeasures.

2. *Economic Policy*: U.S. policy on economic relations with the USSR must serve strategic and foreign policy goals as well as economic interests. In this context, U.S. objectives are:

- Above all, to ensure that East-West economic relations do not facilitate the Soviet military buildup. This requires prevention of the transfer of technology and equipment that would make a substantial contribution directly or indirectly to Soviet military power.

- To avoid subsidizing the Soviet economy or unduly easing the burden of Soviet resource allocation decisions, so as not to dilute pressures for structural change in the Soviet system.

- To seek to minimize the potential for Soviet exercise of reverse leverage on Western countries based on trade, energy supply, and financial relationships.

- To permit mutual beneficial trade — without Western subsidization or the creation of Western dependence — with the USSR in non-strategic areas, such as grains.

The U.S. must exercise strong leadership with its Allies and others to develop a common understanding of the strategic implications of East-West trade, building upon the agreement announced November 13, 1982. This approach should involve efforts to reach agreements with the Allies on specific measures, such as: (a) no incremental deliveries of Soviet gas beyond the amounts contracted for from the first strand of the Siberian pipeline; (b) the addition of critical technologies and equipment to the COCOM [Coordinating Committee for Multilateral Export Controls] list, the harmonization of national licensing procedures for COCOM, and the substantial improvement of the coordination and effectiveness of international enforcement efforts; (c) controls on advanced technology and equipment beyond the expanded COCOM list, including equipment in the oil and gas sector; (d) further restraints on officially-backed credits such as higher down payments, shortened maturities and an established framework to monitor this process; and (e) the strengthening of the role of the OECD [Organization of Economic Cooperation and Development] and NATO in East-West trade analysis and policy.

In the longer term, if Soviet behavior should worsen, e.g., an invasion of Poland, we would need to consider extreme measures. Should Soviet behavior improve, carefully calibrated positive economic signals, including a broadening of government-to-government economic contacts, could be considered as a means of demonstrating to the Soviets the benefits that real restraint in their conduct might bring. Such steps could not, however, alter the basic direction of U.S. policy.

3. *Political Action*: U.S. policy must have an ideological thrust which clearly affirms the superiority of U.S. and Western values of individual dignity and freedom, a free press, free trade unions, free enterprise, and political democracy over the repressive features of Soviet Communism. We need to review and significantly strengthen U.S. instruments of political action including: (a) The President's London initiative to support democratic forces; (b) USG [U.S. government] efforts to highlight Soviet human rights violations; and (c) U.S. radio broadcasting policy. The U.S. should:

- Expose at all available fora the double standards employed by the Soviet Union in dealing with difficulties within its own domain and the outside ("capitalist") world (e.g., treatment of labor, policies toward ethnic minorities, use of chemical weapons, etc.).

- Prevent the Soviet propaganda machine from seizing the semantic high-ground in the battle of ideas through the appropriation of such terms as "peace."

GEOPOLITICAL

1. *The Industrial Democracies*: An effective response to the Soviet challenge requires close partnership among the industrial democracies, including stronger and more effective collective defense arrangements. The U.S. must provide strong leadership and conduct effective consultations to build consensus and cushion the impact of intra-alliance disagreements. While Allied support of U.S. overall strategy is essential, the U.S. may on occasion be forced to act to protect vital interests without Allied support and even in the face of Allied opposition; even in this event, however, [the] U.S. should consult to the maximum extent possible with its Allies.

2. *The Third World*: The U.S. must rebuild the credibility of its commitment to resist Soviet encroachment on U.S. interests and those of its Allies and friends, and to support effectively those Third World states that are willing to resist Soviet pressures or oppose Soviet initiatives

hostile to the United States, or are special targets of Soviet policy. The U.S. effort in the Third World must involve an important role for security assistance and foreign military sales, as well as readiness to use U.S. military forces where necessary to protect vital interests and support endangered Allies and friends. U.S. policy must also involve diplomatic initiatives to promote resolution of regional crises vulnerable to Soviet exploitation, and an appropriate mixture of economic assistance programs and private sector initiatives for Third World countries.

3. *The Soviet Empire*: There are a number of important weaknesses and vulnerabilities within the Soviet empire which the U.S. should exploit. U.S. policies should seek wherever possible to encourage Soviet allies to distance themselves from Moscow in foreign policy and to move toward democratization domestically.

a. *Eastern Europe*: The primary U.S. objective in Eastern Europe is to loosen Moscow's hold on the region while promoting the cause of human rights in individual East European countries. The U.S. can advance this objective by carefully discriminating in favor of countries that show relative independence from the USSR in their foreign policy, or show a greater degree of internal liberalization. U.S. policies must also make clear that East European countries which reverse movements of liberalization, or drift away from an independent stance in foreign policy, will incur significant costs in their relations with the U.S.

b. *Afghanistan*: The U.S. objective is to keep maximum pressure on Moscow for withdrawal and to ensure that the Soviets' political, military, and other costs remain high while the occupation continues.

c. *Cuba*: The U.S. must take strong countermeasures to affect the political/military impact of Soviet arms deliveries to Cuba. The U.S. must also provide economic and military assistance to states in Central America and the Caribbean Basin threatened by Cuban destabilizing activities. Finally, the U.S. will seek to reduce the Cuban presence and influence in southern Africa by energetic leadership of the diplomatic effort to achieve a Cuban withdrawal from Angola, or failing that, by increasing the costs of Cuba's role in southern Africa.

d. *Soviet Third World Alliances*: U.S. policy will seek to limit the destabilizing activities of Soviet Third World allies and clients. It is a further objective to weaken and, where possible, undermine the existing links between them and the Soviet Union. U.S.

policy will include active efforts to encourage democratic movements and forces to bring about political change inside these countries.

4. *China*: China continues to support U.S. efforts to strengthen the world's defenses against Soviet expansionism. The U.S. should over time seek to achieve enhanced strategic cooperation and policy coordination with China, and to reduce the possibility of a Sino-Soviet rapprochement. The U.S. will continue to pursue a policy of substantially liberalized technology transfer and sale of military equipment to China on a case-by-case basis within the parameters of the policy approved by the President in 1981, and defined further in 1982.

5. *Yugoslavia*: It is U.S. policy to support the independence, territorial integrity and national unity of Yugoslavia. Yugoslavia's current difficulties in paying its foreign debts have increased its vulnerability to Soviet pressures. The Yugoslav government, well aware of this vulnerability, would like to reduce its trade dependence on the Soviet Union. It is in our interest to prevent any deterioration in Yugoslavia's economic situation that might weaken its resolve to withstand Soviet pressure.

BILATERIAL [*sic*] RELATIONSHIPS

1. *Arms Control*: The U.S. will enter into arms control negotiations when they serve U.S. national security objectives. At the same time, U.S. policy recognizes that arms control agreements are not an end in themselves but are, in combination with U.S. and Allied efforts to maintain the military balance, an important means for enhancing national security and global stability. The U.S. should make clear to the Allies as well as to the USSR that U.S. ability to reach satisfactory results in arms control negotiations will inevitably be influenced by the international situation, the overall state of U.S.-Soviet relations, and the difficulties in defining areas of mutual agreement with an adversary which often seeks unilateral gains. U.S. arms control proposals will be consistent with necessary force modernization plans and will seek to achieve balanced, significant, and verifiable reductions to equal levels of comparable armaments.

2. *Official Dialogue*: The U.S. should insist that Moscow address the full range of U.S. concerns about Soviet internal behavior and human rights violations, and should continue to resist Soviet efforts to return to a U.S.-Soviet agenda focused primarily on arms control. U.S.-Soviet diplomatic contacts on regional issues can serve U.S. interests if they are used to keep pressure on Moscow for responsible behavior. Such contacts can also be useful in driving home to Moscow that the costs

of irresponsibility are high, and that the U.S. is prepared to work for pragmatic solutions of regional problems if Moscow is willing seriously to address U.S. concerns. At the same time, such contacts must be handled with care to avoid offering the Soviet Union a role in regional questions it would not otherwise secure.

A continuing dialogue with the Soviets at Foreign Minister level facilitates necessary diplomatic communication with the Soviet leadership and helps to maintain Allied understanding and support for [the] U.S. approach to East-West relations. A summit between President Reagan and his Soviet counterpart might promise similarly beneficial results. At the same time, unless it were carefully handled a summit could be seen as registering an improvement in U.S.-Soviet relations without the changes in Soviet behavior which we have insisted upon. It could therefore generate unrealizable expectations and further stimulate unilateral Allied initiatives toward Moscow.

A summit would not necessarily involve signature of major new U.S.-Soviet agreements. Any summit meeting should achieve the maximum possible positive impact with U.S. Allies and the American public, while making clear to both audiences that improvement in Soviet-American relations depends on changes in Soviet conduct. A summit without such changes must not be understood to signal such improvement.

3. *U.S.-Soviet Cooperation Exchanges*: The role of U.S.-Soviet cultural, educational, scientific and other cooperative exchanges should be seen in light of the U.S. intention to maintain a strong ideological component in relations with Moscow. The U.S. should not further dismantle the framework of exchanges; indeed those exchanges which could advance the U.S. objective of promoting positive evolutionary change within the Soviet system should be expanded. At the same time, the U.S. will insist on *full* reciprocity and encourage its Allies to do so as well. This recognizes that unless the U.S. has an effective official framework for handling exchanges, the Soviets will make separate arrangements with private U.S. sponsors, while denying reciprocal access to the Soviet Union. U.S. policy on exchanges must also take into account the necessity to prevent transfer of sensitive U.S. technology to the Soviet Union.

PRIORITIES IN THE U.S. APPROACH: MAXIMIZING RESTRAINING LEVERAGE OVER SOVIET BEHAVIOR

The interrelated tasks of containing and reversing Soviet expansion and promoting evolutionary change within the Soviet Union itself cannot be accomplished quickly. The coming 5–10 years will be a period of considerable uncertainty in which the Soviets may test U.S. resolve by continuing the kind of aggressive international behavior which the U.S. finds unacceptable.

The uncertainties will be exacerbated by the fact that the Soviet Union will be engaged in the unpredictable process of political succession to Brezhnev. The U.S. will not seek to adjust its policies to the Soviet internal conflict, but rather try to create incentives (positive and negative) for the new leadership to adopt policies less detrimental to U.S. interests. The U.S. will remain ready for improved U.S.-Soviet relations if the Soviet Union makes significant changes in policies of concern to it; the burden for any further deterioration in relations must fall squarely on Moscow. The U.S. must not yield to pressures to "take the first step."

The existing and projected gap between finite U.S. resources and the level of capabilities needed to implement U.S. strategy makes it essential that the U.S.: (1) establish firm priorities for the use of limited U.S. resources where they will have the greatest restraining impact on the Soviet Union; and (2) mobilize the resources of Allies and friends which are willing to join the U.S. in containing the expansion of Soviet power.

Underlying the full range of U.S. and Western policies must be a strong military capable of action across the entire spectrum of potential conflicts and guided by a well conceived political and military strategy. The heart of U.S. military strategy is to deter attack by the USSR and its allies against the U.S., its Allies, or other important countries, and to defeat such an attack should deterrence fail. Although unilateral U.S. efforts must lead the way in rebuilding Western military strength to counter the Soviet threat, the protection of Western interests will require increased U.S. cooperation with Allied and other states and greater utilization of their resources. This military strategy will be combined with a political strategy attaching high priority to the following objectives:

- *Sustaining steady, long-term growth in U.S. defense spending and capabilities — both nuclear and conventional.* This is the most important way of conveying to the Soviets U.S. resolve and political staying-power.

- *Creating a long-term Western consensus for dealing with the Soviet Union.* This will require that the U.S. exercise strong leadership in developing policies to deal with the multifaceted Soviet threat to Western interests. It will require that the U.S. take Allied concerns into account, and also that U.S. Allies take into equal account U.S. concerns. In this connection, and in addition to pushing Allies to spend more on defense, the U.S.

must make a serious effort to negotiate arms control agreements consistent with U.S. military strategy and necessary force modernization plans, and should seek to achieve balanced, significant and verifiable reductions to equal levels of comparable armaments. The U.S. must also develop, together with the Allies, a unified Western approach to East-West economic relations, implementing the agreement announced on November 13, 1982.

* *Maintenance of a strategic relationship with China, and efforts to minimize opportunities for a Sino-Soviet rapprochement.*

* *Building and sustaining a major ideological/political offensive which, together with other efforts, will be designed to bring about evolutionary change of the Soviet system.* This must be a long-term and sophisticated program, given the nature of the Soviet system.

* *Effective opposition to Moscow's efforts to consolidate its position in Afghanistan.* This will require that the U.S. continue efforts to promote Soviet withdrawal in the context of a negotiated settlement of the conflict. At the same time, the U.S. must keep pressure on Moscow for withdrawal and ensure that Soviet costs on the ground are high.

* *Blocking the expansion of Soviet influence in the critical Middle East and Southwest Asia regions.* This will require both continued efforts to seek a political solution to the Arab-Israeli conflict and to bolster U.S. relations with moderate states in the region, and a sustained U.S. defense commitment to deter Soviet military encroachments.

* *Maintenance of international pressure on Moscow to permit a relaxation of the current repression in Poland and a longer-term increase in diversity and independence throughout Eastern Europe.* This will require that the U.S. continue to impose costs on the Soviet Union for its behavior in Poland. It will also require that the U.S. maintain a U.S. policy of differentiation among East European countries.

* *Neutralization and reduction of the threat to U.S. national security interests posed by the Soviet-Cuban relationship.* This will require that the U.S. use a variety of instruments, including diplomatic efforts and U.S. security and economic assistance. The U.S. must also retain the option of using its military forces to protect vital U.S. security interests against threats which may arise from the Soviet-Cuban connection.

**ARTICULATING THE U.S. APPROACH: SUSTAINING PUBLIC AND
CONGRESSIONAL SUPPORT**

The policy outlined above is one for the long haul. It is unlikely to yield
a rapid breakthrough in bilateral relations with the Soviet Union. In the
absence of dramatic near-term victories in the U.S. effort to moderate
Soviet behavior, pressure is likely to mount for change in U.S. policy.
There will be appeals from important segments of domestic opinion
for a more "normal" U.S.-Soviet relationship, particularly in a period of
political transition in Moscow.

It is therefore essential that the American people understand and
support U.S. policy. This will require that official U.S. statements and
actions avoid generating unrealizable expectations for near-term progress in U.S.-Soviet relations. At the same time, the U.S. must demonstrate credibly that its policy is not a blueprint for an open-ended, sterile
confrontation with Moscow, but a serious search for a stable and constructive long-term basis for U.S.-Soviet relations.

RONALD REAGAN

33

RONALD REAGAN

"Evil Empire" Speech
March 8, 1983

*Reagan used moralistic language to describe the cold war, distinguishing
himself from earlier politicians who had sought a more pragmatic tone
toward the Soviet Union. Reagan rooted this speech, which he delivered
at a meeting of the National Association of Evangelicals, in arguments he
had made for decades about the moral underpinnings of the war against
communism. By giving a hawkish foreign policy address to a group of
religious leaders, Reagan was solidifying connections among different
parts of the Republican coalition.*

From Ronald Reagan, "Remarks at the Annual Convention of the National Association of
Evangelicals in Orlando, Florida," in *Public Papers of the Presidents of the United States:
Ronald Reagan, 1983* (Washington, D.C.: U.S. Government Printing Office, 1984),
1:359–64.

I'm pleased to be here today with you who are keeping America great by keeping her good. Only through your work and prayers and those of millions of others can we hope to survive this perilous century and keep alive this experiment in liberty, this last, best hope of man. . . .

. . . There's a great spiritual awakening in America, a renewal of the traditional values that have been the bedrock of America's goodness and greatness. . . .

There is sin and evil in the world, and we're enjoined by Scripture and the Lord Jesus to oppose it with all our might. Our nation, too, has a legacy of evil with which it must deal. The glory of this land has been its capacity for transcending the moral evils of our past. For example, the long struggle of minority citizens for equal rights, once a source of disunity and civil war, is now a point of pride for all Americans. We must never go back. There is no room for racism, anti-Semitism, or other forms of ethnic and racial hatred in this country. . . .

. . . In this century, America has kept alight the torch of freedom, but not just for ourselves but for millions of others around the world.

. . . During my first press conference as President, in answer to a direct question, I pointed out that, as good Marxist-Leninists, the Soviet leaders have openly and publicly declared that the only morality they recognize is that which will further their cause, which is world revolution. I think I should point out I was only quoting Lenin, their guiding spirit, who said in 1920 that they repudiate all morality that proceeds from supernatural ideas—that's their name for religion—or ideas that are outside class conceptions. Morality is entirely subordinate to the interests of class war. And everything is moral that is necessary for the annihilation of the old, exploiting social order and for uniting the proletariat.

Well, I think the refusal of many influential people to accept this elementary fact of Soviet doctrine illustrates an historical reluctance to see totalitarian powers for what they are. We saw this phenomenon in the 1930's. We see it too often today.

This doesn't mean we should isolate ourselves and refuse to seek an understanding with them. I intend to do everything I can to persuade them of our peaceful intent, to remind them that it was the West that refused to use its nuclear monopoly in the forties and fifties for territorial gain and which now proposes [a] 50-percent cut in strategic ballistic missiles and the elimination of an entire class of land-based, intermediate-range nuclear missiles.

At the same time, however, they must be made to understand we will never compromise our principles and standards. We will never give away our freedom. We will never abandon our belief in God. And we will never stop searching for a genuine peace. But we can assure none of these things America stands for through the so-called nuclear freeze solutions proposed by some.

The truth is that a freeze now would be a very dangerous fraud, for that is merely the illusion of peace. The reality is that we must find peace through strength.

I would agree to a freeze if only we could freeze the Soviets' global desires. A freeze at current levels of weapons would remove any incentive for the Soviets to negotiate seriously in Geneva [at the summit] and virtually end our chances to achieve the major arms reductions which we have proposed. Instead, they would achieve their objectives through the freeze.

A freeze would reward the Soviet Union for its enormous and unparalleled military buildup. It would prevent the essential and long overdue modernization of United States and allied defenses and would leave our aging forces increasingly vulnerable. And an honest freeze would require extensive prior negotiations on the systems and numbers to be limited and on the measures to ensure effective verification and compliance. And the kind of a freeze that has been suggested would be virtually impossible to verify. Such a major effort would divert us completely from our current negotiations on achieving substantial reductions. . . .

. . . Let us pray for the salvation of all of those who live in that totalitarian darkness—pray they will discover the joy of knowing God. But until they do, let us be aware that while they preach the supremacy of the state, declare its omnipotence over individual man, and predict its eventual domination of all peoples on the Earth, they are the focus of evil in the modern world. . . .

. . . If history teaches anything, it teaches that simple-minded appeasement or wishful thinking about our adversaries is folly. It means the betrayal of our past, the squandering of our freedom.

So, I urge you to speak out against those who would place the United States in a position of military and moral inferiority. . . . In your discussions of the nuclear freeze proposals, I urge you to beware the temptation of pride—the temptation of blithely declaring yourselves above it all and label both sides equally at fault, to ignore the facts of history and the aggressive impulses of an evil empire, to simply call the arms race a giant misunderstanding and thereby remove yourself from the struggle between right and wrong and good and evil.

I ask you to resist the attempts of those who would have you withhold your support for our efforts, this administration's efforts, to keep

America strong and free, while we negotiate real and verifiable reductions in the world's nuclear arsenals and one day, with God's help, their total elimination.

While America's military strength is important, let me add here that I've always maintained that the struggle now going on for the world will never be decided by bombs or rockets, by armies or military might. The real crisis we face today is a spiritual one; at root, it is a test of moral will and faith. . . .

I believe we shall rise to the challenge. I believe that communism is another sad, bizarre chapter in human history whose last pages even now are being written. I believe this because the source of our strength in the quest for human freedom is not material, but spiritual. And because it knows no limitation, it must terrify and ultimately triumph over those who would enslave their fellow man. For in the words of Isaiah: "He giveth power to the faint; and to them that have no might He increased strength. . . . But they that wait upon the Lord shall renew their strength; they shall mount up with wings as eagles; they shall run, and not be weary."

34

RONALD REAGAN

Address to the Nation on Defense and National Security

March 23, 1983

Seeking to counteract the nuclear freeze movement, Reagan offered his own vision for achieving security in the United States. In this speech, Reagan proposed the Strategic Defense Initiative (SDI), which would create a shield over the country to protect it from incoming missiles. The shield had been sought by conservatives for several decades. Most prominent scientists—with some notable exceptions, such as the physicist and father of the hydrogen bomb, Edward Teller—believed that the shield

From Ronald Reagan, "Address to the Nation on Defense and National Security," in *Public Papers of the Presidents of the United States: Ronald Reagan, 1983* (Washington, D.C.: U.S. Government Printing Office, 1984), 1:437–43.

would never work and would create a more dangerous situation through the illusion that nuclear war could be prevented. While Reagan hoped that the announcement of SDI would reassure Americans about their safety, critics redubbed the program "Star Wars" as a way of suggesting its unfeasibility.

My fellow Americans, thank you for sharing your time with me tonight. . . .

At the beginning of this year, I submitted to the Congress a defense budget which reflects my best judgment of the best understanding of the experts and specialists who advise me about what we and our allies must do to protect our people in the years ahead. That budget is much more than a long list of numbers, for behind all the numbers lies America's ability to prevent the greatest of human tragedies and preserve our free way of life in a sometimes dangerous world. It is part of a careful, long-term plan to make America strong again after too many years of neglect and mistakes. . . .

The budget request that is now before the Congress has been trimmed to the limits of safety. Further deep cuts cannot be made without seriously endangering the security of the Nation. The choice is up to the men and women you've elected to the Congress, and that means the choice is up to you.

Tonight, I want to explain to you what this defense debate is all about and why I'm convinced that the budget now before the Congress is necessary, responsible, and deserving of your support. And I want to offer hope for the future.

But first, let me say what the defense debate is not about. It is not about spending arithmetic. I know that in the last few weeks you've been bombarded with numbers and percentages. Some say we need only a 5-percent increase in defense spending. The so-called alternate budget backed by liberals in the House of Representatives would lower the figure to 2 to 3 percent, cutting our defense spending by $163 billion over the next 5 years. The trouble with all these numbers is that they tell us little about the kind of defense program America needs or the benefits and security and freedom that our defense effort buys for us.

What seems to have been lost in all this debate is the simple truth of how a defense budget is arrived at. It isn't done by deciding to spend a certain number of dollars. Those loud voices that are occasionally heard charging that the Government is trying to solve a security problem by throwing money at it are nothing more than noise based on ignorance.

We start by considering what must be done to maintain peace and review all the possible threats against our security. Then a strategy for strengthening peace and defending against those threats must be agreed upon. And, finally, our defense establishment must be evaluated to see what is necessary to protect against any or all of the potential threats. The cost of achieving these ends is totaled up, and the result is the budget for national defense. . . .

The defense policy of the United States is based on a simple premise: The United States does not start fights. We will never be an aggressor. We maintain our strength in order to deter and defend against aggression—to preserve freedom and peace. . . .

For 20 years the Soviet Union has been accumulating enormous military might. They didn't stop when their forces exceeded all requirements of a legitimate defensive capability. And they haven't stopped now. During the past decade and a half, the Soviets have built up a massive arsenal of new strategic nuclear weapons—weapons that can strike directly at the United States. . . .

As the Soviets have increased their military power, they've been emboldened to extend that power. They're spreading their military influence in ways that can directly challenge our vital interests and those of our allies. . . .

On the small island of Grenada, at the southern end of the Caribbean chain, the Cubans, with Soviet financing and backing, are in the process of building an airfield with a 10,000-foot runway. Grenada doesn't even have an air force. Who is it intended for? The Caribbean is a very important passageway for our international commerce and military lines of communication. More than half of all American oil imports now pass through the Caribbean. The rapid buildup of Grenada's military potential is unrelated to any conceivable threat to this island country of under 110,000 people and totally at odds with the pattern of other eastern Caribbean States, most of which are unarmed.

The Soviet-Cuban militarization of Grenada, in short, can only be seen as power projection into the region. And it is in this important economic and strategic area that we're trying to help the Governments of El Salvador, Costa Rica, Honduras, and others in their struggles for democracy against guerrillas supported through Cuba and Nicaragua. . . .

. . . The Soviet Union is also supporting Cuban military forces in Angola and Ethiopia. They have bases in Ethiopia and South Yemen, near the Persian Gulf oil fields. . . .

Some people may still ask: Would the Soviets ever use their formidable military power? Well, again, can we afford to believe they won't?

There is Afghanistan. And in Poland, the Soviets denied the will of the people and in so doing demonstrated to the world how their military power could also be used to intimidate.

. . . The Soviet Union is acquiring what can only be considered an offensive military force. . . .

When I took office in January 1981, I was appalled by what I found. . . .

There was a real question then about how well we could meet a crisis. And it was obvious that we had to begin a major modernization program to ensure we could deter aggression and preserve the peace in the years ahead.

We had to move immediately to improve the basic readiness and staying power of our conventional forces, so they could meet—and therefore help deter—a crisis. We had to make up for lost years of investment by moving forward with a long-term plan to prepare our forces to counter the military capabilities our adversaries were developing for the future. . . .

This adds up to a major effort, and it isn't cheap. It comes at a time when there are many other pressures on our budget and when the American people have already had to make major sacrifices during the recession. But we must not be misled by those who would make defense once again the scapegoat of the Federal budget. . . .

This is why I'm speaking to you tonight—to urge you to tell your Senators and Congressmen that you know we must continue to restore our military strength. If we stop in midstream, we will send a signal of decline, of lessened will, to friends and adversaries alike. Free people must voluntarily, through open debate and democratic means, meet the challenge that totalitarians pose by compulsion. It's up to us, in our time, to choose and choose wisely between the hard but necessary task of preserving peace and freedom and the temptation to ignore our duty and blindly hope for the best while the enemies of freedom grow stronger day by day.

The solution is well within our grasp. But to reach it, there is simply no alternative but to continue this year, in this budget, to provide the resources we need to preserve the peace and guarantee our freedom.

Now, thus far tonight I've shared with you my thoughts on the problems of national security we must face together. My predecessors in the Oval Office have appeared before you on other occasions to describe the threat posed by Soviet power and have proposed steps to address that threat. But since the advent of nuclear weapons, those steps have been increasingly directed toward deterrence of aggression through the promise of retaliation.

This approach to stability through offensive threat has worked. We and our allies have succeeded in preventing nuclear war for more than three decades. In recent months, however, my advisers, including in particular the Joint Chiefs of Staff, have underscored the necessity to break out of a future that relies solely on offensive retaliation for our security. . . .

. . . Wouldn't it be better to save lives than avenge them? . . . Let me share with you a vision of the future which offers hope. It is that we embark on a program to counter the awesome Soviet missile threat with measures that are defensive. Let us turn to the very strengths in technology that spawned our great industrial base and that have given us the quality of life we enjoy today.

What if free people could live secure in the knowledge that their security did not rest upon the threat of instant U.S. retaliation to deter a Soviet attack, that we could intercept and destroy strategic ballistic missiles before they reached our own soil or that of our allies?

I know this is a formidable, technical task, one that may not be accomplished before the end of this century. Yet, current technology has attained a level of sophistication where it's reasonable for us to begin this effort. It will take years, probably decades of effort on many fronts. There will be failures and setbacks, just as there will be successes and breakthroughs. And as we proceed, we must remain constant in preserving the nuclear deterrent and maintaining a solid capability for flexible response. But isn't it worth every investment necessary to free the world from the threat of nuclear war? We know it is. . . .

. . . I call upon the scientific community in our country, those who gave us nuclear weapons, to turn their great talents now to the cause of mankind and world peace, to give us the means of rendering these nuclear weapons impotent and obsolete.

. . . I'm taking an important first step. I am directing a comprehensive and intensive effort to define a long-term research and development program to begin to achieve our ultimate goal of eliminating the threat posed by strategic nuclear missiles. . . .

My fellow Americans, tonight we're launching an effort which holds the promise of changing the course of human history. There will be risks, and results take time. But I believe we can do it. As we cross this threshold, I ask for your prayers and your support.

Setbacks and Victories in Foreign Affairs, 1983–1984

35

ROBERT C. BYRD AND THOMAS P. O'NEILL JR.

Letter to President Reagan

July 28, 1983

*Reagan relied on a strategy whereby the executive branch would deter-
mine foreign policy. Frustrated with Democratic control of the House
and the willingness of Democrats to challenge the White House on foreign
policy, Reagan embraced presidential power as a way to achieve his
administration's conservative goals. In this letter from Robert Byrd, Democratic leader in the Senate, and House Speaker Tip O'Neill, Democrats
raised early concerns that the White House was circumventing the legislative branch when making policy, especially regarding Central America.*

Dear Mr. President:

We want to express formally in this letter to you our concerns regarding the necessity for Congress to be kept fully and currently informed,
in advance, of significant actions or events involving the military forces
of the United States.

In particular, neither of us, nor to the best of our knowledge were
any of our Chairmen or Ranking Members on the key Congressional
Committees notified about the planned military deployments in Honduras and off the coast of Central America—activities which could pose

From White House Office of Records Management: Subject File Foreign Affairs 003–02,
Ronald Reagan Library.

a great danger of direct military engagement of United States combat forces.

Accordingly, we were surprised when you indicated during your press conference of July 26 that your Administration was keeping the Congress apprised of our government's actions in Central America.

Even apart from the possible applicability of the Congressional consultation provisions of the War Powers Resolution, we are most concerned that officials of your Administration did not foresee the need to consult with the Congress prior to initiating such serious actions. We do not know of anyone in the Congress who would deny you the full and unequivocal support which you must have when combat troops are deployed to protect the legitimate national security interest of this country. But we also can assure you that the Members of Congress, on both sides of the aisle, must feel confident, that upon providing that support we do so based upon full, accurate, and timely information. We deeply regret that no such information was provided in this case, and that virtually all of our information has been derived from published reports in the news media. . . .

In view of the foregoing it seems clear to us that we need to fashion cooperatively an ongoing system of timely briefings for the Congressional Leadership and the key Committee Chairmen and Ranking Members. . . .

Therefore, we urge you to raise this matter with those officials in your Administration whom you have charged with the responsibility to implement a continuing program of keeping the Congressional Leadership and appropriate Committees fully informed on a timely basis. We would appreciate your instructing them to meet and provide us a timely briefing, prior to the August recess, at which time details could be worked out governing the future consultation process.

Thank you very much for your kind and prompt attention to our concerns.

Sincerely,

THOMAS P. O'NEILL, JR.

The Speaker

ROBERT C. BYRD
Senate Democratic Leader

36

CBS NEWS/NEW YORK TIMES

Poll on Grenada and Lebanon Conflicts
October 28, 1983

The invasion of Grenada in October 1983 boosted Reagan's standing with the public. Reagan had won election as a candidate who promised to restore American strength abroad. Although the public was aware of political motivations that might have been a factor in the president's decision to invade Grenada, the public was happy with the quick and decisive victory as captured in this public opinion poll conducted by CBS News and the New York Times. Yet as the reaction to the earlier attack on the Marine barracks in Lebanon, where Reagan had sent peace- keeping troops, revealed, Americans were weary of committing troops and resources to spread democracy or keep the peace in volatile parts of the world.

Grenada and the President

A majority of Americans interviewed after President Reagan's address to the country last night approved of the decision that sent U.S. troops to the island of Grenada. Nearly two-thirds of those who watched or lis- tened to the speech approved. Before the speech Americans were more evenly divided. Almost half the public (46%) heard him speak.

In his speech, the President claimed that Cuba intended to take over Grenada and use it as a military base. Two-thirds of the public believed him. However, the public is no more likely now than it was in June to favor American intervention in another Cuban-influenced neighboring country — Nicaragua. Only one in five thinks the U.S. should help the people in Nicaragua who are trying to overthrow the government there; three out of five disapprove of such action.

Reagan also said that the government has a responsibility to go to the aid of its citizens when they are in danger. After the speech, two-thirds of the public agreed that the Americans in Grenada were in

From Christopher M. Lehman Files, Box 2, file: Central America, Ronald Reagan Library.

danger. Fewer believed that the day before; however, the public might not have needed Reagan's speech to convince them after the televised reports about the rescued medical students. Indeed, as many of those who didn't hear the speech as those who did, believed the Americans in Grenada were in danger.

The President's gain in support for sending American troops to Grenada translates neither into increased support for his Presidency nor his foreign policy. Even though Presidents usually gain support during a time of international crisis, there has been no improvement for Reagan. His overall approval rating is virtually unchanged since the last CBS News/*New York Times* Poll in late September. Similarly, there was little change in the proportion thinking he deserves to be re-elected.

Americans were more likely to believe that decisions about dealing with crises were being made by Reagan's advisers rather than by the President himself. Moreover, majorities believed the administration is too quick to use force and did not spend enough time looking for diplomatic solutions. . . .

Lebanon

A majority of the public does not believe the Marines can keep the peace in Lebanon. And they are divided about having the Marines there at all. Even so, Americans, now more than in September, do lean slightly more towards approving of the government sending troops to Lebanon for peacekeeping purposes. In September, only a third of the public approved of sending Marines to Lebanon on a peacekeeping mission. Now, almost half approve.

The President's speech last night did help convince some Americans that it is possible for the Marines to help keep the peace. Only 33% thought so before the speech. Thursday night, after the speech, 42% believed this was possible. Before the speech, only 28% thought the government had tried hard enough to explain why the Marines and Navy had been sent to Lebanon; after the speech, 40% agreed.

Other attitudes about Lebanon showed little change after the speech. About a third of the public favor withdrawal of all Marines now in Lebanon. About a third were willing to blame the Iranian government for the attack on the barracks. On the whole, the American public leans more towards thinking that the Marine officers in Lebanon didn't take enough security precautions rather than believe terrorists are unstoppable.

There was another area where the President has more convincing to do: The public is as likely to believe that Grenada was the assertion of

U.S. military strength by the administration to counter reaction to the bombing in Beirut as they are to believe the action in Grenada on Tuesday was really necessary.

37

WILLIAM I. GREENER III

Upcoming Movie on ABC
November 17, 1983

In November 1983, ABC planned to air the television film The Day After, *which depicted a fictitious war between the United States and the Soviet Union resulting in the nuclear attack and military devastation of both countries. The Reagan administration realized that the apocalyptic film would increase public anxiety about nuclear war and give momentum to the nuclear freeze movement. To counteract any negative publicity resulting from the film, the administration designed a public relations strategy based on this memo from the director of communications for the Republican National Committee to Reagan's communications director. In fact, many of the 100 million Americans who watched the film found it startling and even traumatizing. In response, the administration continued to sell SDI as a technology that would prevent such a nuclear holocaust.*

MEMORANDUM TO DAVID R. GERGEN

Per our conversation of last evening, I am providing you with a set of the information that we will be using in contacting Party leaders so that they might be better equipped to discuss the ABC movie dealing with nuclear war to be aired this Sunday evening.

The key points we are trying to make are:

1. Everyone agrees nuclear war would be horrible, beyond anyone's ability to imagine.

2. The movie raises the question as to what the best way to prevent such horror actually is.

From David Gergen Files, Box 3, file: The Day After, Ronald Reagan Library.

3. The movie seems to suggest that one policy would increase the likelihood of such a horror happening.

4. The ABC people certainly are entitled to represent that viewpoint with the movie, but we disagree that the policies in the movie would increase the likelihood of such a horror.

5. We believe the President's approach of reducing weapons after we have achieved parity is the best way to prevent such a war. . . .

. . . You can be assured that no one, most especially the Chairman, has any plans to attack the right of ABC to do what they have done. We do plan to make certain that we strongly support the notion that President Reagan's policies are the best way to prevent a nuclear war.

38

RONALD REAGAN

Remarks at a Ceremony Commemorating the Fortieth Anniversary of the Normandy Invasion, D-Day

June 5, 1984

Reagan delivered one of his most famous addresses in Normandy in June 1984. Appealing to the patriotic sentiment of Americans, he spoke about the heroic accomplishments of the Allies during World War II. He also reminded his American audience watching on television back home of the importance of U.S. commitment to the NATO alliance as a way to prevent the outbreak of another world war and check Soviet power in Eastern Europe. With this stirring speech, Reagan helped to build popular support for a buildup of the U.S. military.

We're here to mark that day in history when the Allied armies joined in battle to reclaim this continent to liberty. . . .

From Ronald Reagan, "Text of Remarks to the French People on the 40th Anniversary of the Normandy Invasion, D-Day," in *Public Papers of the Presidents of the United States: Ronald Reagan, 1984* (Washington, D.C.: U.S. Government Printing Office, 1986), 1:815.

Behind me is a memorial that symbolizes the Ranger daggers that were thrust into the top of these cliffs. And before me are the men who put them there.

These are the boys of Pointe du Hoc [key site of the Normandy invasion]. These are the men who took the cliffs. These are the champions who helped free a continent. These are the heroes who helped end a war.

Gentlemen, I look at you and I think of the words of Stephen Spender's poem. You are men who in your "lives fought for life . . . and left the vivid air signed with your honor." . . .

Forty summers have passed since the battle that you fought here. You were young the day you took these cliffs; some of you were hardly more than boys, with the deepest joys of life before you. Yet, you risked everything here. Why? Why did you do it? What impelled you to put aside the instinct for self-preservation and risk your lives to take these cliffs? What inspired all the men of the armies that met here? We look at you, and somehow we know the answer. It was faith and belief; it was loyalty and love.

The men of Normandy had faith that what they were doing was right, faith that they fought for all humanity, faith that a just God would grant them mercy on this beachhead or on the next. It was the deep knowledge—and pray God we have not lost it—that there is a profound, moral difference between the use of force for liberation and the use of force for conquest. You were here to liberate, not to conquer, and so you and those others did not doubt your cause. And you were right not to doubt.

You all knew that some things are worth dying for. One's country is worth dying for, and democracy is worth dying for, because it's the most deeply honorable form of government ever devised by man. All of you loved liberty. All of you were willing to fight tyranny, and you knew the people of your countries were behind you. . . .

In spite of our great efforts and successes, not all that followed the end of the war was happy or planned. Some liberated countries were lost. The great sadness of this loss echoes down to our own time in the streets of Warsaw, Prague, and East Berlin. Soviet troops that came to the center of this continent did not leave when peace came. They're still there, uninvited, unwanted, unyielding, almost 40 years after the war. Because of this, allied forces still stand on this continent. Today, as 40 years ago, our armies are here for only one purpose—to protect and defend democracy. The only territories we hold are memorials like this one and graveyards where our heroes rest.

We in America have learned bitter lessons from two World Wars: It is better to be here ready to protect the peace, than to take blind shelter across the sea, rushing to respond only after freedom is lost. We've learned that isolationism never was and never will be an acceptable response to tyrannical governments with an expansionist intent.

But we try always to be prepared for peace; prepared to deter aggression; prepared to negotiate the reduction of arms; and, yes, prepared to reach out again in the spirit of reconciliation. In truth, there is no reconciliation we would welcome more than a reconciliation with the Soviet Union, so, together, we can lessen the risks of war, now and forever. . . .

We will pray forever that someday that . . . will come. But for now, particularly today, it is good and fitting to renew our commitment to each other, to our freedom, and to the alliance that protects it.

39

Debate between Ronald Reagan and Walter Mondale

October 21, 1984

In a presidential campaign debate with Reagan, Democratic candidate Walter Mondale was extremely critical of the president's foreign policies, from the intervention in Central America to the nuclear buildup. Mondale warned that the president had brought the world closer to the brink of war. As much as the public worried about the implementation of an aggressive foreign policy, Reagan's confident and strong stand against communism and in favor of democracy resonated with Americans, who reelected him in a landslide victory.

Mr. Kondracke:[1] Mr. Mondale, in an address earlier this year you said that before this country resorts to military force, and I'm quoting, "American interests should be sharply defined, publicly supported, congressionally sanctioned, militarily feasible, internationally defensible, open

[1]Morton Kondracke, executive editor of the *New Republic*.

From "Debate between the President and Former Vice President Walter F. Mondale in Kansas City, Missouri," in *Public Papers of the Presidents of the United States: Ronald Reagan, 1984* (Washington, D.C.: U.S. Government Printing Office, 1987), 2:1589–1608.

to independent scrutiny, and alert to regional history." Now, aren't you setting up such a gauntlet of tests here that adversaries could easily suspect that as President you would never use force to protect American interests?

Mr. Mondale: No. As a matter of fact, I believe every one of those standards is essential to the exercise of power by this country. And we can see that in both Lebanon and in Central America.

In Lebanon, this President exercised American power, all right, but the management of it was such that our marines were killed, we had to leave in humiliation, the Soviet Union became stronger, terrorists became emboldened. And it was because they did not think through how power should be exercised, did not have the American public with them on a plan that worked, that we ended up the way we did.

Similarly, in Central America: What we're doing in Nicaragua with this covert war—which the Congress, including many Republicans, have tried to stop—is finally end up with a public definition of American power that hurts us, where we get associated with political assassins and the rest. We have to decline, for the first time in modern history, jurisdiction in the World Court because they'll find us guilty of illegal actions. And our enemies are strengthened from all of this.

We need to be strong, we need to be prepared to use that strength, but we must understand that we are a democracy. We are a government by the people, and when we move, it should be for very severe and extreme reasons that serve our national interests and end up with a stronger country behind us. It is only in that way that we can persevere. . . .

The Nicaraguans must know that it is the policy of our government that [their] leadership must stay behind the boundaries of their nation, not interfere in other nations. And by working with all of the nations in the region—unlike the policies of this administration and unlike the President said, they have not supported negotiations in that region—we will be much stronger, because we'll have the moral authority that goes with those efforts.

International Negotiations and Covert Missions, 1985–1986

40

RONALD REAGAN

Letter to Mikhail Gorbachev

March 11, 1985

and

ALEXANDER YAKOVLEV

Memo on Reagan

March 12, 1985

In 1985, when Mikhail Gorbachev became general secretary of the Communist party of the Soviet Union, he represented a new voice in the Soviet leadership, one eager for internal reform and negotiation with the United States. Reagan responded to Gorbachev by inviting him, in this letter, to begin a conversation about improved relations between the two countries, including a discussion of arms limitation. Soviet officials believed that Reagan was serious in his intentions, as the memo by Gorbachev's propaganda chief, Alexander Yakovlev, makes clear. In November, the two would meet in Geneva for the first of four summits, during which they developed a productive working relationship.

From Margaret Thatcher Foundation; and from Yakovlev Collection, State Archive of the Russian Federation, Moscow, in National Security Archive, George Washington University.

Letter to Gorbachev

Dear Mr General Secretary,

As you assume your new responsibilities, I would like to take this opportunity to underscore my hope that we can in the months and years ahead develop a more stable and constructive relationship between our two countries. Our differences are many, and we will need to proceed in a way that takes both differences and common interests into account in seeking to resolve problems and build a new measure of trust and confidence. But history places on us a very heavy responsibility for maintaining and strengthening peace, and I am convinced we have before us new opportunities to do so. Therefore I have requested the Vice President to deliver this letter to you.

I believe our differences can and must be resolved through discussion and negotiation. The international situation demands that we redouble our efforts to find political solutions to the problems we face. I valued my correspondence with Chairman Chernenko,[1] and believe my meetings with First Deputy Prime Minister Gromyko and Mr. Shcherbitsky[2] here in Washington were useful in clarifying views and issues and making it possible to move forward to deal with them in a practical and realistic fashion.

In recent months we have demonstrated that it is possible to resolve problems to mutual benefit. We have had useful exchanges on certain regional issues, and I am sure you are aware that American interest in progress on humanitarian issues remains as strong as ever. In our bilateral relations, we have signed a number of new agreements, and we have promising negotiations underway in several important fields. Most significantly, the negotiations we have agreed to begin in Geneva provide us with a genuine chance to make progress toward our common ultimate goal of eliminating nuclear weapons.

It is important for us to build on these achievements. You can be assured of my personal commitment to work with you and the rest of the Soviet leadership in serious negotiations. In that spirit, I would like to invite you to visit me in Washington at your earliest convenient opportunity. I recognize that an early answer may not be possible, but I want you to know that I look forward to a meeting that could yield results of

[1] Konstantin Chernenko, previous leader of the Communist party and Soviet premier.
[2] Vladimir Shcherbitsky, Politburo member.

benefit to both our countries and to the international community as a whole.

Sincerely,
RONALD REAGAN

Memo on Reagan

MEMORANDUM PREPARED ON REQUEST FROM M. S. GORBACHEV

ABOUT REAGAN

Starting positions — they are not so simple.

1. Everything points to the fact that Reagan is trying persistently to capture the initiative in international affairs, to create an image of America as a country that is purposefully striving to improve relations with the Soviet Union and to improve the global political climate.

He would like to solve a number of problems in the context of [his] dream about a "great peace-maker President" and "great America," although currently the psychological situation is not in his favor.

2. Reagan had outlined and partially carried out the plans to militarize America; and he has given practically everything that he had promised to the military business, therefore, now he can move on to diplomacy "at the highest level," which in any case would be a prestigious course, which would raise [his] political stock, which is what Reagan needs right now.

3. He is constrained now by the budget deficit, which might lead to economic difficulties. This deficit has to be either *justified by an external threat, or decreased.*

4. Notwithstanding the appearance of relative solidarity in NATO and among other allies, there is no unity [among them], or it is not all that solid. The USA *is trying to hold on to the crest of the centripetal tendency and to prevent the development of the centrifugal tendency by all means.*

The invitation for a meeting should, obviously, be understood in this context. A lot of issues can be seen here: the aspiration *to confine our relations with the West to the Soviet-American framework* (the USA is watching its allies with concern); the awareness of the anti-war mood both in the Congress and outside of it; the desire to feel out the Soviet position on key international issues once again.

Undoubtedly, this action, apart from its political aims, carries a significant propaganda content. He does not lose anything if we refuse to meet [with him] ("you see, I wanted to, but . . ."), just the same if the meeting is a failure ("the Russians are uncooperative, as always . . .").

In other words, from Reagan's point of view, his proposal is well thought-through, precisely calculated, and does not contain [any] political risk.

Conclusion. Meeting with Reagan is in the national interest of the Soviet Union. We should agree to it, but without haste. We should not help create an impression that it is Reagan solely, who pushes the buttons of world development.

Goals of the meeting. (a) to get a personal impression of the American leader; (b) to give a clear signal that the USSR is genuinely prepared to negotiate, but only on the basis of strict reciprocity; (c) to let Reagan know in a very straightforward form that the USSR would not let [anyone] manipulate itself, and would not yield on [the matters of] its national interests; we should continue to point out in a delicate way that the world does not end with the USA, but at the same time not to lose real opportunities in terms of improving relations with the USA, because in the next quarter of a century the USA will remain the strongest power in the world.

It would be hard to expect any unanticipated changes of a *principal character* in the American policy. And this is not only due to the anti-Communist dogmatism of Reagan himself; the U.S. harsh policy is dictated by the *character of the transitional period for the United States — from its absolute dominance in the capitalist world, to a position of dominant partnership, and subsequently to a relative equality.*

The painful nature of this process, even if one ignores the traditional geopolitical claims of the USA, is obvious: it will continue to affect [its] foreign policy for a long time.

It is precisely this *transitional period* that dictates that we should undertake a certain re-orientation of our foreign policy in terms of gradually and consistently developing relations with *Western Europe, Japan and China.*

However, this should not lead to a decreasing attention to U.S.-Soviet relations in their substance, but to the contrary — they should be given increased attention.

Timing. Possibly after the Congress [of the Communist Party]. It would be better [if it took place] after some economic reforms, or other practical initiatives and achievements, which would demonstrate the dynamism of our country. Practical actions are the best to persuade the Americans; they will become more cooperative.

Location. Not in the USA; some place in Europe.

Alternative. As has been mentioned above, we should use all possible factors of possible political pressure on the United States, and first among them all is the interest of the Europeans in a relaxation of tensions, which was clearly felt during the recent discussions in Moscow; [we should] confirm our position of initiative.

For that, we would need a powerful countermove.

For example, in connection with the 10th anniversary of the Helsinki Conference[3] (August 1 of this year), we could put forward a proposal to hold a summit of heads of states, who put their signatures under the Final Act in the capital of Finland. By promoting this idea, we could focus attention on the need to introduce elements of trust into international relations and to revive the process of détente in the political as well as in the military sphere.

As a first step, this idea could be raised in a personal letter from the General Secretary of the Central Committee to the President of the USA, noting that in Helsinki they could establish personal contact and exchange ideas about the timing and the general framework of a U.S.-Soviet summit.

Regardless of the American reaction, we could inform our allies about the step, which we took, and talk to them about conducting appropriate work with Western European countries. . . . Most importantly — not only would we have *confirmed our active approach to reviving the détente processes — but we would have also put our own base under the Soviet-American meeting at the highest level.*

A. YAKOVLEV.

---

[3] International meeting in 1975 that resulted in a declaration of principles of relations among the participating countries, including the United States and the Soviet Union.

41

OLIVER NORTH

Fallback Plan for the Nicaraguan Resistance
March 16, 1985

Congress opposed Reagan's assistance to Nicaragua by approving a series of amendments to defense appropriations bills passed between 1982 and 1984. These amendments, known as the Boland Amendments, placed restrictions on the president. For one thing, they prohibited the use of federal funds for the military overthrow of the Nicaraguan government by the contra rebels. In this memo, NSC staffer Oliver North mapped out a plan to raise money privately for the Nicaraguan contras as a way around congressional opposition. North would also raise money covertly through the sale of arms to Iran and the diversion of these funds to the contras.

MEMORANDUM FOR ROBERT C. McFARLANE

The plan attached [here] has been developed, pursuant to our discussion on Friday regarding fallback options. It is premised on the assumption of a major Congressional budget battle and an assessment that the Congress will not rescind the restrictions in Section 8066 of the FY-85 C.R. Should you determine in your meeting with Senators [David] Durenburger and [Richard] Lugar (Tuesday, March 19, 0730) that the Congress will not endorse a resumption of USG [U.S. government] support to the resistance, the plan . . . provides a workable alternative.

Secrecy for the plan is paramount. We could not implement such an option if it became known in advance and it also mandates that present donors continue their relationship with the resistance beyond the current funding figure. The plan would require the President to make a major public pronouncement which, in turn, must be supported by other Administration officials, resistance leaders, and regional Heads of State once it has been announced. . . .

From National Security Archive, George Washington University.

Fallback Option Plan for the Nicaraguan Resistance

Assumptions.   The Congress is unwilling to support release of $14M in USG funds for the purpose of supporting, directly or indirectly, military or paramilitary operations in Nicaraguan [*sic*]. The FY-86 budget is seriously jeopardized by Congressional action and will require a major effort on the part of the President immediately after the [vote on the MX missile] through mid-July. There will be insufficient time or assets available to organize the kind of Administration-wide effort required to achieve an affirmative vote in both Houses on the Nicaraguan resistance program.

Section 8066 of the law expires on October 1, 1985. There are currently $28M requested in the FY-86 intelligence budget for the purpose of supporting paramilitary operations by the Nicaraguan resistance. The current funding relationship which exists between the resistance and its donors is sufficient to purchase arms and munitions between now and October—if additional monies are provided for non-military supplies (e.g., food, clothing, medical items, etc.). The current donors will have to be convinced of the need to continue their funding for munitions after October 1, 1985. A commitment for another $25–30M from the donors will be necessary for munitions in 1986 in anticipation that the $28M requested in the intelligence budget is not approved.

Concept.   In lieu of forwarding the report to the Congress required by Section 8066 of PL 98-473, the President would announce on or about April 2 that the American people should contribute funds ("... send your check or money order to the Nicaraguan Freedom Fighters, Box 1776, Gettysburg, PA ...") to support liberty and democracy in the Americas. He would note that the monies raised would be used to support the humanitarian needs of those struggling for freedom against Communist tyranny in Central America. By necessity, the speech must be dramatic and a surprise. It *cannot* be leaked in advance.

Prior to the speech, the following steps must be taken:

- Calero, Cruz, and Robelo (the principle [*sic*] leadership of the Nicaraguan armed and unarmed resistance) must be covertly advised of this plan and must assure their support.
- The Nicaraguan Freedom Fund, Inc., a 501(c)3 tax exempt corporation, must be established and obtain a Post Office Box 1776 in Gettysburg, Philadelphia, Valley Forge, or Yorktown. (This process is already underway.)

- Presidents Suazo [Honduras], Monge [Costa Rica], and Duarte [El Salvador] (and the appropriate leadership of each of those countries) must be apprised of this plan 1–2 days in advance of the announcement. They must be prepared to fully support the President's proclamation.

- The current donors must be apprised of the plan and agree to provide additional $25–30M to the resistance for the purchase of arms and munitions.

- Public groups and political action committees already mobilized for the Congressional campaign to relieve the 8066 constraints will have to be mobilized for the new approach (advertising, posters, mailings, phonecalls, etc.) several hours before the President speaks.

- Assuming a Presidential speech on or about April 2 at 8:00 p.m., a briefing for senior Administration officials should be held at 7:00 p.m. that day in Room 450 OEOB [Old Executive Office Building] to ensure that public commentary after the speech by these official[s] is supportive of this proclamation[.]

Additional Requirements.

- Informal contact several months ago with a lawyer sympathetic to our cause indicated that such a procedure would be within the limits of the law. Fred Fielding [White House counsel] should be asked to . . . conduct a very *private* evaluation of the President's role in making such a request.

- The name of one of several existing non-profit foundations, [which] we have established in the course of the last year, will be changed to Nicaraguan Freedom Fund, Inc. Several reliable American citizens must be contacted to serve as its corporate leadership on its board of directors along with Cruz, Calero, and Robelo[.]

- Calero, Cruz, and Robelo *will* support support [*sic*] such an option if properly approached. They should then be photo-graphed with the President on the day of his announcement and [be] prepared to appear on U.S. and other media supporting the President's program.

- You will have to make a quick (one day) trip to the region, preferably the day before announcement in order to brief Heads of State and regional leaders. For obvious reasons, this must be a very secret trip.

- The President's speech must be prepared in total secrecy much the same as [speechwriter] Ben Elliott worked on the Grenada announcements.

42

Memo on Conversation between Reagan and Gorbachev

and

Meeting While Leaders Walk

November 19, 1985

The first meeting between Reagan and Gorbachev, which took place in Geneva, fostered a good rapport between them. Each came away with a sense that the other was committed to reform, and the meeting laid the groundwork for continued negotiations and future summits. However, deep divisions over issues, particularly SDI, prevented the achievement of any deal. In the meeting that followed, Soviet officials (foreign minister Eduard Shevardnadze and Soviet ambassador Anatoly Dobrynin) insisted to Secretary of State George Shultz that the United States drop its SDI plans. They argued that SDI would result in a military space race and that it would never work. Although Gorbachev refused to see the space shield as defensive, he came away with an appreciation of Reagan's deep commitment to the program.

Memo between Reagan and Gorbachev

The President and the General Secretary emerged from their tete-a-tete and greeted each member of the others [*sic*] delegation. There was then a photo opportunity. The two delegations were then seated.

From Robert E. Linhard Files, Box 92178, file: Geneva Summit Records (3 of 4), Ronald Reagan Library.

The President opened the meeting by stating to the General Secretary that we are pleased that we are now underway. He noted that the two of them had had a good discussion. He then turned the floor over to the General Secretary.

Gorbachev thanked the President. He noted that he and the President had agreed that it was important to have a constructive exchange of views at this meeting. He had said already during their one on one meeting that the Soviet Union attaches a lot of importance to this meeting, to that fact that it is taking place after almost seven years since the last Summit. A lot of things had changed in the world and in developments in our two countries. Many problems had come up which were of concern to the American people, to the Soviet people and to their leaders. In this context they regarded this meeting as a positive event.

The General Secretary continued that there is the question of how to proceed and at what level. The Soviet Union wishes to proceed to make our bilateral relationship one based more on trust. We need to think together about a mechanism for implementing this idea. This should include a political dialogue at various levels. It is not good when for extended periods our relationship is reduced to having our entire dialogue take place via the press. . . .

The General Secretary stated that he was hopeful that . . . both sides could express their views about war and peace and disarmament. He would like in conclusion of his overview of the world's situation to state that the Soviet Union believes that the central question is how to halt the arms race and to disarm. For their part the Soveit [*sic*] Union would not put forward proposals which would be detrimental to the United States. They are for equal security. If anything detrimental to the United States was proposed, this would not be acceptable to the Soviet Union because it would not make for stability. The Soviet Union has no ulterior motives. What the President had said about equal security, no superiority and movement toward halting the arms race were the conditions for building a cooperative relationship. The United States is losing a big market in the Soviet Union; the Soviets have good economic cooperation with other countries.

Gorbachev continued that we can live in this world only together, so both must think how to put their relations on a new track. If the United States thinks that by saying these things, Gorbachev is showing weakness, that the Soviet Union is more interested than the United States, then this will all come to nothing. The Soviet Union will not permit an unequal approach but if there is on the U.S. side a positive will, the United States will find the Soviets an active participant in the process.

President Reagan then began his presentation. He said that as he had noted earlier, if the two sides are to get down to reducing the mountains of weapons, that both must get at the cause of the distrust which has led to them. Why does the distrust and suspicion exist? . . .

The President stated that this is the first time that the United States is seeking with the Soviet Union to actually reduce the mountains of these weapons. The other meetings, eighteen so far, merely addressed regulating the increase in these weapons. In 1980 the President had said he could not support this approach. He would stay as long as needed with the policy of insisting on reductions. The President recalled that the Soviet government had talked about a one world communist state and had been inspiring revolutions around the world. The United States saw the Soviet military build up, including in nuclear weapons. This came after dozens of United States proposals. The United States has fewer nuclear weapons than in 1969. The Soviet Union has had the largest military in history. Yes, he had made a promise to refurbish the American military and this has been done, but the United States is still behind. The Soviet Union has 5.4 milion [sic] men in their armed forces: The U.S. has 2.4 million men. The United States also sees an expansionist Soviet Union. It has a satellite in Cuba just 90 miles off our shores. We had problems there with nuclear missiles but this was settled. Now we see Afghanistan, Ethopia [sic], Angola and Yemen—with for example 35,000 Cubans in Angola.

The President stated that he was setting all of this as the basis for American concern and distrust. With regard to American industry and our military policy, or any effort to incite our people to more military sales, the budget of the United States government for elderly and handicapped and other social needs is bigger than the military budget. Two thirds of our military spending pays for man power; only a small percentage is spent on weapons. This is a very small percentage of our GNP; of course we would be better off without it. The basic interest of our industry is consumer products, for example the automobile and airplane industry. The United States has no interest in carrying on an arms race.

The President said that now the two sides have come to this meeting he had said frankly why the American people are concerned. Maybe the Soviets did not want war but it seemed to want to get its way. The United States has seen violations of arms control agreements already signed. The United States is ready to try to meet the Soviet Union's concerns if the Soviet Union is ready to meet ours. But more than words are needed. The two sides need to get on to deeds. If the two sides just get in bargaining over a particular type of weapon we will just go on trying to keep advantages. But if we can go on the basis of trust, then those mountains of weapons will disappear quickly as we will be confident that they are not needed.

The President continued that no other nations in the world can do what the Soviet Union and the United States can. They are the only ones which can bring about a world war. The only ones. That is a measure of their responsibility. The two must remove the causes of distrust. History since World War II has shown that if the United States had any hostile designs it was in a position to impose its will with little danger to itself. Indeed the United States had restrained its own programs[.]

The President continued that today he wanted to talk about one specific question. Gorbachev had said that the United States had indicated an interest in achieving a first strike capability by having an anti-missile shield which would destroy missiles before they hit the target. The United States did not know whether this would be possible. The United States had a research program. The Soviet Union had the same kind of program. The United States has some hope that it might be possible. If both sides continue their research and if one or both come up with such a system then they should sit down and make it available to everyone so no one would have a fear of a nuclear strike. A mad man might come along with a nuclear weapon. If we could come up with a shield and share it, then nobody would worry about the mad man. He didn't even want to call this a weapon; it was a defensive system.

The President said that he hoped he had made clear that it is the sincerest desire of the United States to eliminate suspicion. When he thinks of our two great powers, and of how many areas we could cooperate in helping the world, he thinks about how we must do this with deeds. This is the best way for both sides to assure the other that they have no hostile intent.

Meeting While Leaders Walk

SHULTZ: Do you wish to talk on guidelines? No need to let the time pass. There are some points of intersection. We could try to narrow it down. President Reagan is doing that. Do you have suggestions?

SHEVARDNADZE: The General Secretary has outlined our approach: a ban of space weapons, and an exploration of the gap between our two proposals.

DOBRYNIN: This would provide short, good guidelines.

SHULTZ: We will not stop our research. President Reagan is ready to talk about what we can do if progress is made—and we are ready to talk about this now.

SHEVARDNADZE: I can't understand the purpose of this.

SHULTZ: Our purpose is to move the concept of deterrence into a more stable and humane posture. It will also serve to deal with unstabilization of offensive arms brought about by increasing accuracy and mobility. Those developments bring us to the need for a shield. Stability can be enhanced if it is not a race, but is a cooperative effort. Unilateral actions are not stable. A negotiated transition would be more stable.

SHEVARDNADZE: What you are proposing, cooperating in unknown area, is more like science fiction. The General Secretary has said if we can agree on a ban, then on that basis, and on proposals put forth by both, there is a realistic way forward. You have said that what is destabilizing today is offensive forces, but I say it is your SDI. But for this program, we could have serious progress in Geneva. One more point, not mentioned earlier, you have been saying in the context of explaining your SDI program that the USSR has similar research and that we are somewhere ahead of you. This is being asserted by your press and your official spokesman. If that is so, why are we now proposing a ban on a space strike?

SHULTZ: I am confident your research is parallel to ours, and I can tell you why we feel it exists.

NITZE: In the area of lasers, there is no doubt.

SHEVARDNADZE: If you have invited us to talk to convince us of the utility of SDI, I doubt you can do it. As the General Secretary has said, our arguments are not made of thin air. We have worked this issue with our experts. As a result, we hold deep convictions that the development of space strike arms will usher in [a] new era of the arms race. Any talk of regulating this process by treaty is not realistic. In fact it is most unrealistic. The right decision is not to allow a new cycle of the arms race.

43

OLIVER NORTH AND JOHN M. POINDEXTER

Covert Action Finding Regarding Iran

January 17, 1986

*Administration officials completed their covert plan to provide military
assistance to the contras in Nicaragua by authorizing the sale of U.S.
weapons to Iran. They hoped that the sale would help free American
hostages in Lebanon taken by the Iranian-supported terrorist organization Hezbollah (or Hizballah) and that it would nurture moderate
elements in the Iranian regime. In a handwritten note at the end of the
memo, Poindexter, Reagan's national security adviser, noted that the
president was "briefed verbally from this paper." He also noted that Vice
President Bush was present.*

MEMORANDUM FOR THE PRESIDENT

Prime Minister [Shimon] Peres of Israel secretly dispatched his special
advisor on terrorism with instructions to propose a plan by which Israel,
with limited assistance from the U.S., can create conditions to help bring
about a more moderate government in Iran. The Israelis are very concerned that Iran's deteriorating position in the war with Iraq, the potential for further radicalization in Iran, and the possibility of enhanced
Soviet influence in the Gulf all pose significant threats to the security
of Israel. They believe it is essential that they act to at least preserve a
balance of power in the region.

The Israeli plan is premised on the assumption that moderate elements
in Iran can come to power if these factions demonstrate their credibility
in defending Iran against Iraq and in deterring Soviet intervention. To
achieve the strategic goal of a more moderate Iranian government, the
Israelis are prepared to unilaterally commence selling military material
to Western-oriented Iranian factions. It is their belief that by so doing
they can achieve a heretofore unobtainable penetration of the Iranian
governing hierarchy. The Israelis are convinced that the Iranians are
so desperate for military materiel, expertise and intelligence that the
provision of these resources will result in favorable long-term changes

From Arthur B. Culvahouse Files, Ronald Reagan Library.

in personnel and attitudes within the Iranian government. Further, once the exchange relationship has commenced, a dependency would be established on those who are providing the requisite resources, thus allowing the provider(s) to coercively influence near-term events. Such an outcome is consistent with our policy objectives and would present significant advantages for U.S. national interests. As described by the Prime Minister's emissary, the only requirement the Israelis have is an assurance that they will be allowed to purchase U.S. replenishments for the stocks that they sell to Iran. We have researched the legal problems of Israel's selling U.S. manufactured arms to Iran. Because of the requirement in U.S. law for recipients of U.S. arms to notify the U.S. government of transfers to third countries, I do not recommend that you agree with the specific details of the Israeli plan. However, there is another possibility. Some time ago Attorney General William French Smith determined that under an appropriate finding you could authorize the CIA to sell arms to countries outside of the provisions of the laws and reporting requirements for foreign military sales. The objectives of the Israeli plan could be met if the CIA, using an authorized agent as necessary, purchased arms from the Department of Defense under the Economy Act and then transferred them to Iran directly after receiving appropriate payment from Iran.

The Covert Action Finding . . . provides the latitude for the transactions indicated above to proceed. The Iranians have indicated an immediate requirement for 4,000 basic TOW weapons for use in the launchers they already hold.

The Israeli's [*sic*] are also sensitive to a strong U.S. desire to free our Beirut hostages and have insisted that the Iranians demonstrate both influence and good intent by an early release of the five Americans. Both sides have agreed that the hostages will be immediately released upon commencement of this action. Prime Minister Peres had his emissary pointedly note that they well understand our position on not making concessions to terrorists. They also point out, however, that terrorist groups, movements, and organizations are significantly easier to influence through governments than they are by direct approach. In that we have been unable to exercise any suasion over Hizballah during the course of nearly two years of kidnappings, this approach through the government of Iran may well be our *only* way to achieve the release of the Americans held in Beirut. It must again be noted that since this dialogue with the Iranians began in September, Reverend Weir[1] has been

---

[1] Reverend Benjamin Weir, one of the original hostages.

released and there have been no Shia terrorist attacks against American or Israeli persons, property, or interests.

Therefore it is proposed that Israel make the necessary arrangements for the sale of 4000 TOW weapons to Iran. Sufficient funds to cover the sale would be transferred to an agent of the CIA. The CIA would then purchase the weapons from the Department of Defense and deliver the weapons to Iran through the agent. If all of the hostages are not released after the first shipment of 1000 weapons, further transfers would cease.

On the other hand, since hostage release is in some respects a byproduct of a larger effort to develop ties to potentially moderate forces in Iran, you may wish to redirect such transfers to other groups within the government at a later time.

The Israelis have asked for our urgent response to this proposal so that they can plan accordingly. They note that conditions inside both Iran and Lebanon are highly volatile. The Israelis are cognizant that this entire operation will be terminated if the Iranians abandon their goal of moderating their government or allow further acts of terrorism. You have discussed the general outlines of the Israeli plan with Secretaries Shultz and Weinberger, Attorney General Meese and Director Casey. The Secretaries do not recommend you proceed with this plan. Attorney General Meese and Director Casey believe the short-term and long-term objectives of the plan warrant the policy risks involved and recommend you approve the attached Finding. Because of the extreme sensitivity of this project, it is recommended that you exercise your statutory prerogative to withhold notification of the Finding to the Congressional oversight committees until such time that you deem it to be appropriate.

Prepared by:
OLIVER L. NORTH

44

RONALD REAGAN

Address to the Nation on the Situation in Nicaragua

March 16, 1986

*White House officials conducted a covert operation to assist the Nicara-
guan contras by diverting funds from the secret sale of arms to Iran. At
the same time, Reagan mounted a public campaign to put pressure on
Congress to support American assistance in Central America. He referred
to the contras as "freedom fighters" to win sympathy for them. Reagan's
campaign was having an effect, as Democratic opposition was starting
to weaken. However, in the 1986 midterm elections, the Democrats took
back control of the Senate, making a change in policy less likely. The
revelation of the covert operation soon after the election would further
undermine White House efforts to win popular support.*

I must speak to you tonight about a mounting danger in Central America
that threatens the security of the United States. This danger will not go
away; it will grow worse, much worse, if we fail to take action now. I'm
speaking of Nicaragua, a Soviet ally on the American mainland only 2
hours' flying time from our own borders. With over a billion dollars in
Soviet-bloc aid, the Communist government of Nicaragua has launched
a campaign to subvert and topple its democratic neighbors. Using
Nicaragua as a base, the Soviets and Cubans can become the dominant
power in the crucial corridor between North and South America. Established there, they will be in a position to threaten the Panama Canal,
interdict our vital Caribbean sea-lanes, and, ultimately, move against
Mexico. Should that happen, desperate Latin peoples by the millions
would begin fleeing north into the cities of the southern United States
or to wherever some hope of freedom remained.

From Ronald Reagan, "Address to the Nation on the Situation in Nicaragua," in *Public
Papers of the Presidents of the United States: Ronald Reagan, 1986* (Washington, D.C.:
U.S. Government Printing Office, 1988), 1:352–57.

The United States Congress has before it a proposal to help stop this threat. The legislation is an aid package of $100 million for the more than 20,000 freedom fighters struggling to bring democracy to their country and eliminate this Communist menace at its source. But this $100 million is not an additional 100 million. We're not asking for a single dime in new money. We are asking only to be permitted to switch a small part of our present defense budget to the defense of our own southern frontier. . . .

For our own security, the United States must deny the Soviet Union a beachhead in North America. But let me make one thing plain: I'm not talking about American troops. They are not needed; they have not been requested. The democratic resistance fighting in Nicaragua is only asking America for the supplies and support to save their own country from communism. The question the Congress of the United States will now answer is a simple one: Will we give the Nicaraguan democratic resistance the means to recapture their betrayed revolution, or will we turn our backs and ignore the malignancy in Managua until it spreads and becomes a mortal threat to the entire New World? Will we permit the Soviet Union to put a second Cuba, a second Libya, right on the doorstep of the United States? . . .

. . . Through this crucial part of the Western Hemisphere passes almost half our foreign trade, more than half our imports of crude oil, and a significant portion of the military supplies we would have to send to the NATO alliance in the event of a crisis. These are the chokepoints where the sea-lanes could be closed. Central America is strategic to our Western alliance, a fact always understood by foreign enemies. In World War II only a few German U-boats, operating from bases 4,000 miles away in Germany and occupied Europe, inflicted crippling losses on U.S. shipping right off our southern coast. Today Warsaw Pact engineers are building a deep water port on Nicaragua's Caribbean coast, similar to the naval base in Cuba for Soviet-built submarines. They are also constructing, outside Managua, the largest military airfield in Central America—similar to those in Cuba, from which Russian Bear Bombers patrol the U.S. east coast from Maine to Florida. . . .

Clearly, the Soviet Union and the Warsaw Pact have grasped the great stakes involved, the strategic importance of Nicaragua. The Soviets have made their decision—to support the Communists. Fidel Castro has made his decision—to support the Communists. Arafat, Qadhafi, and the Ayatollah Khomeini[1] have made their decision—to support the

---

[1] Yasir Arafat, head of the Palestine Liberation Organization (PLO); Muammar al-Qaddafi, leader of Libya; and Ayatollah Ruholla Khomeini, leader of Iran.

Communists. Now we must make our decision. With Congress' help, we can prevent an outcome deeply injurious to the national security of the United States. If we fail, there will be no evading responsibility—history will hold us accountable. This is not some narrow partisan issue; it is a national security issue, an issue on which we must act not as Republicans, not as Democrats, but as Americans. . . .

So, tonight I ask you to do what you've done so often in the past. Get in touch with your Representative and Senators and urge them to vote yes; tell them to help the freedom fighters. Help us prevent a Communist takeover of Central America.

I have only 3 years left to serve my country; 3 years to carry out the responsibilities you entrusted to me; 3 years to work for peace. Could there be any greater tragedy than for us to sit back and permit this cancer to spread, leaving my successor to face far more agonizing decisions in the years ahead? The freedom fighters seek a political solution. They are willing to lay down their arms and negotiate to restore the original goals of the revolution, a democracy in which the people of Nicaragua choose their own government. That is our goal also, but it can only come about if the democratic resistance is able to bring pressure to bear on those who have seized power.

We still have time to do what must be done so history will say of us: We had the vision, the courage, and good sense to come together and act—Republicans and Democrats—when the price was not high and the risks were not great. We left America safe, we left America secure, we left America free—still a beacon of hope to mankind, still a light unto the nations.

National Security Scandal and Success, 1986–1988

45

CASPAR WEINBERGER

Oval Office Meeting on Iran-Contra

November 10, 1986

In a meeting in early November, in which Secretary of Defense Caspar Weinberger took notes, Reagan administration officials began to discuss what their response should be to the revelation of the covert arms-for-hostages program they had been running. The president appeared on national television on November 13 and denied that any such deals had been made. He acknowledged a "secret diplomatic initiative," which he defended as "honorable" for the sake of renewing relations with Iran, ending the Iran-Iraq War, and freeing American hostages. He maintained, as he had previously, that the United States would not negotiate with terrorists. Later revelations proved these assertions to be untrue. Some of the memo (shown as three asterisks, * * *) is redacted for national security concerns.

* * * The President said we did not do any trading with the enemy for our hostages. We do need to note that * * * (Khomeni) [*sic*] will be gone someday, and we want better leverage with the new government and with their military. That is why we felt it necessary to give them some small defensive weapons.

We can discuss that publicly, but no way could we ever disclose it all without getting our hostages executed. (We must make it plain that we are not doing business with terrorists. We aren't paying them or dealing with them.) We are trying to get better relations with Iran, and we can't discuss the details of this publicly without endangering the people

From National Security Archive, George Washington University.

we are working through and with in Iran. I pointed out we must bear in mind we have given the Isralies [*sic*] and the Iranians the opportunity to blackmail us by reporting selectively bits and pieces of the total story. I also pointed out that Congress could—and probably would—hold legislative hearings. Admiral Poindexter pointed out that we do want a better relationship with Iran.

In [Jan]* 1986, the President [apparently]* made a formal finding under Section 501 of the Arms Export Control Act which directes [*sic*] the DCI [director of central intelligence] not to notify Congress until further notice, and authorizes discussion with friendly groups which are trying to get a better government in Iran. I had not known of this finding before [illegible text here]—Shultz said he had not known of it either. We needed to help those elements to get a more pro-U.S. government in Iran. Poindexter continued that we assisted Israel initially because we found Israel was sending arms to Iran * * * and also wanted the Iran-Iraq war to end as soon as possible. . . .

I reminded John [Poindexter] that he had always told me that there would be no more weapons sent to Iran, after the first 500 TOWS, until *after all* of the hostages were returned, but unfortunate[ly] we did send a second 500 because it "seemed the only way to get the hostages out," according to Poindexter.

Poindexter pointed out the hostage taking had stopped for a year. I pointed out that they took three more quite recently. Poindexter pointed out that this was not done by the same people or Iranians. . . .

The President said this is what you had to do to reward Iran for the efforts of those who could help. Actually the captors do not benefit at all. We buy the support and the oportunity [*sic*] to persuade the Iranians.

I again pointed out we will have to answer many questions and have Congressional hearings. The President said we need to point out any discussion [that] endangers our source in Iran and our plan, because we do want to get additional hostages released. Mr. Shultz spoke up for the first time, saying that it is the responsibility of the government to look after its citizens, but once you do deal for hostages, you expose everyone to future capture. He said we don't know, but we have to assume the captors will get someone. He said he felt the Isralies [*sic*] sucked us up into their operation so we could not object to their sales to Iran. He pointed out there will be a lot of questions after any statement, even after a statement such as Mr. Casey proposed to read. The President said we should release the statement, but not take any questions. Mr. Regan said we are being hung out to dry, our credibility is at stake, and we have to say enough.

---

* Bracketed material appears in handwriting in original document.

46

RONALD REAGAN

Address to the Nation on the Iran Arms and Contra Aid Controversy

March 4, 1987

In this speech, Reagan attempted to calm the political storm that emerged as a result of the Iran-contra scandal, claiming that he had made mistakes but insisting that he had not broken the law. The scandal had a damaging effect on the administration, as Reagan's approval ratings plummeted. The president was consumed with trying to defend himself from the congressional investigation. Many White House officials feared that the scandal would take over the rest of his presidency, with some even worried about the possibility of impeachment.

My fellow Americans:

I've spoken to you from this historic office on many occasions and about many things. The power of the Presidency is often thought to reside within this Oval Office. Yet it doesn't rest here; it rests in you, the American people, and in your trust. Your trust is what gives a President his powers of leadership and his personal strength, and it's what I want to talk to you about this evening.

For the past 3 months, I've been silent on the revelations about Iran. And you must have been thinking: "Well, why doesn't he tell us what's happening? Why doesn't he just speak to us as he has in the past when we've faced troubles or tragedies?" Others of you, I guess, were thinking: "What's he doing hiding out in the White House?" Well, the reason I haven't spoken to you before now is this: You deserve the truth. And as frustrating as the waiting has been, I felt it was improper to come to you with sketchy reports, or possibly even erroneous statements, which would then have to be corrected, creating even more doubt and confusion. There's been enough of that. I've paid a price for my silence in terms of your trust and confidence. But I've had to wait, as you have, for

From Ronald Reagan, "Address to the Nation on the Iran Arms and Contra Aid Controversy," in *Public Papers of the Presidents of the United States: Ronald Reagan, 1987* (Washington, D.C.: U.S. Government Printing Office, 1989), 1:208–11.

the complete story. That's why I appointed Ambassador David Abshire as my Special Counsellor to help get out the thousands of documents to the various investigations. And I appointed a Special Review Board, the Tower board, which took on the chore of pulling the truth together for me and getting to the bottom of things. It has now issued its findings.

I'm often accused of being an optimist, and it's true I had to hunt pretty hard to find any good news in the Board's report. As you know, it's well-stocked with criticisms, which I'll discuss in a moment; but I was very relieved to read this sentence: "the Board is convinced that the President does indeed want the full story to be told." And that will continue to be my pledge to you as the other investigations go forward. . . .

I've studied the Board's report. Its findings are honest, convincing, and highly critical; and I accept them. And tonight I want to share with you my thoughts on these findings and report to you on the actions I'm taking to implement the Board's recommendations. First, let me say I take full responsibility for my own actions and for those of my administration. As angry as I may be about activities undertaken without my knowledge, I am still accountable for those activities. As disappointed as I may be in some who served me, I'm still the one who must answer to the American people for this behavior. And as personally distasteful as I find secret bank accounts and diverted funds — well, as the Navy would say, this happened on my watch.

Let's start with the part that is the most controversial. A few months ago I told the American people I did not trade arms for hostages. My heart and my best intentions still tell me that's true, but the facts and the evidence tell me it is not. As the Tower board reported, what began as a strategic opening to Iran deteriorated, in its implementation, into trading arms for hostages. This runs counter to my own beliefs, to administration policy, and to the original strategy we had in mind. There are reasons why it happened, but no excuses. It was a mistake. I undertook the original Iran initiative in order to develop relations with those who might assume leadership in a post-Khomeini government.

It's clear from the Board's report, however, that I let my personal concern for the hostages spill over into the geopolitical strategy of reaching out to Iran. I asked so many questions about the hostages' welfare that I didn't ask enough about the specifics of the total Iran plan. Let me say to the hostage families: We have not given up. We never will. And I promise you we'll use every legitimate means to free your loved ones from captivity. But I must also caution that those Americans who freely remain in such dangerous areas must know that they're responsible for their own safety.

Now, another major aspect of the Board's findings regards the transfer of funds to the Nicaraguan contras. The Tower board wasn't able to find out what happened to this money, so the facts here will be left to the continuing investigations of the court appointed Independent Counsel and the two congressional investigating committees. I'm confident the truth will come out about this matter, as well. As I told the Tower board, I didn't know about any diversion of funds to the contras. But as President, I cannot escape responsibility.

47

RONALD REAGAN

Remarks on East-West Relations at the Brandenburg Gate in West Berlin

June 12, 1987

Even as Reagan continued negotiations with Gorbachev on an arms agreement, the president delivered a forceful message to the Soviets at the Brandenburg Gate in front of the Berlin Wall. The Soviet-backed government of East Germany had erected the wall in 1961 to prevent people from moving to West Germany, which was a democracy and an ally of the United States. While some of the president's advisers worried about the harsh tone of the appeal to Gorbachev to dismantle the wall, Reagan believed that such a message would keep pressure on the Soviet leadership to soften its grip on Eastern Europe. This tough stance would also strengthen Reagan's credibility with conservatives in the United States.

Behind me stands a wall that encircles the free sectors of this city, part of a vast system of barriers that divides the entire continent of Europe. From the Baltic, south, those barriers cut across Germany in a gash of barbed wire, concrete, dog runs, and guard towers. Farther south, there may be no visible, no obvious wall. But there remain armed guards and

From Ronald Reagan, "Remarks on East-West Relations at the Brandenburg Gate in West Berlin," in *Public Papers of the Presidents of the United States: Ronald Reagan, 1987* (Washington, D.C.: U.S. Government Printing Office, 1989), 1:634–38.

checkpoints all the same—still a restriction on the right to travel, still an instrument to impose upon ordinary men and women the will of a totalitarian state. Yet it is here in Berlin where the wall emerges most clearly; here, cutting across your city, where the news photo and the television screen have imprinted this brutal division of a continent upon the mind of the world. Standing before the Brandenburg Gate, every man is a German, separated from his fellow men. Every man is a Berliner, forced to look upon a scar.

President [Richard] von Weizsacker [of West Germany] has said: "The German question is open as long as the Brandenburg Gate is closed." Today I say: As long as this gate is closed, as long as this scar of a wall is permitted to stand, it is not the German question alone that remains open, but the question of freedom for all mankind. Yet I do not come here to lament. For I find in Berlin a message of hope, even in the shadow of this wall, a message of triumph. . . .

Where four decades ago there was rubble, today in West Berlin there is the greatest industrial output of any city in Germany—busy office blocks, fine homes and apartments, proud avenues, and the spreading lawns of park land. Where a city's culture seemed to have been destroyed, today there are two great universities, orchestras and an opera, countless theaters, and museums. . . .

. . . In the West today, we see a free world that has achieved a level of prosperity and well-being unprecedented in all human history. In the Communist world, we see failure, technological backwardness, declining standards of health, even want of the most basic kind—too little food. Even today, the Soviet Union still cannot feed itself. After these four decades, then, there stands before the entire world one great and inescapable conclusion: Freedom leads to prosperity. Freedom replaces the ancient hatreds among the nations with comity and peace. Freedom is the victor.

And now the Soviets themselves may, in a limited way, be coming to understand the importance of freedom. We hear much from Moscow about a new policy of reform and openness. Some political prisoners have been released. Certain foreign news broadcasts are no longer being jammed. Some economic enterprises have been permitted to operate with greater freedom from state control. Are these the beginnings of profound changes in the Soviet state? Or are they token gestures, intended to raise false hopes in the West, or to strengthen the Soviet system without changing it? We welcome change and openness; for we believe that freedom and security go together, that the advance of human liberty can only strengthen the cause of world peace.

There is one sign the Soviets can make that would be unmistakable, that would advance dramatically the cause of freedom and peace. General Secretary Gorbachev, if you seek peace, if you seek prosperity for the Soviet Union and Eastern Europe, if you seek liberalization: Come here to this gate! Mr. Gorbachev, open this gate! Mr. Gorbachev, tear down this wall! . . .

As I looked out a moment ago from the Reichstag [the building housing the German parliament], that embodiment of German unity, I noticed words crudely spray-painted upon the wall, perhaps by a young Berliner, "This wall will fall. Beliefs become reality." Yes, across Europe, this wall will fall. For it cannot withstand faith; it cannot withstand truth. The wall cannot withstand freedom.

48

RONALD REAGAN

Address to the Nation on the Iran Arms and Contra Aid Controversy and Administration Goals

August 12, 1987

Reagan continued to find himself on the defensive in 1987 as the Iran-contra scandal escalated. Congress convened joint hearings on Iran-contra, which millions of Americans watched on television. Reagan's approval ratings were falling quickly. There were serious fears within the White House about how far Congress might go in its investigations and how much damage might be caused to the presidency. The hearings ended on August 3, 1987, after more than 250 hours of testimony from twenty-eight witnesses. In this speech, Reagan attempted to contain the political damage by speaking directly to the American people.

From Ronald Reagan, "Address to the Nation on the Iran Arms and Contra Aid Controversy and Administration Goals," in *Public Papers of the Presidents of the United States: Ronald Reagan, 1987* (Washington, D.C.: U.S. Government Printing Office, 1989), 2:942–45.

My fellow Americans:

As I said to you in March, I let my preoccupation with the hostages intrude into areas where it didn't belong. The image—the reality—of Americans in chains, deprived of their freedom and families so far from home, burdened my thoughts. And this was a mistake.

My fellow Americans, I've thought long and often about how to explain to you what I intended to accomplish, but I respect you too much to make excuses. The fact of the matter is that there's nothing I can say that will make the situation right. I was stubborn in my pursuit of a policy that went astray.

The other major issue of the hearings, of course, was the diversion of funds to the Nicaraguan contras. Colonel North and Admiral Poindexter believed they were doing what I would have wanted done—keeping the democratic resistance alive in Nicaragua. I believed then and I believe now in preventing the Soviets from establishing a beachhead in Central America. Since I have been so closely associated with the cause of the contras, the big question during the hearings was whether I knew of the diversion. I was aware the resistance was receiving funds directly from third countries and from private efforts, and I endorsed those endeavors wholeheartedly; but—let me put this in capital letters—I did not know about the diversion of funds. Indeed, I didn't know there were excess funds.

Yet the buck does not stop with Admiral Poindexter, as he stated in his testimony; it stops with me. I am the one who is ultimately accountable to the American people. The admiral testified that he wanted to protect me; yet no President should ever be protected from the truth. No operation is so secret that it must be kept from the Commander in Chief. I had the right, the obligation, to make my own decision. I heard someone the other day ask why I wasn't outraged. Well, at times, I've been mad as a hornet. Anyone would be—just look at the damage that's been done and the time that's been lost. But I've always found that the best therapy for outrage and anger is action.

I've tried to take steps so that what we've been through can't happen again, either in this administration or future ones. But I remember very well what the Tower board said last February when it issued this report. It said the failure was more in people than in process. We can build in every precaution known to the world. We can design that best system ever devised by man. But in the end, people are going to have to run it. And we will never be free of human hopes, weaknesses, and enthusiasms. . . .

The problem goes deeper . . . than policies and personnel. Probably the biggest lesson we can draw from the hearings is that the executive and legislative branches of government need to regain trust in each other. We've seen the results of that mistrust in the form of lies, leaks, divisions, and mistakes. We need to find a way to cooperate while realizing foreign policy can't be run by committee. And I believe there's now the growing sense that we can accomplish more by cooperating. And in the end, this may be the eventual blessing in disguise to come out of the Iran-contra mess.

49

ARTHUR B. CULVAHOUSE

Iran-Contra Congressional Reports
November 16, 1987

The congressional Iran-Contra Committee produced its report in the fall of 1987. As this memo from the president's counsel makes clear, the majority argued that there was no evidence that Reagan had consciously violated the law. But it also asserted that the administration had conducted an operation that blurred ethical boundaries in authorizing and then covering up the arms-for-hostages deal and diverting funds to the contras. The Democratic majority also insisted that the administration had overstepped the authority of the executive office and infringed on the foreign policy powers of Congress.

MEMORANDUM FOR THE PRESIDENT

On Wednesday, November 18, 1987, the congressional committees investigating the Iran/Contra matter will issue their reports. The majority report was signed by all of the Democrat members of the House and Senate Select Committees, as well as by Republican Senators [Warren] Rudman, [Paul] Trible and [William] Cohen. Senators [Orrin] Hatch and [James] McClure joined with all of the House Republicans to sign the minority report. Various committee members also signed their own additional views. . . .

From Ken Duberstein Files, Box 2, file: Iran Contra Issues (1), Ronald Reagan Library.

Majority Report

The majority report reaches harsh conclusions and is short on objectivity. It does not reveal any substantial new facts beyond those previously discussed in the Tower Board Report. The report adds considerable detail, however, to the public record regarding operations of the so-called "Enterprise" (the group of companies and individuals assisting in the arms sales to Iran and in the Contra resupply effort). The "Enterprise" was allegedly run by Major General (Ret.) Richard V. Secord and naturalized American citizen Albert Hakim, under the direction of Lt. Col. Oliver L. North.

The Select Committees appear to have successfully accounted for the funds paid to the "Enterprise" as an intermediary for the Iran arms sales including amounts which were later used for supporting the freedom fighters in Nicaragua. The report concludes that the Enterprise received approximately $16.1 million in profits from the Iran arms sales by marking up the price charged to Iran over the price paid to the U.S. Government. According to the majority report, approximately $3.8 million was "diverted" from the arms proceeds to the freedom fighters. . . .

The majority report states that you cooperated with the investigation and recognizes that you did not assert executive privilege. The majority does not find that you had prior knowledge of or approved the diversion. Nonetheless, the report concludes that "the ultimate responsibility for the events in the Iran/Contra affair must rest with the President. If the President did not know what his national security advisers were doing, he should have."

The report finds that a number of laws and constitutional principles were violated, but does not assign criminal culpability to particular individuals. The majority report criticizes the Administration for allegedly subverting the constitutional principle that the power of the purse shall be controlled by Congress. It states that "when members of the executive branch raised money from third countries and private citizens, took control of that money through the Enterprise, and used it to support the Contras' war in Nicaragua, they bypassed this crucial safeguard in the Constitution." [The report also states:]

> The Constitution contemplates that the government will conduct its affairs only with funds appropriated by Congress. By resorting to funds not appropriated by Congress, and indeed denied the executive branch by Congress, the Administration committed a transgression far more basic than a violation of the Boland Amendment.

The majority report also found that the statutory transfer and reporting requirements of the Arms Export Control Act were violated by the August/September 1985 shipment of TOW missiles from Israel to Iran, as well as the November 1985 shipment of HAWK missiles. According to the majority, the failure to notify the House and Senate Intelligence Committees of the Findings authorizing the sale of arms to Iran violated the reporting requirements under the National Security Act.

The majority report concludes that:

> The Iran/Contra affair resulted from the failure of individuals to observe the law, not from deficiencies in existing law or in our system of governance. . . . The principal recommendations emerging from the investigation are not for new laws but for a renewal of the commitment to constitutional government and sound processes of decision-making.

The majority report contends that Congress' role in foreign policy must be recognized and maintains that "excessive secrecy in the making of important policy decisions is profoundly anti-Democratic and rarely promotes sound policy decisions." Thus, legislation tightening the approval, consulting and reporting requirements for covert actions is recommended.

50

CONGRESSIONAL COMMITTEES INVESTIGATING THE IRAN-CONTRA AFFAIR

Introduction to Iran-Contra Minority Report

1987

The minority report of the Iran-Contra Committee's activities argued that the investigation into Iran-contra had been a partisan attack on a popular Republican president. The Republicans on the committee said that the Democrats had conducted a "witch hunt." The minority not only justified the administration's actions as lawful and necessary but also offered a strong defense of using executive power in the realm of national security.

From *Report of the Congressional Committees Investigating the Iran-Contra Affair, with Supplemental, Minority, and Additional Views*, 100th Cong., 1st sess., 1987, H. Rep. 100–433; S. Rep. 100–216, 437–38, 441–42, 450.

The argument for executive authority would influence many Republicans, including the ranking House Republican on the committee, Richard Cheney, over the next few decades by offering an intellectual rationale for expanded presidential power.

President Reagan and his staff made mistakes in the Iran-Contra Affair. It is important at the outset, however, to note that the President himself has already taken the hard step of acknowledging his mistakes and reacting precisely to what went wrong. He has directed the National Security Council staff not to engage in covert operations. He has changed the procedures for notifying Congress when an intelligence activity does take place. Finally, he has installed people with seasoned judgment to be White House Chief of Staff, National Security Adviser, and Director of Central Intelligence.

The bottom line, however, is that the mistakes of the Iran-Contra Affair were just that—mistakes in judgment, and nothing more. There was no constitutional crisis, no systematic disrespect for "the rule of law," no grand conspiracy, and no Administration-wide dishonesty or coverup. In fact, the evidence will not support any of the more hysterical conclusions the Committees' Report tries to reach.

No one in the government was acting out of corrupt motives. To understand what they did, it is important to understand the context within which they acted. The decisions we have been investigating grew out of:

- Efforts to pursue important U.S. interests both in Central America and in the Middle East;
- A compassionate, but disproportionate, concern for the fate of American citizens held hostage in Lebanon by terrorists, including one CIA station chief who was killed as a result of torture;
- A legitimate frustration with abuses of power and irresolution by the legislative branch; and
- An equally legitimate frustration with leaks of sensitive national security secrets coming out of both Congress and the executive branch.

Understanding this context can help explain and mitigate the resulting mistakes. It does not explain them away, or excuse their having happened.

The Committees' Report and the Ongoing Battle

The excesses of the Committees' Report are reflections of something far more profound. Deeper than the specifics of the Iran-Contra Affair lies an underlying and festering institutional wound these Committees have been unwilling to face. In order to support rhetorical overstatements about democracy and the rule of law, the Committees have rested their case upon an aggrandizing theory of Congress' foreign policy powers that is itself part of the problem. Rather than seeking to heal, the Committees' hearings and Report betray an attitude that we fear will make matters worse. The attitude is particularly regrettable in light of the unprecedented steps the President took to cooperate with the Committees and in light of the actions he already has taken to correct past errors.

A substantial number of the mistakes of the Iran-Contra Affair resulted directly from an ongoing state of political guerilla warfare over foreign policy between the legislative and executive branches. We would include in this category the excessive secrecy of the Iran initiative that resulted from a history and legitimate fear of leaks. We also would include the approach both branches took toward the so-called Boland Amendments. Congressional Democrats tried to use vaguely worded and constantly changing laws to impose policies in Central America that went well beyond the law itself. For its own part, the Administration tried to work within the letter of the law covertly, instead of forcing a public and principled confrontation that would have been healthier in the long run.

Given these kinds of problems, a sober examination of legislative-executive branch relations in foreign policy was sorely needed. It still is. Judgments about the Iran-Contra Affair ultimately must rest upon one's views about the proper roles of Congress and the President in foreign policy. There were many statements during the public hearings, for example, about the rule of law. But the fundamental law of the land is the Constitution. Unconstitutional statutes violate the rule of law every bit as much as do willful violations of constitutional statutes. It is essential, therefore, to frame any discussion of what happened with a proper analysis of the Constitutional allocation of legislative and executive power in foreign affairs.

The country's future security depends upon a modus vivendi in which each branch recognizes the other's legitimate and constitutionally sanctioned sphere of activity. Congress must recognize that an effective foreign policy requires, and the Constitution mandates, the President to be the country's foreign policy leader. At the same time, the President must recognize that his preeminence rests upon personal leadership, public education, political support, and interbranch comity. Interbranch comity does not require Presidential obsequiousness, of course. Presidents are elected to lead and to persuade. But Presidents must also have Congressional support for the tools to make foreign policy effective. No President can ignore Congress and be successful over the long term. Congress must realize, however, that the power of the purse does not make it supreme. Limits must be recognized by both branches, to protect the balance that was intended by the Framers, and that is still needed today for effective policy. This mutual recognition has been sorely lacking in recent years. . . .

"The Rule of Law"

Finally, the Committees' Report tries—almost as an overarching thesis—to portray the Administration as if it were behaving with wanton disregard for the law. In our view, *every single one* of the Committees' legal interpretations is open to serious question. On some issues—particularly the ones involving the statutes governing covert operations—we believe the law to be clearly on the Administration's side. In every other case, the issue is at least debatable. In some, such as the Boland Amendment, we are convinced we have by far the better argument. In a few others—such as who owns the funds the Iranians paid Gen. Richard Secord and Albert Hakim—we see the legal issue as being close. During the course of our full statement, we shall indicate which is which.

What the Committees' Report has done with the legal questions, however, is to issue a one-sided brief that pretends the Administration did not even have worthwhile arguments to make. As if that were not enough, the Report tries to build upon these one-sided assertions to present a politicized picture of an Administration that behaved with contempt for the law. If nothing else would lead readers to view the Report with extreme skepticism, the adversarial tone of the legal discussion should settle the matter.

Our View of the Iran-Contra Affair

The main issues raised by the Iran-Contra Affair are not legal ones, in our opinion. This opinion obviously does have to rest on some legal conclusions, however. We have summarized our legal conclusions at the end of this introductory chapter. The full arguments appear in subsequent chapters. In our view, the Administration did proceed legally in pursuing both its Contra policy and the Iran arms initiative. We grant that the diversion does raise some legal questions, as do some technical and relatively insubstantial matters relating to the Arms Export Control Act. It is important to stress, however, that the Administration could have avoided every one of the legal problems it inadvertently encountered, while continuing to pursue the exact same policies as it did.

The fundamental issues, therefore, have to do with the policy decisions themselves, and with the political judgments underlying the way policies were implemented. When these matters are debated as if they were legal—and even criminal—concerns, it is a sign that interbranch intimidation is replacing and debasing deliberation. That is why we part company not only with the Committees Report's answers, but with the very questions it identifies as being the most significant. . . .

The Presidency

The Constitution created the Presidency to be a separate branch of government whose occupant would have substantial discretionary power to act. He was not given the power of an 18th century monarch, but neither was he meant to be a creature of Congress. The country needs a President who can exercise the powers the Framers intended. As long as any President has those powers, there will be mistakes. It would be disastrous to respond to the possibility of error by further restraining and limiting the powers of the office. Then, instead of seeing occasional actions turn out to be wrong, we would be increasing the probability that future Presidents would be unable to act decisively, thus guaranteeing ourselves a perpetually paralyzed, reactive, and unclear foreign policy in which mistake by inaction would be the order of the day.

If Congress can learn something about democratic responsibility from the Iran-Contra Affair, future Presidents can learn something too. The Administration would have been better served over the long run by insisting on a principled confrontation over those strategic issues that can be debated publicly. Where secrecy is necessary, as it often must be, the Administration should have paid more careful attention to consultation and the need for consistency between what is public and what is covert. Inconsistency carries a risk to a President's future ability to persuade, and persuasion is at the heart of a vigorous, successful presidency.

A President's most important priorities, the ones that give him a chance to leave an historic legacy, can be attained only through persistent leadership that leads to a lasting change in the public's understanding and opinions. President Reagan has been praised by his supporters as a "communicator" and criticized by his opponents as an ideologue. The mistakes of the Iran-Contra Affair, ironically, came from a lack of communication and an inadequate appreciation of the importance of ideas. During President Reagan's terms of office, he has persistently taken two major foreign policy themes to the American people: a strong national defense for the United States, and support for the institutions of freedom abroad. The 1984 election showed his success in persuading the people to adopt his fundamental perspective. The events since then have threatened to undermine that achievement by shifting the agenda and refocusing the debate. If the President's substantial successes are to be sustained, it is up to him, and those of us who support his objectives, to begin once again with the task of democratic persuasion.

51

Meeting of Ronald Reagan and Mikhail Gorbachev

December 8, 1987

Gorbachev traveled to Washington, D.C., to meet with Reagan in December 1987 for their third summit, during which they reached a historic agreement to reduce nuclear weapons, the INF Treaty. Americans greeted Gorbachev like a celebrity, revealing how people's attitudes had changed toward the Soviet Union. Reagan's success in these negotiations revitalized his public standing, which had been deeply damaged by Iran-contra. While 80 percent of Americans approved of the treaty, conservatives denounced it as a sellout to the nation's number one enemy. Conservative pundit William F. Buckley called the treaty a "suicide pact." [1]

---

[1] In Steven Hayward, *The Age of Reagan: The Conservative Counterrevolution, 1980–1989* (New York: Crown, 2009), 591.

From National Security Online Archive, George Washington University.

Gorbachev observed that the two leaders had covered a long road from their first to this third meeting between them, a road marked by important and difficult issues. During that time, their dialogue had become much more profound, had begun to contain elements of trust between the two parties. There was an improved ability to address questions quietly and productively, a greater willingness to deal with political responses on each side, and political will to move ahead. . . .

Gorbachev said it was not oversimplifying to claim that there had been a true change for the better in US-Soviet relations. Exchanges and discussions resolving important problems were underway. We would now sign the first agreement ever eliminating nuclear weapons, a fact of historic importance. We recognized, he said, that the process was not easy, that we had different views. Questions were being asked about prospects for ratification. The General Secretary said he was himself being asked to explain why the Soviet Union was to dismantle four times the number of weapons NATO and the US side would. He said he would succeed in explaining the value of the treaty to the Soviet people as the President would to the American people. He then referred to a letter from a student pleading that he and the President not become captives of emotion.

The President suggested that ministers be invited to join the meeting at this point. The *General Secretary* agreed. *The President* said that he and the General Secretary were doing something very important for the future. . . . *Gorbachev* said he personally felt that a very important aspect of the current steps being taken in the US-Soviet relationship was the mental or psychological change being made in the minds of men, which he deeply felt. *The President* agreed. This had somehow to be captured, responded the General Secretary.

The President expressed gratitude to Gorbachev for his efforts in improving a relationship that was far from easy. *Gorbachev* agreed that striving for cooperation was not easy, but that we should not be afraid to do it. He expressed pleasure at the President's remarks at the welcoming ceremony. He expressed the view that, if there was no gap between what the President said and the actions that were taken, then there would be practical progress and he would find the Soviet side to be a good partner.

. . . Launching into a general statement on next steps in arms control, the *General Secretary* expressed thanks to the people who had worked on the INF Treaty. He said the signing of this treaty radically changed the whole situation, activated the discussion, and increased international pressure for new progress. . . .

The President noted the late hour, and *Secretary Shultz* remarked that it might be time for a larger meeting in the Cabinet Room. But first the Secretary wanted to make another point or two to guide working group activity. With regard to mobile missiles, he said, the US had no problem in principle with allowing them. But the verification problems were exceptionally difficult and the working group had to focus on them.

Gorbachev agreed with the President that it was about time to break off this part of the meeting, but he too wanted to add one more point, on nuclear testing. He noted that we were now negotiating about new limits on testing as part of a process leading to nuclear disarmament. This was good; we had momentum. We had already decided to exchange visits of monitoring experts and to conduct experiments in yield measurement. He had an idea he wanted the President and others to think about. Since the negotiations now underway were aimed at the ultimate result of a total prohibition on all nuclear testing, why not, now, declare a bilateral moratorium on testing for the duration of these negotiations. This would be an act of enormous importance the whole world would support. He asked that the President and his colleagues not respond immediately to this idea but think it over carefully. Then noting that time was short and the matter of forging instructions to negotiators for future arms talks paramount, he passed to the President a Soviet paper containing the tentative proposals of the Soviet side, as discussed at the last ministerial [meeting] in Geneva. *The President* passed to the General Secretary a comparable US document covering START and Defense and Space issues.

52

RONALD REAGAN

Remarks at the University of Virginia in Charlottesville

December 16, 1988

In this speech, Reagan's warm words about U.S.-Soviet relations indicated how much his attitudes had changed since he started his presidency. At the same time, Reagan offered a vigorous defense of executive power, arguing that his national security policies had been responsible for the arms agreement with the Soviets. In 1988, conservatives were very unhappy with the president for his softening stance toward the Soviet Union. But once the Soviet Union collapsed, they would credit Reagan with victory.

Consider for just a moment the sights we've seen this year: an American President with his Soviet counterpart strolling through Red Square and talking to passers-by about war and peace; an American President there in the Lenin Hills of Moscow speaking to the students of Moscow State University, young people like yourselves, about the wonder and splendor of human freedom; an American President, only last week, with a future American President and the President of the Soviet Union standing in New York Harbor, looking up at Lady Liberty, hearing again the prayer on the lips of all those millions who once passed that way in hope of a better life and future—a prayer of peace and freedom for all humanity. . . .

One of those visuals you've seen in the last year is the signing of accords between Mr. Gorbachev and me and the destruction of American and Soviet missiles. It was more than just good television, more than just action news. The INF treaty is the first accord in history to eliminate an entire class of U.S. and Soviet nuclear missiles. . . .

. . . What happens in the next few years, whether all this progress is continued or ended—this is, in large part, up to us. It's why now, more

From Ronald Reagan, "Remarks and a Question-and-Answer Session at the University of Virginia in Charlottesville," in *Public Papers of the Presidents of the United States: Ronald Reagan, 1988–89* (Washington, D.C.: U.S. Government Printing Office, 1991), 2:1631–41.

than ever, we must not falter. American power must be exercised morally, of course, but it must also be exercised, and exercised effectively. For the cause of peace and freedom in the eighties, that power made all the difference. The nineties will prove no different.

. . . It's precisely where Congress and the President have worked together—as in Afghanistan and Cambodia, or resolved differences, as in Angola, the Persian Gulf, and many aspects of U.S.-Soviet relations—precisely there, our policies have succeeded, and we see progress. But where Congress and the President have engaged each other as adversaries, as over Central America, U.S. policies have faltered and our common purposes have not been achieved.

Congress' on-again, off-again indecisiveness on resisting Sandinista tyranny and aggression has left Central America a region of continuing danger. Sometimes congressional actions in foreign affairs have had the effect of institutionalizing that kind of adversarial relationship. We see it in the War Powers Resolution, in the attempted restrictions on the President's power to implement treaties, and on trade policy. We see it in the attempt to manage complex issues of foreign policy by the blunt instrument of legislation—such as unduly restrictive intelligence oversight, limits on arms transfers, and earmarking of 95 percent of our foreign assistance—denying a President the ability to respond flexibly to rapidly changing conditions. Even in arms reduction, a President's ability to succeed depends on congressional support for military modernization—sometimes attempts are made to weaken my hand. . . .

Well, the President and the Vice President are elected by all the people. So, too, is the Congress as a collegial body. All who are elected to serve in these coordinate departments of our National Government have one unmistakable and undeniable mandate: to preserve, protect, and defend the Constitution. To this—this foremost—they must always be attentive. For a President, it means protecting his office and its place in our constitutional framework. In doing that, the President is accountable to the people in the most direct way, accountable to history and to his own conscience.

The President and Congress, to be sure, share many responsibilities. But their roles are not the same. Congress alone, for example, has the power of the purse. The President is chief executive, chief diplomat, and commander in chief. How these great branches of government perform their legitimate roles is critically important to the Nation's ability to succeed, nowhere more so than in the field of foreign affairs. They need each other and must work together in common cause with all deference, but within their separate spheres.

Today we live in a world in which America no longer enjoys preponderant power, but must lead by example and persuasion; a world of pressing new challenges to our economic prosperity; a world of new opportunities for peace and of new dangers. In such a world, more than ever, America needs strong and consistent leadership, and the strength and resilience of the Presidency are vital.

I think if we can keep these concerns in mind during the coming years public debate and support will be enhanced and America's foreign policy will continue to prosper. All of us know the terrible importance of maintaining the progress we've made in the decade of the eighties. We're moving away from war and confrontation toward peace and freedom, and today toward a future beyond the imaginings of the past. These are the stakes. Some may find such prospects daunting. I think you should find them challenging and exciting. And I think you can see that in all of this you and your country will have a special role to play.

Legacies, 1988–2009

53

GEORGE H. W. BUSH

Acceptance Speech at the 1988 Republican National Convention
August 18, 1988

In his 1988 presidential campaign, Vice President George H. W. Bush defined himself as the candidate who would continue the Reagan legacy of conservatism. In one of the most famous campaign promises in American history, Bush vowed that he would not increase taxes. When Bush later reversed himself by accepting tax increases in 1990, conservative Republicans such as Newt Gingrich were livid.

I seek the presidency for a single purpose, a purpose that has motivated millions of Americans across the years and the ocean voyages. I seek the presidency to build a better America. It is that simple—and that big.

I'm a man who sees life in terms of missions—missions defined and missions completed. And when I was a torpedo bomber pilot they defined the mission for us. And before we took off we all understood that no matter what, you try to reach the target. There have been other missions for me—Congress, China, the CIA. But I am here tonight—and I am your candidate—because the most important work of my life is to complete the mission that we started in 1980. How do we complete it? We build on it. . . .

From David Hoffman Collection, 1988 Campaign Files, file: Bush/New Orleans Acceptance Speech, George H. W. Bush Library.

Eight years ago, eight years ago, I stood here with Ronald Reagan and we promised, together, to break with the past and return America to her greatness. Eight years later look at what the American people have produced: the highest level of economic growth in our entire history—and the lowest level of world tensions in more than fifty years. . . .

An election, an election, that's about ideas and values is also about philosophy. And I have one.

At the bright center is the individual. And radiating out from him or her is the family, the essential unit of closeness and of love. For it's the family that communicates to our children—to the 21st century—our culture, our religious faith, our traditions and history.

From the individual to the family to the community, and then on out to the town, the church and the school, and, still echoing out, to the county, the state, and the nation—each doing only what it does well, and no more. And I believe that power must always be kept close to the individual—close to the hands that raise the family and run the home. . . .

Should public school teachers be required to lead our children in the pledge of allegiance? My opponent says no—and I say yes.

Should society be allowed to impose the death penalty on those who commit crimes of extraordinary cruelty and violence? My opponent says no—but I say yes.

And should our children have the right to say a voluntary prayer, or even observe a moment of silence in the schools? My opponent says no—but I say yes.

And should, should free men and women have the right to own a gun to protect their home? My opponent says no—but I say yes.

And is it right to believe in the sanctity of life and protect the lives of innocent children? My opponent says no—but I say yes.

You see, we must, we must change, we've got to change from abortion—to adoption. And let me tell you this: Barbara and I have an adopted granddaughter. And the day of her christening we wept with joy. I thank God that her parents chose life.

I'm, I'm the one who believes it is a scandal to give a weekend furlough to a hardened first degree killer who hasn't even served enough time to be eligible for parole.

I'm the one, I'm the one, who says a drug dealer who is responsible for the death of a policeman should be subject to capital punishment.

And I'm the one who will not raise taxes. My opponent, my opponent now says, my opponent now says, he'll raise them as a last resort, or a third resort. But when a politician talks like that, you know that's one resort he'll be checking into. My opponent won't rule out raising taxes. But I will. And the Congress will push me to raise taxes, and I'll say no, and they'll push, and I'll say no, and they'll push again, and I'll say, to them, "Read my lips: no new taxes."

54

GEORGE H. W. BUSH

"New World Order" Speech

September 11, 1990

As the cold war came to an end, Republicans struggled to define what the new challenges in foreign relations would be. During George H. W. Bush's presidency, rogue states such as Iraq would emerge as the major threat facing the country. Since this threat was harder to define than a Communist superpower, Bush struggled to explain to Americans what his foreign policy vision was. In 1990, Bush achieved an important victory when he led an international coalition that removed Iraqi forces from Kuwait. In the wake of that victory, Bush proposed the concept of a new world order to outline what America's role might be in this new era.

We gather tonight, witness to events in the Persian Gulf as significant as they are tragic. In the early morning hours of August 2d, following negotiations and promises by Iraq's dictator Saddam Hussein not to use force, a powerful Iraqi army invaded its trusting and much weaker neighbor, Kuwait. Within 3 days, 120,000 Iraqi troops with 850 tanks had poured into Kuwait and moved south to threaten Saudi Arabia. It was then that I decided to act to check that aggression. . . .

. . . Tonight I want to talk to you about what's at stake—what we must do together to defend civilized values around the world and maintain our economic strength at home.

From George H. W. Bush, "Address before a Joint Session of the Congress on the Persian Gulf Crisis and the Federal Budget Deficit," in *Public Papers of the Presidents of the United States: George H. W. Bush, 1990* (Washington, D.C.: U.S. Government Printing Office, 1991), 2:1218–22.

Our objectives in the Persian Gulf are clear, our goals defined and familiar: Iraq must withdraw from Kuwait completely, immediately, and without condition. . . .

As you know, I've just returned from a very productive meeting with Soviet President Gorbachev. And I am pleased that we are working together to build a new relationship. . . . Clearly, no longer can a dictator count on East-West confrontation to stymie concerted United Nations action against aggression. A new partnership of nations has begun.

We stand today at a unique and extraordinary moment. The crisis in the Persian Gulf, as grave as it is, also offers a rare opportunity to move toward an historic period of cooperation. Out of these troubled times . . . a new world order can emerge: a new era—freer from the threat of terror, stronger in the pursuit of justice, and more secure in the quest for peace. An era in which the nations of the world, East and West, North and South, can prosper and live in harmony. A hundred generations have searched for this elusive path to peace, while a thousand wars raged across the span of human endeavor. And today that new world is struggling to be born, a world quite different from the one we've known. A world where the rule of law supplants the rule of the jungle. A world in which nations recognize the shared responsibility for freedom and justice. A world where the strong respect the rights of the weak. This is the vision that I shared with President Gorbachev in Helsinki. He and other leaders from Europe, the Gulf, and around the world understand that how we manage this crisis today could shape the future for generations to come.

The test we face is great, and so are the stakes. This is the first assault on the new world that we seek, the first test of our mettle. Had we not responded to this first provocation with clarity of purpose, if we do not continue to demonstrate our determination, it would be a signal to actual and potential despots around the world. America and the world must defend common vital interests—and we will. America and the world must support the rule of law—and we will. America and the world must stand up to aggression—and we will. And one thing more: In the pursuit of these goals America will not be intimidated.

55

REPUBLICAN PARTY LEADERS

Contract with America

1994

In 1994, congressional Republicans ran a successful national campaign attacking Democrats as corrupt and President Bill Clinton as an extreme liberal. Two years earlier, Clinton had campaigned as a centrist Democrat who sought to move his party beyond the orthodoxies of the New Deal and the Great Society. In 1993 and 1994, however, Republicans had used the contentious debate over a new national health care plan, which went down to defeat, as a way to depict Clinton as a proponent of big-government liberalism. Republicans realized that if they could run a coordinated national campaign in the 1994 midterm elections—one that was united and ideological—they could potentially take control of Congress for the first time since 1952. Promising that they would complete the Reagan Revolution, they signed the Contract with America, outlining several key proposals that a new Republican majority in Congress would pursue. The Republicans took back the Senate from the Democrats, who had returned to power in 1986, and they also recaptured the House for the first time since 1954.

As Republican Members of the House of Representatives and as citizens seeking to join that body we propose not just to change its policies, but even more important, to restore the bonds of trust between the people and their elected representatives.

That is why, in this era of official evasion and posturing, we offer instead a detailed agenda for national renewal, a written commitment with no fine print.

This year's election offers the chance, after four decades of one-party control, to bring to the House a new majority that will transform the way

---

"Republican Contract with America," http://www.house.gov/house/Contract/CONTRACT.html.

Congress works. That historic change would be the end of government that is too big, too intrusive, and too easy with the public's money. It can be the beginning of a Congress that respects the values and shares the faith of the American family.

Like Lincoln, our first Republican president, we intend to act "with firmness in the right, as God gives us to see the right." To restore accountability to Congress. To end its cycle of scandal and disgrace. To make us all proud again of the way free people govern themselves.

On the first day of the 104th Congress, the new Republican majority will immediately pass the following major reforms, aimed at restoring the faith and trust of the American people in their government:

FIRST, require all laws that apply to the rest of the country also apply equally to the Congress;

SECOND, select a major, independent auditing firm to conduct a comprehensive audit of Congress for waste, fraud or abuse;

THIRD, cut the number of House committees, and cut committee staff by one-third;

FOURTH, limit the terms of all committee chairs;

FIFTH, ban the casting of proxy votes in committee;

SIXTH, require committee meetings to be open to the public;

SEVENTH, require a three-fifths majority vote to pass a tax increase;

EIGHTH, guarantee an honest accounting of our Federal Budget by implementing zero base-line budgeting.

Thereafter, within the first 100 days of the 104th Congress, we shall bring to the House Floor the following bills, each to be given full and open debate, each to be given a clear and fair vote and each to be immediately available this day for public inspection and scrutiny.

1. THE FISCAL RESPONSIBILITY ACT

A balanced budget/tax limitation amendment and a legislative line-item veto to restore fiscal responsibility to an out-of-control Congress, requiring them to live under the same budget constraints as families and businesses.

2. THE TAKING BACK OUR STREETS ACT

An anti-crime package including stronger truth-in-sentencing, "good faith" exclusionary rule exemptions, effective death penalty provisions, and cuts in social spending from this summer's "crime" bill to fund prison construction and additional law enforcement to keep people secure in their neighborhoods and kids safe in their schools.

3. THE PERSONAL RESPONSIBILITY ACT

Discourage illegitimacy and teen pregnancy by prohibiting welfare to minor mothers and denying increased AFDC for additional children while on welfare, cut spending for welfare programs, and enact a tough two-years-and-out provision with work requirements to promote individual responsibility.

4. THE FAMILY REINFORCEMENT ACT

Child support enforcement, tax incentives for adoption, strengthening rights of parents in their children's education, stronger child pornography laws, and an elderly dependent care tax credit to reinforce the central role of families in American society.

5. THE AMERICAN DREAM RESTORATION ACT

A $500 per child tax credit, begin repeal of the marriage tax penalty, and creation of American Dream Savings Accounts to provide middle class tax relief.

6. THE NATIONAL SECURITY RESTORATION ACT

No U.S. troops under U.N. command and restoration of the essential parts of our national security funding to strengthen our national defense and maintain our credibility around the world.

7. THE SENIOR CITIZENS FAIRNESS ACT

Raise the Social Security earnings limit which currently forces seniors out of the work force, repeal the 1993 tax hikes on Social Security benefits and provide tax incentives for private long-term care insurance to let Older Americans keep more of what they have earned over the years.

8. THE JOB CREATION AND WAGE ENHANCEMENT ACT

Small business incentives, capital gains cut and indexation, neutral cost recovery, risk assessment/cost-benefit analysis, strengthening the Regulatory Flexibility Act and unfunded mandate reform to create jobs and raise worker wages.

9. THE COMMON SENSE LEGAL REFORM ACT

"Loser pays" laws, reasonable limits on punitive damages and reform of product liability laws to stem the endless tide of litigation.

10. THE CITIZEN LEGISLATURE ACT

A first-ever vote on term limits to replace career politicians with citizen legislators.

Further, we will instruct the House Budget Committee to report to the floor and we will work to enact additional budget savings, beyond the budget cuts specifically included in the legislation described above, to ensure that the Federal budget deficit will be less than it would have been without the enactment of these bills.

Respecting the judgment of our fellow citizens as we seek their mandate for reform, we hereby pledge our names to this Contract with America.

56

WILLIAM J. CLINTON

Statement on Signing the Personal Responsibility and Work Opportunity Reconciliation Act of 1996

August 22, 1996

Bill Clinton's decision to sign a welfare reform act in 1996 signaled to many liberals that Clinton had accepted key components of conservatism. Clinton had responded to the Republican takeover of Congress by emphasizing his centrism and focusing on areas where he could push for a reduction in the role of government. Welfare, which had been a focus of conservative attack since World War II, emerged as Clinton's prime target. Moderate Democrats agreed with the conservative criticism that the existing welfare system made many poor Americans dependent on government services rather than helping them to achieve self-sufficiency. Although Clinton signed on to this historic reform, he continued to engage in bruising political battles with his Republican opponents in Congress over other parts of the welfare state.

From William J. Clinton, "Statement on Signing the Personal Responsibility and Work Opportunity Reconciliation Act of 1996," in *Public Papers of the Presidents of the United States: William J. Clinton, 1996* (Washington, D.C.: U.S. Government Printing Office, 1998), 2:1328–30.

Today, I have signed into law H.R. 3734, the "Personal Responsibility and Work Opportunity Reconciliation Act of 1996." While far from perfect, this legislation provides an historic opportunity to end welfare as we know it and transform our broken welfare system by promoting the fundamental values of work, responsibility, and family.

This Act honors my basic principles of real welfare reform. It requires work of welfare recipients, limits the time they can stay on welfare, and provides child care and health care to help them make the move from welfare to work. It demands personal responsibility, and puts in place tough child support enforcement measures. It promotes family and protects children.

This bipartisan legislation is significantly better than the bills that I vetoed. The Congress has removed many of the worst provisions of the vetoed bills and has included many of the improvements that I sought. I am especially pleased that the Congress has preserved the guarantee of health care for the poor, the elderly, and the disabled.

Most important, this Act is tough on work. Not only does it include firm but fair work requirements, it provides $4 billion more in child care than the vetoed bills—so that parents can end their dependency on welfare and go to work—and maintains health and safety standards for day care providers. The bill also gives States positive incentives to move people into jobs and holds them accountable for maintaining spending on welfare reform. In addition, it gives States the ability to create subsidized jobs and to provide employers with incentives to hire people off welfare.

The Act also does much more to protect children than the vetoed bills. It cuts spending on childhood disability programs less deeply and does not unwisely change the child protection programs. It maintains the national nutritional safety net, by eliminating the Food Stamp annual spending cap and the Food Stamp and School Lunch block grants that the vetoed bills contained. In addition, it preserves the Federal guarantee of health care for individuals who are currently eligible for Medicaid through the AFDC program or are in transition from welfare to work.

Furthermore, this Act includes the tough personal responsibility and child support enforcement measures that I proposed 2 years ago. It requires minor mothers to live at home and stay in school as a condition of assistance. It cracks down on parents who fail to pay child support by garnishing their wages, suspending their driver's licenses, tracking them across State lines, and, if necessary, making them work off what they owe.

For these reasons, I am proud to have signed this legislation. The current welfare system is fundamentally broken, and this may be our last best chance to set it straight. I am doing so, however, with strong objections to certain provisions, which I am determined to correct.

First, while the Act preserves the national nutritional safety net, its cuts to the Food Stamp program are too deep. . . .

Second, I am deeply disappointed that this legislation would deny Federal assistance to legal immigrants and their children, and give States the option of doing the same. . . .

I have concerns about other provisions of this legislation as well. It fails to provide sufficient contingency funding for States that experience a serious economic downturn, and it fails to provide Food Stamp support to childless adults who want to work, but cannot find a job or are not given the opportunity to participate in a work program. In addition, we must work to ensure that States provide in-kind vouchers to children whose parents reach the 5-year Federal time limit without finding work.

This Act gives States the responsibility that they have sought to reform the welfare system. This is a profound responsibility, and States must face it squarely. We will hold them accountable, insisting that they fulfill their duty to move people from welfare to work and to do right by our most vulnerable citizens, including children and battered women. I challenge each State to take advantage of its new flexibility to use money formerly available for welfare checks to encourage the private sector to provide jobs.

The best antipoverty program is still a job. Combined with the newly increased minimum wage and the Earned Income Tax Credit—which this legislation maintains—H.R. 3734 will make work pay for more Americans.

I am determined to work with the Congress in a bipartisan effort to correct the provisions of this legislation that go too far and have nothing to do with welfare reform. But, on balance, this bill is a real step forward for our country, for our values, and for people on welfare. It should represent not simply the ending of a system that too often hurts those it is supposed to help, but the beginning of a new era in which welfare will become what it was meant to be: a second chance, not a way of life. It is now up to all of us—States and cities, the Federal Government, businesses and ordinary citizens—to work together to make the promise of this new day real.

57

GEORGE W. BUSH

Acceptance Speech at the 2000 Republican National Convention

August 3, 2000

In 2000, George W. Bush ran as a Republican who wanted to continue what Ronald Reagan had started. Yet he also sought to expand the Republican coalition by promising a form of compassionate conservatism. According to Bush, this translated to Republicans using government to deal with certain problems in American life, such as education reform and assistance to faith-based institutions. Although Bush started his presidency focusing on this theme, it was quickly eclipsed by the 9/11 terrorist attacks, which turned public attention to the war on terrorism.

In Midland, Texas, where I grew up, the town motto was "the sky is the limit," and we believed it.

There was a restless energy, a basic conviction that, with hard work, anybody could succeed, and everybody deserved a chance.

Our sense of community was just as strong as that sense of promise.

Neighbors helped each other. There were dry wells and sandstorms to keep you humble, and lifelong friends to take your side, and churches to remind us that every soul is equal in value and equal in need.

This background leaves more than an accent, it leaves an outlook. Optimistic. Impatient with pretense. Confident that people can chart their own course.

That background may lack the polish of Washington. Then again, I don't have a lot of things that come with Washington.

I don't have enemies to fight. And I have no stake in the bitter arguments of the last few years. I want to change the tone of Washington to one of civility and respect. . . .

From George W. Bush, "Address Accepting the Presidential Nomination at the Republican National Convention in Philadelphia," in John T. Woolley and Gerhard Peters, *The American Presidency Project* [online], Santa Barbara, CA: University of California (hosted), Gerhard Peters (database), http://www.presidency.ucsb.edu/ws/?pid=25954.

Big government is not the answer. But the alternative to bureaucracy is not indifference.

It is to put conservative values and conservative ideas into the thick of the fight for justice and opportunity.

This is what I mean by compassionate conservatism. And on this ground we will lead our nation.

We will give low-income Americans tax credits to buy the private health insurance they need and deserve.

We will transform today's housing rental program to help hundreds of thousands of low-income families find stability and dignity in a home of their own.

And, in the next bold step of welfare reform, we will support the heroic work of homeless shelters and hospices, food pantries and crisis pregnancy centers—people reclaiming their communities block-by-block and heart-by-heart. . . .

Government cannot do this work. It can feed the body, but it cannot reach the soul. Yet government can take the side of these groups, helping the helper, encouraging the inspired.

My administration will give taxpayers new incentives to donate to charity, encourage after-school programs that build character, and support mentoring groups that shape and save young lives.

We must give our children a spirit of moral courage, because their character is our destiny.

We must tell them, with clarity and confidence, that drugs and alcohol can destroy you, and bigotry disfigures the heart.

Our schools must support the ideals of parents, elevating character and abstinence from afterthoughts to urgent goals.

We must help protect our children, in our schools and streets, by finally and strictly enforcing our nation's gun laws.

Most of all, we must teach our children the values that defeat violence. I will lead our nation toward a culture that values life—the life of the elderly and the sick, the life of the young, and the life of the unborn. Good people can disagree on this issue, but surely we can agree on ways to value life by promoting adoption and parental notification, and when Congress sends me a bill against partial-birth abortion, I will sign it into law.

58

GEORGE W. BUSH

Address on the U.S. Response to the Terrorist Attacks of September 11

September 20, 2001

After the terrorist attacks of September 11, 2001, Bush told Americans that the war against terrorism would be the new defining national security challenge. The tragic attacks by al-Qaeda terrorists, which led to the collapse of New York's World Trade Center and damage to the Pentagon, focused public attention on this international network as public enemy number one. Just as the cold war shaped conservatism during the Reagan era, the war on terrorism would do the same after 9/11.

Mr. Speaker, Mr. President Pro Tempore, Members of Congress, and Fellow Americans:

On September 11th, enemies of freedom committed an act of war against our country. Americans have known wars, but for the past 136 years, they have been wars on foreign soil, except for one Sunday in 1941. Americans have known the casualties of war, but not at the center of a great city on a peaceful morning. Americans have known surprise attacks but never before on thousands of civilians. All of this was brought upon us in a single day, and night fell on a different world, a world where freedom itself is under attack.

Americans have many questions tonight. Americans are asking, who attacked our country? The evidence we have gathered all points to a collection of loosely affiliated terrorist organizations known as Al Qaida. . . .

The terrorists practice a fringe form of Islamic extremism that has been rejected by Muslim scholars and the vast majority of Muslim clerics, a fringe movement that perverts the peaceful teachings of Islam. The terrorists' directive commands them to kill Christians and Jews, to

From George W. Bush, "Address before a Joint Session of the Congress on the United States Response to the Terrorist Attacks of September 11," in *Public Papers of the Presidents of the United States: George W. Bush, 2001* (Washington, D.C.: U.S. Government Printing Office, 2003), 2:1140–44.

kill all Americans, and make no distinctions among military and civilians, including women and children. . . .

. . . The enemy of America is not our many Muslim friends; it is not our many Arab friends. Our enemy is a radical network of terrorists and every government that supports them.

Our war on terror begins with Al Qaida, but it does not end there. It will not end until every terrorist group of global reach has been found, stopped, and defeated.

Americans are asking, why do they hate us? They hate what we see right here in this Chamber, a democratically elected government. Their leaders are self-appointed. They hate our freedoms—our freedom of religion, our freedom of speech, our freedom to vote and assemble and disagree with each other. . . .

We are not deceived by their pretenses to piety. We have seen their kind before. They are the heirs of all the murderous ideologies of the 20th century. By sacrificing human life to serve their radical visions, by abandoning every value except the will to power, they follow in the path of fascism and Nazism and totalitarianism. And they will follow that path all the way, to where it ends, in history's unmarked grave of discarded lies.

Americans are asking, how will we fight and win this war? We will direct every resource at our command, every means of diplomacy, every tool of intelligence, every instrument of law enforcement, every financial influence, and every necessary weapon of war, to the disruption and to the defeat of the global terror network. . . .

. . . Every nation, in every region, now has a decision to make. Either you are with us, or you are with the terrorists. From this day forward, any nation that continues to harbor or support terrorism will be regarded by the United States as a hostile regime.

Our Nation has been put on notice: We are not immune from attack. We will take defensive measures against terrorism to protect Americans. Today dozens of Federal departments and agencies, as well as State and local governments, have responsibilities affecting homeland security. These efforts must be coordinated at the highest level.

So tonight I announce the creation of a Cabinet-level position reporting directly to me, the Office of Homeland Security. And tonight I also announce a distinguished American to lead this effort to strengthen American security, a military veteran, an effective Governor, a true patriot, a trusted friend, Pennsylvania's Tom Ridge. He will lead, oversee, and coordinate a comprehensive national strategy to safeguard our country against terrorism and respond to any attacks that may come.

59

GEORGE W. BUSH

Eulogy at the National Funeral Service for Ronald Reagan

June 11, 2004

At the beginning of the twenty-first century, conservatives looked back to Ronald Reagan as the transformative president of the twentieth century. As is evident in this eulogy delivered by President George W. Bush, conservatives would downplay the challenges that Reagan faced in fulfilling conservative objectives, the compromises that he made while in power, and the divisions that existed between the Reagan White House and the right. Instead, Reagan was remembered as an icon of conservatism and an example of how the right could govern successfully.

Ronald Reagan's moment arrived in 1980. . . . What followed was one of the decisive decades of the century, as the convictions that shaped the President began to shape the times.

He came to office with great hopes for America, and more than hopes—like the President he had revered and once saw in person, Franklin Roosevelt, Ronald Reagan matched an optimistic temperament with bold, persistent action. President Reagan was optimistic about the great promise of economic reform, and he acted to restore the reward and spirit of enterprise. He was optimistic that a strong America could advance the peace, and he acted to build the strength that mission required. He was optimistic that liberty would thrive wherever it was planted, and he acted to defend liberty wherever it was threatened.

And Ronald Reagan believed in the power of truth in the conduct of world affairs. When he saw evil camped across the horizon, he called that evil by its name. There were no doubters in the prisons and gulags, where dissidents spread the news, tapping to each other in code what the American President had dared to say. There were no doubters in the

From George W. Bush, "Eulogy at the National Funeral Service for President Ronald Reagan," in *Public Papers of the Presidents of the United States: George W. Bush, 2004* (Washington, D.C.: U.S. Government Printing Office, 2007), 1:1030–33.

shipyards and churches and secret labor meetings, where brave men and women began to hear the creaking and rumbling of a collapsing empire. And there were no doubters among those who swung hammers at the hated wall that the first and hardest blow had been struck by President Ronald Reagan.

The ideology he opposed throughout his political life insisted that history was moved by impersonal ties and unalterable fates. Ronald Reagan believed instead in the courage and triumph of free men. And we believe it, all the more, because we saw that courage in him.

As he showed what a President should be, he also showed us what a man should be. Ronald Reagan carried himself, even in the most powerful office, with a decency and attention to small kindnesses that also defined a good life. . . .

Sure, our 40th President wore his title lightly, and it fit like a white Stetson. In the end, through his belief in our country and his love for our country, he became an enduring symbol of our country. We think of his steady stride, that tilt of a head and snap of a salute, the big-screen smile, and the glint in his Irish eyes when a story came to mind.

60

MICHAEL SCHERER

Right-Wingers Turn against Bush
February 9, 2006

During his presidency, George W. Bush grappled with many of the same types of problems Reagan faced. Bush, too, found that there were significant limits to how far he could push a conservative agenda, and he often found himself in conflict with the right wing of his party. In a 2006 article for Salon *magazine, journalist Michael Scherer examined the divisions between the White House and conservatives, which flared the year before Democrats retook control of Congress.*

From Michael Scherer, "Right-Wingers Turn against Bush," *Salon*, February 9, 2006, http://www.salon.com/news/feature/2006/02/09/right_backlash/index.html.

After George W. Bush delivered his State of the Union last week, White House aides arranged a private conference call with the president's top conservative allies. The goal was to rally cheerleading pundits with talking points, but right-wing leaders called in with a heavy sense of foreboding.

"I listened in on several White House calls before and after, boosting the troops," said Richard Viguerie, the 72-year-old direct mail pioneer who rose to fame and fortune working on Ronald Reagan's 1980 campaign. "They all sang the same song—'Oh boy, we hit a home run.'" Viguerie wasn't buying it. "Look at the treatment conservative issues got in the State of the Union. It was just perfunctory. It almost wasn't there. It was very disappointing."

Instead of shoring up the conservative base, Bush's bland rhetoric and ticky-tacky domestic initiatives—more switchgrass, less malaria—only confirmed conservatives' ever-growing concern: Far from an heir to the legacy of Ronald Reagan, the president has become just another free-spending, big-government politician.

The governor who wooed conservatives in 2000 became a president who increased federal education spending, signed a pork-laden 2002 farm bill, and passed the largest new entitlement since the days of Lyndon Johnson, the Medicare prescription drug bill. After becoming a champion of leave-us-alone libertarians, he went on to authorize a vast expansion of executive power with the Patriot Act and warrantless wiretapping of Americans. And after promising to appoint another Supreme Court justice like Antonin Scalia or Clarence Thomas, he nominated his own ideologically unknown lawyer, Harriet Miers, to the job.

As Viguerie put it, "When there are no microphones around, when it is just us there, people are really, really ticked and frustrated." With the 2006 elections just over the horizon and the 2008 presidential race already underway, activists like Viguerie are no longer content to just sit by and shake their pompoms. . . .

Listen carefully and one can hear the slap of a new gauntlet being thrown down at the feet of the president and the GOP leaders in Congress: Change course or face a depleted, if not disastrous, conservative turnout in the 2006 midterm elections. "Winning can be overrated sometimes," explained Viguerie, who began his career comfortably on the right-wing fringes of the Republican Party. "There have been times when we have advanced the cause in a major way when we lose."

61

DAN BALZ AND HAYNES JOHNSON

A Political Odyssey

August 2, 2009

In 2008, many Republicans wondered whether the conservative era had come to an end. Some thought that the coalition that had brought Reagan to power had fractured and that the movement no longer had defining ideas. Others disagreed, seeing Democratic victories in 2008 as a setback but not a permanent reversal. President Barack Obama himself rejected the idea that Reagan's conservatism had vanished from American life. This article, published during Obama's first year in office, explored these themes.

Did [Obama] believe that his election marked the end of the Reagan era?

"What Reagan ushered in was a skepticism toward government solutions to every problem, a suspicion of command-and-control, top-down social engineering," he said. "I don't think that has changed. I think that's a lasting legacy of the Reagan era and the conservative movement, starting with Goldwater. But I do think [what we're seeing] is an end to the knee-jerk reaction toward the New Deal and big government."

Added Obama: "What we don't known yet is whether my administration and this next generation of leadership is going to be able to hew to a new, more pragmatic approach that is less interested in whether we have big government or small government, [but is] more interested in whether we have a smart, effective government."

And what had he learned about the American people from his campaign?

"I have to tell you," he said, "and this is in no way an indication of overconfidence—I was not surprised by the campaign. I felt that, and I said this on the stump, I felt vindicated in my faith in the American people."

From Dan Balz and Haynes Johnson, "A Political Odyssey: How Obama's Team Forged a Path That Surprised Everyone, Even the Candidate," *Washington Post*, August 2, 2009.

Drawing on his legal background, he offered "a theory of the case" that he said guided his campaign.

"For at least a decade, maybe longer," he said, Americans have been "frustrated with a government that was unresponsive; that their economic life was becoming more difficult despite the surface prosperity; that wages and incomes had flat-lined and that in this new globalized world people were feeling more and more insecure; that we had never replaced or updated the structures for security that the New Deal had provided with something that made sense for this new economy; that people were weary of culture wars as a substitute for policy; that people were tired of only focusing on what divides instead of what brought us together; that the 50-plus-one electoral strategies that were generally pursued in national elections were completely inadequate to solve big problems like health care and energy that would require a broader consensus; that people were embarrassed by the decline in America's standing in the eyes of the world and that that would have political relevance to voters who normally might not care that much about foreign policy; and that the American people were decent and good and would be open to a different tone to politics.

So that was the theory that we started with. What was remarkable in my mind about our campaign was we never really changed our theory. You could read the speech we gave the day I announced and then read my speech on election night, and it was pretty consistent."

A Chronology of Ronald Reagan and Conservatism (1911–2004)

1911   *February*   Ronald Wilson Reagan born in Tampico, Illinois, to John and Nelle Wilson Reagan.

1932   *June*   Reagan graduates from Eureka College in Eureka, Illinois.

1937   *June*   Reagan begins working for Warner Brothers.

1942   *April*   Reagan reports for duty in the U.S. Army at Fort Mason, California.

1947   *March*   Reagan elected president of the Screen Actors Guild.

1952   *Fall*   Reagan campaigns as a registered Democrat for Eisenhower. He would similarly support Eisenhower's reelection bid in 1956.

1954   *August*   Reagan begins delivering speeches for General Electric at their plants.

      September   Reagan begins hosting *General Electric Theater.*

1955   *November*   Conservative William F. Buckley publishes the first issue of the *National Review.*

1960   *Fall*   Reagan campaigns as a registered Democrat for Nixon.

1962   *Fall*   Reagan changes his voter registration to Republican.

1964   *October*   Reagan's "A Time for Choosing" speech in support of Barry Goldwater broadcast on television.

1967   *January*   Reagan delivers his first inaugural address as governor of California.

1970   *November*   Reagan reelected as governor of California.

1975   *November*   Reagan announces his candidacy for president.

1976   *November*   After a difficult primary fight with Ronald Reagan, Republican Gerald Ford loses his bid for the presidency to Democrat Jimmy Carter, governor of Georgia.

1979   *November*   Sixty-six Americans taken hostage by Iranian revolutionaries at the U.S. embassy in Tehran. Fourteen released over the next few months.

      December   The Soviet Union invades Afghanistan.

1980 *July*   Reagan wins the presidential nomination at the Republican National Convention.

November   Reagan wins the presidential election in a landslide victory over incumbent Jimmy Carter, and the Republicans retake control of the Senate for the first time since 1954.

1981 *January*   The fifty-two remaining American hostages released in Iran minutes after Reagan inaugurated as the fortieth president of the United States.

February   Reagan sends to Congress his economic plan, titled "America's New Beginning: A Program for Economic Recovery."

March   Reagan shot by John Hinckley Jr. in an attempted assassination outside a Washington, D.C., hotel.

July   Congress passes the Economic Recovery Tax Act, which reduces taxes by 25 percent, not the 30 percent Reagan initially proposed.

August   Professional Air Traffic Controllers Organization (PATCO) workers go on strike, and Reagan fires all strikers who do not return to work within forty-eight hours.

September   Sandra Day O'Connor sworn in as the first female Supreme Court justice.

December   The *Atlantic Monthly* publishes William Greider's article about David Stockman and the challenges of Reaganomics.

1982 *August*   U.S. Marines arrive on a peacekeeping mission in Beirut, Lebanon, where Christian and Muslim groups are engaged in violent conflict.

Fall   The U.S. economy slides deeper into recession, and the unemployment rate soars to 10.8 percent, its highest level since the Great Depression.

November   Soviet leader Leonid Brezhnev dies and is succeeded by Yuri Andropov.

1983 *March*   Reagan delivers his "Evil Empire" speech to the National Association of Evangelicals convention in Orlando, Florida.

Reagan announces his plan for the Strategic Defense Initiative (SDI).

April   Reagan signs the Social Security Amendments of 1983.

September   The Soviet Union shoots down the Korean airliner KAL 007, killing all 269 passengers on board.

October   The truck bombing of the U.S. Marine barracks in Beirut kills 241.

U.S. forces invade Grenada.

1984   *January*   Reagan delivers an address on U.S.-USSR relations that emphasizes the importance of arms talks.

June   Reagan delivers a speech to mark the fortieth anniversary of the D-Day invasion of Normandy.

August   Reagan accepts the presidential nomination at the Republican National Convention.

November   Reagan reelected in a landslide victory over Democratic candidate Walter Mondale.

1985   *January*   Reagan sworn in for his second term as president.

March   Soviet leader Konstantin Chernenko dies and is succeeded by Mikhail Gorbachev.

June   Congress votes to approve economic aid to the Nicaraguan contras, who are fighting against the Communist Sandinista government.

November   Reagan and Gorbachev meet in Geneva and agree to continue talks and to work toward a reduction of nuclear armaments.

December   Reagan signs the Gramm-Rudman-Hollings Balanced Budget and Emergency Deficit Control Act.

1986   *September*   Antonin Scalia and William Rehnquist sworn in as justice and chief justice, respectively, of the Supreme Court.

October   Reagan and Gorbachev meet in Reykjavik, but their disagreement over Reagan's SDI program ends the summit.

Reagan signs the Tax Reform Act of 1986.

November   Democrats regain control of the Senate with a 55–45 majority.

Reagan appears before a national television audience to assure Americans that the United States did not send arms to Iran in exchange for the release of hostages. Later that month, Attorney General Edwin Meese reveals that the United States did divert profits from the sale of arms to Iran to the contras in Nicaragua, and a formal investigation of the Iran-contra affair begins.

1987   *June*   Reagan delivers a speech at the Brandenburg Gate calling on Gorbachev to tear down the Berlin Wall.

July   Congress holds televised hearings on the Iran-contra scandal.

October   The stock market loses $500 billion in the largest one-day percentage drop (22.6 percent) in history.

Judge Robert Bork denied Senate confirmation for his nomination to the Supreme Court.

December   Gorbachev travels to Washington, D.C., where he and Reagan sign the INF Treaty.

1988   *February*   Anthony Kennedy sworn in as Supreme Court justice.

March   A federal grand jury indicts key Iran-contra figures Oliver North and John Poindexter for their roles in diverting funds to the Nicaraguan contras.

June   Reagan and Gorbachev ratify the INF Treaty in Moscow.

November   Vice President George H. W. Bush wins the presidential election, defeating Democratic nominee Michael Dukakis.

1989   *January*   Reagan delivers his farewell address to the nation.

April   A movement for democratic reform shakes the USSR.

June   Hungary, Czechoslovakia, Bulgaria, and Romania become democratic.

November   The Berlin Wall torn down.

1991   *January–February*   Iraqi forces expelled from Kuwait in the Gulf War.

December   The Soviet Union dissolved.

1992   *November*   Democrat Bill Clinton elected president.

1994   *Fall*   Congressional Republicans led by Newt Gingrich publish their Contract with America.

November   Republicans sweep to victory in the midterm elections, retaking control of the House for the first time in forty years.

Reagan reveals in a letter to the American public that he has Alzheimer's disease.

1996   *November*   Clinton wins reelection over Republican challenger Bob Dole.

2000   *December*   In *Bush v. Gore*, the U.S. Supreme Court ends the recount of votes in Florida, and George W. Bush becomes president.

2001   *September*   Terrorists hijack four planes and attack the World Trade Center and the Pentagon.

2003   *March*   The United States announces Operation Iraqi Freedom, and U.S. forces initiate military action that begins the Iraq War.

December   Iraqi ruler Saddam Hussein captured.

2004   *June*   Reagan dies at his home in California.

Questions for Consideration

1. Was there a Reagan Revolution?
2. What were the main ideas and objectives of conservatism in the late twentieth century?
3. How did the numerous crises of the 1960s and 1970s shape Reagan and other conservatives?
4. What were the main challenges that Republicans encountered after winning control of the White House and Senate in 1980?
5. What were the main strategies that Reagan and congressional Republicans used to overcome these challenges? Were they successful?
6. Did Republicans in Congress assist or obstruct Reagan's domestic agenda? How did Democrats in the House respond, and how did their strategies change over time?
7. What concerns did conservative activists outside of government express about Reagan?
8. How did U.S.-Soviet relations change during the Reagan years?
9. What was the impact of the Iran-contra scandal? What kind of threat did it pose to Reagan's presidency and to conservatism?
10. What was Reagan's reaction to the emergence of Gorbachev? What steps did he take to facilitate negotiations?
11. How did conservatives respond to Reagan's relationship with Gorbachev?
12. Did Reagan end the cold war?
13. How have different political and intellectual constituencies remembered the legacy of the Reagan Revolution?
14. What were the most lasting effects of the Reagan presidency?
15. How does learning about Reagan's experience help us to understand the presidency of George W. Bush and conservative government from 2002 to 2006?

Selected Bibliography

CONSERVATIVES AND CONSERVATISM

For the origins and development of American conservatism, see Godfrey Hodgson, *The World Turned Right Side Up: A History of the Conservative Ascendancy in America* (Boston: Houghton Mifflin, 1996); Godfrey Hodgson, *More Equal Than Others: America from Nixon to the New Century* (Princeton, N.J.: Princeton University Press, 2004); Jonathan M. Schoenwald, *A Time for Choosing: The Rise of Modern American Conservatism* (New York: Oxford University Press, 2001); and William C. Berman, *America's Right Turn: From Nixon to Clinton* (Baltimore: Johns Hopkins University Press, 1998).

Studies about pivotal conservative leaders and organizations include Dan T. Carter, *The Politics of Rage: George Wallace, the Origins of the New Conservatism, and the Transformation of American Politics* (New York: Simon and Schuster, 1995); Donald T. Critchlow, *Phyllis Schlafly and Grassroots Conservatism: A Woman's Crusade* (Princeton, N.J.: Princeton University Press, 2005); Rick Perlstein, *Before the Storm: Barry Goldwater and the Unmaking of the American Consensus* (New York: Hill and Wang, 2001); Rick Perlstein, *Nixonland: The Rise of a President and the Fracturing of America* (New York: Scribner, 2008); and John A. Andrew, *The Other Side of the Sixties: Young Americans for Freedom and the Rise of Conservative Politics* (New Brunswick, N.J.: Rutgers University Press, 1997).

A collection of essays about conservatism and the 1970s is Bruce J. Schulman and Julian E. Zelizer, eds., *Rightward Bound: Making America Conservative in the 1970s* (Cambridge, Mass.: Harvard University Press, 2008). The best general introduction to the decade is Bruce J. Schulman, *The Seventies: The Great Shift in American Culture, Society, and Politics* (New York: Free Press, 2001).

On the relationship between conservatism and the GOP, see Donald T. Critchlow, *The Conservative Ascendancy: How the GOP Right Made Political History* (Cambridge, Mass.: Harvard University Press, 2007). The best intellectual history of conservatism remains George H. Nash, *The Conservative Intellectual Movement in America since 1945* (New York: Basic Books, 1976).

There is an expanding scholarly literature on the rise of the American right. On the role of big business, see Kimberly Phillips-Fein, *Invisible Hands: The Making of the Conservative Movement from the New Deal to Reagan* (New York: Norton, 2009). For two studies of conservatism in suburban America, see Lisa McGirr, *Suburban Warriors: The Origins of the New American Right* (Princeton, N.J.: Princeton University Press, 2001), and Matthew D. Lassiter, *The Silent Majority: Suburban Politics in the Sunbelt South* (Princeton, N.J.: Princeton University Press, 2006). On racial and regional politics, see Kevin M. Kruse, *White Flight: Atlanta and the Making of Modern Conservatism* (Princeton, N.J.: Princeton University Press, 2005); Joseph Crespino, *In Search of Another Country: Mississippi and the Conservative Counterrevolution* (Princeton, N.J.: Princeton University Press, 2007); Joseph E. Lowndes, *From the New Deal to the New Right: Race and the Southern Origins of Modern Conservatism* (New Haven, Conn.: Yale University Press, 2008); and Dan T. Carter, *From George Wallace to Newt Gingrich: Race in the Conservative Counterrevolution, 1963–1994* (Baton Rouge: Louisiana State University Press, 1996).

On conservatism and Congress, see Julian E. Zelizer, *On Capitol Hill: The Struggle to Reform Congress and Its Consequences, 1948–2000* (New York: Cambridge University Press, 2004).

Some of the best memoirs written from the perspective of participants in the Reagan administration include Martin Anderson, *Revolution: The Reagan Legacy* (Stanford, Calif.: Hoover Institution Press, Stanford University, 1990); Donald T. Regan, *For the Record: From Wall Street to Washington* (San Diego: Harcourt Brace Jovanovich, 1988); David A. Stockman, *The Triumph of Politics: Why the Reagan Revolution Failed* (New York: Harper and Row, 1986); and Michael K. Deaver, *Behind the Scenes*, with Mickey Herskowitz (New York: Morrow, 1987).

THE REAGAN YEARS

Two recent works about the significance of Ronald Reagan and the 1980 presidential election are Matthew Dallek, *The Right Moment: Ronald Reagan's First Victory and the Decisive Turning Point in American Politics* (New York: Free Press, 2000), and Andrew E. Busch, *Reagan's Victory: The Presidential Election of 1980 and the Rise of the Right* (Lawrence: University Press of Kansas, 2005).

Several books have been published about the Reagan era and presidency: Gil Troy, *The Reagan Revolution: A Very Short Introduction* (New York: Oxford University Press, 2009); John Ehrman, *The Eighties: America in the Age of Reagan* (New Haven, Conn.: Yale University Press, 2005); Gil Troy, *Morning in America: How Ronald Reagan Invented the 1980s* (Princeton, N.J.: Princeton University Press, 2005); Michael Schaller, *Right Turn: American Life in the Reagan-Bush Era, 1980–1992* (New York: Oxford University Press, 2007); Michael Schaller, *Reckoning with Reagan: America and*

Its President in the 1980s (New York: Oxford University Press, 1992); Jules Tygiel, *Ronald Reagan and the Triumph of American Conservatism* (New York: Pearson Longman, 2004); Robert M. Collins, *Transforming America: Politics and Culture during the Reagan Years* (New York: Columbia University Press, 2007); Cheryl Hudson and Gareth Davies, eds., *Ronald Reagan and the 1980s: Perceptions, Policies, Legacies* (New York: Palgrave Macmillan, 2008); Haynes Johnson, *Sleepwalking through History: America in the Reagan Years* (New York: Norton, 1991); W. Elliot Brownlee and Hugh Davis Graham, eds., *The Reagan Presidency: Pragmatic Conservatism and Its Legacies* (Lawrence: University Press of Kansas, 2003); Robert Dallek, *Ronald Reagan: The Politics of Symbolism* (Cambridge, Mass.: Harvard University Press, 1984); Jane Mayer and Doyle McManus, *Landslide: The Unmaking of the President, 1984–1988* (Boston: Houghton Mifflin, 1988); Jack W. Germond and Jules Witcover, *Wake Us When It's Over: Presidential Politics of 1984* (New York: Macmillan, 1985); and Gerald M. Pomper et al., *The Election of 1984: Reports and Interpretations* (Chatham, N.J.: Chatham House Publishers, 1985).

For histories of the 1988 presidential election, see Sidney Blumenthal, *Pledging Allegiance: The Last Campaign of the Cold War* (New York: HarperCollins, 1990); Jack W. Germond and Jules Witcover, *Whose Broad Stripes and Bright Stars? The Trivial Pursuit of the Presidency, 1988* (New York: Warner Books, 1989); and Gerald M. Pomper, et al., *The Election of 1988: Reports and Interpretations* (Chatham, N.J.: Chatham House Publishers, 1989).

There are numerous biographical accounts of Reagan's life. Some of the best are John Patrick Diggins, *Ronald Reagan: Fate, Freedom, and the Making of History* (New York: Norton, 2007); Lou Cannon, *Governor Reagan: His Rise to Power* (New York: Public Affairs, 2003); and Lou Cannon, *President Reagan: The Role of a Lifetime* (New York: Simon and Schuster, 1991).

Reagan's diaries, speeches, and letters have been collected in several publications: Ronald Reagan, *The Reagan Diaries*, ed. Douglas Brinkley (New York: HarperCollins, 2007); Kiron K. Skinner, Annelise Anderson, and Martin Anderson, eds., *Reagan, in His Own Hand: The Writings of Ronald Reagan That Reveal His Revolutionary Vision for America* (New York: Free Press, 2001); and Kiron K. Skinner, Annelise Anderson, and Martin Anderson, eds., *Reagan: A Life in Letters* (New York: Free Press, 2003). For Reagan's account, see Ronald Reagan, *Where's the Rest of Me?* with Richard G. Hubler (New York: Duell, Sloan and Pearce, 1965), and Ronald Reagan, *An American Life* (New York: Simon and Schuster, 1990).

LIBERALS

For histories of post-1960s liberalism, see Alonzo L. Hamby, *Liberalism and Its Challengers: From F.D.R. to Bush*, 2nd ed. (New York: Oxford University Press, 1992); Tip O'Neill, *Man of the House: The Life and Political Memoirs of*

Speaker Tip O'Neill, with William Novak (New York: Random House, 1987); Daniel P. Moynihan, *Came the Revolution: Argument in the Reagan Era* (San Diego: Harcourt Brace Jovanovich, 1988); and Adam Clymer, *Edward M. Kennedy: A Biography* (New York: Morrow, 1999).

ECONOMIC POLICY

Ronald Reagan's economic policies have been examined in John W. Sloan, *The Reagan Effect: Economics and Presidential Leadership* (Lawrence: University Press of Kansas, 1999); Anthony S. Campagna, *The Economy in the Reagan Years: The Economic Consequences of the Reagan Administrations* (Westport, Conn.: Greenwood Press, 1994); Paul Krugman, *Peddling Prosperity: Economic Sense and Nonsense in the Age of Diminished Expectations* (New York: Norton, 1994); Kevin P. Phillips, *The Politics of Rich and Poor: Wealth and the American Electorate in the Reagan Aftermath* (New York: Random House, 1990); Kevin P. Phillips, *Wealth and Democracy: A Political History of the American Rich* (New York: Broadway Books, 2002); and Alan Greenspan, *The Age of Turbulence: Adventures in a New World* (New York: Penguin, 2007). There has been some work on deregulatory policy: Roger E. Meiners and Bruce Yandle, eds., *Regulation and the Reagan Era: Politics, Bureaucracy, and the Public Interest* (New York: Holmes and Meier, 1989); Martha Derthick and Paul J. Quirk, *The Politics of Deregulation* (Washington, D.C.: Brookings Institution, 1985); and Nelson Lichtenstein, *State of the Union: A Century of American Labor* (Princeton, N.J.: Princeton University Press, 2002).

SOCIAL POLICY

There has been a significant amount of work on cultural and social issues: James Davison Hunter, *Culture Wars: The Struggle to Define America* (New York: Basic Books, 1991); Michael B. Katz, *The Undeserving Poor: From the War on Poverty to the War on Welfare* (New York: Pantheon, 1990); Claudia Goldin, *Understanding the Gender Gap: An Economic History of American Women* (New York: Oxford University Press, 1990); Susan Faludi, *Backlash: The Undeclared War against American Women* (New York: Crown, 1991); Paul Pierson, *Dismantling the Welfare State? Reagan, Thatcher and the Politics of Retrenchment* (New York: Cambridge University Press, 1994); Steven A. Shull, *A Kinder, Gentler Racism? The Reagan-Bush Civil Rights Legacy* (Armonk, N.Y.: M. E. Sharpe, 1993); and Randy Shilts, *And the Band Played On: Politics, People, and the AIDS Epidemic* (New York: St. Martin's Press, 1987).

NATIONAL SECURITY

Some of the best work on national security policy includes John Ehrman, *The Rise of Neoconservatism: Intellectuals and Foreign Affairs, 1945–1994* (New Haven, Conn.: Yale University Press, 1995); Beth A. Fischer, *The*

Reagan Reversal: Foreign Policy and the End of the Cold War (Columbia: University of Missouri Press, 1997); James M. Scott, *Deciding to Intervene: The Reagan Doctrine and American Foreign Policy* (Durham, N.C: Duke University Press, 1996); Coral Bell, *The Reagan Paradox: U.S. Foreign Policy in the 1980s* (New Brunswick, N.J.: Rutgers University Press, 1989); Lloyd C. Gardner, *The Long Road to Baghdad: A History of U.S. Foreign Policy from the 1970s to the Present* (New York: New Press, 2008); Daniel Wirls, *Buildup: The Politics of Defense in the Reagan Era* (Ithaca, N.Y.: Cornell University Press, 1992); Frances FitzGerald, *Way Out There in the Blue: Reagan, Star Wars, and the End of the Cold War* (New York: Simon and Schuster, 2000); and Paul Lettow, *Ronald Reagan and His Quest to Abolish Nuclear Weapons* (New York: Random House, 2005).

SOVIET UNION

Some books about U.S.-Soviet relations and the end of the cold war are James Mann, *The Rebellion of Ronald Reagan: A History of the End of the Cold War* (New York: Viking, 2009); Don Oberdorfer, *From the Cold War to a New Era: The United States and the Soviet Union, 1983–1991* (Baltimore: Johns Hopkins University Press, 1998); Raymond L. Garthoff, *The Great Transition: American-Soviet Relations and the End of the Cold War* (Washington, D.C.: Brookings Institution, 1994); Michael R. Beschloss and Strobe Talbott, *At the Highest Levels: The Inside Story of the End of the Cold War* (Boston: Little, Brown, 1993); and Jay Winik, *On the Brink: The Dramatic, Behind-the-Scenes Saga of the Reagan Era and the Men and Women Who Won the Cold War* (New York: Simon and Schuster, 1996). For a memoir by a career diplomat, see Jack F. Matlock Jr., *Reagan and Gorbachev: How the Cold War Ended* (New York: Random House, 2004); and Martin Anderson and Annelise Anderson, *Reagan's Secret War: The Untold Story of His Fight to Save the World from Nuclear Disaster* (New York: Crown, 2009).

LATIN AMERICA

For historical accounts of U.S. foreign policy in Latin America, see Lars Schoultz, *Beneath the United States: A History of U.S. Policy toward Latin America* (Cambridge, Mass.: Harvard University Press, 1998); Michael Grow, *U.S. Presidents and Latin American Interventions: Pursuing Regime Change in the Cold War* (Lawrence: University Press of Kansas, 2008); and William M. LeoGrande, *Our Own Backyard: The United States in Central America, 1977–1992* (Chapel Hill: University of North Carolina Press, 1998).

IRAN-CONTRA

There have been a few interesting works on the Iran-contra affair, including Theodore Draper, *A Very Thin Line: The Iran-Contra Affairs* (New York:

Hill and Wang, 1991), and David P. Thelen, *Becoming Citizens in the Age of Television: How Americans Challenged the Media and Seized Political Initiative during the Iran-Contra Debate* (Chicago: University of Chicago Press, 1996). The official findings of the White House Special Review Board were published as John Tower, Edmund S. Muskie, and Brent Scowcroft, *The Tower Commission Report: The Full Text of the President's Special Review Board* (New York: Bantam Books, 1987).

MIDDLE EAST

On the Middle East, see Steven A. Yetiv, *The Absence of Grand Strategy: The United States in the Persian Gulf, 1972–2005* (Baltimore: Johns Hopkins University Press, 2008); William B. Quandt, ed., *The Middle East: Ten Years after Camp David* (Washington, D.C.: Brookings Institution, 1988); Bruce W. Jentleson, *With Friends Like These: Reagan, Bush, and Saddam, 1982–1990* (New York: Norton, 1994); and Rachel Bronson, *Thicker Than Oil: America's Uneasy Partnership with Saudi Arabia* (New York: Oxford University Press, 2006).

LEGACY

For books that place Reagan and conservatism, and their legacy, in a broader historical context, see Sean Wilentz, *The Age of Reagan: A History, 1974–2008* (New York: HarperCollins, 2008); James T. Patterson, *Restless Giant: The United States from Watergate to* Bush v. Gore (New York: Oxford University Press, 2005); Andrew J. Bacevich, *The New American Militarism: How Americans Are Seduced by War* (New York: Oxford University Press, 2005); Paul Pierson and Theda Skocpol, eds., *The Transformation of American Politics: Activist Government and the Rise of Conservatism* (Princeton, N.J.: Princeton University Press, 2007); and Julian E. Zelizer, *Arsenal of Democracy: The Politics of National Security — From World War II to the War on Terrorism* (New York: Basic Books, 2010).

Index